Kelvin Sampson

The OU Basketball Story

T0159229

Kelvin Sampson

The OU Basketball Story

Second Edition

Steve Richardson

Republic of Texas Press
Plano, Texas

Library of Congress Cataloging-in-Publication Data

Richardson, Steve.
  Kelvin Sampson : the OU basketball story. 2nd Ed. / Steve Richardson.-- 2nd ed.
      p. cm.
  Includes index.
  ISBN 1-55622-946-1 (alk. paper)
  1. Sampson, Kelvin. 2. Basketball coaches--United States--
  Biography. 3. University of Oklahoma--Basketball-History.
  I. Title.

  GV884.S33 R53 2002   2002006610
  796.323'092--dc21   CIP

Republic of Texas Press is an imprint of Wordware Publishing, Inc.

Printed in the United States of America

ISBN 1-55622-946-1
10 9 8 7 6 5 4 3 2 1
0205

All inquiries for volume purchases of this book should be addressed to
Wordware Publishing, Inc., at 2320 Los Rios Boulevard, Plano, Texas 75074.
Telephone inquiries may be made by calling:

(972) 423-0090

Contents

Foreword

by Jason Rabedeaux
University of Texas-El Paso head basketball coach

My interview to become a graduate assistant coach at Washington State occurred in the summer of 1989. I was working a camp for Kelvin Sampson and at the time was an assistant coach at a Division III school. After two minutes of small talk, Coach Sampson pulled out a folder of applications.

"Jason, I have a stack of applications of guys who want this job, but I am going to hire you because you are nobody and I think you will work hard," Coach Sampson told me.

That's how I became a part of his staff for eleven years, first at Washington State and then at Oklahoma. I was a graduate assistant like he was for Jud Heathcote at Michigan State ten years earlier. There were a lot more guys in that folder with better pedigrees than I had. There were guys who have played Division I basketball and guys who had even coached on the Division I level. But that's the way Coach operates. Look at his staff now. Bennie Seltzer is a former player from Washington State and Jim Shaw is from Western Oregon. It goes back to where he comes from, Pembroke, North Carolina, and how he grew up.

I have been back to Pembroke two or three times. Pembroke is a small town in southeast North Carolina. I have driven up and down those streets. I have been in the college gymnasium. I have been in his mom and dad's house. I have been with him to see his grandmother. So, I know where the Coach comes from. The first time I went back to Pembroke I remember we were recruiting Terrell McIntyre, who was from Raeford, North Carolina, and wound up going to Clemson. After I went back to Pembroke, even having been with Coach five or six years, I had a much greater appreciation and understanding of who he was and the things he had to do to get to where he is.

This was rural North Carolina. But they are almost like family to me. I wanted to see some of these things. I remember going to convenience stores back there to get a Diet Coke and there would be a pool hall in the background.

One of Coach's favorite sayings is, "Don't forget where you came from." When he says that, it is from his own experience. That is one of his greatest assets. He hasn't forgotten he worked in the tobacco market as a kid, that he was a small-college player at Pembroke State, that he was a head coach at Montana Tech, making long drives in vans and buses. And he carries that over to how he coaches his team.

Coach has a great penchant for getting his teams to have a "backs-against-the-wall" mentality. When I was at Oklahoma and we would go play Texas in Austin, he had our players thinking the Longhorns lived up on the hill in the big house and we were the farmers down in the valley. And this was our chance to go in there and take something from them. "We don't have McDonald's All-Americas like these other schools have," Coach Sampson would say. "This is what we have." He created the belief we were going to go in there as a unit and as a staff and win.

The last three or four years I was at OU, Coach and I would always go for walks after shoot-arounds or practices on the road. We would always walk back to the hotel. We would talk and visit. One time we were in Texas and walking back from the Erwin Center to the Marriott. He picked up the school newspaper and read a comment by the Texas coach that Oklahoma had a nice Top 50 program. Coach didn't like that at all. I remember him having that paper with him prior to the start of the game and reading it to the team and wadding it up and throwing it away. He took it as a slam to the OU program. Coach Sampson viewed Texas and Oklahoma as being on the same plane in basketball. All of sudden the team was feeding off him. I remember Ryan Minor made two free throws in overtime to win the game. Coach was very good at motivating a team like that.

It was a great eleven-year ride I had with him before becoming the coach at UTEP in 1999. I started as a graduate assistant for a Washington State team that went 7-22 and lost seventeen straight games in the Pac-10. I left him after he had made six straight NCAA Tournaments and advanced to the Sweet 16. I saw him develop as a coach.

When you cut into Kelvin Sampson after he is dead and gone, loyalty is going to run thick in his blood. You may not be the most talented player or coach. You may not be the smartest. But if you're loyal and bust your butt, you have a place in his family. And you have a place in his heart.

June 4, 2001

A Message from Joe Castiglione, University of Oklahoma Athletic Director

The University of Oklahoma has something very special in Kelvin Sampson (and Karen too for that matter). After working with him for four years, I know he is a uniquely talented leader who repeatedly demonstrates his outstanding teaching skills and ability to inspire. What impresses me most about Kelvin Sampson is the consistent high quality of program he develops and how well his student-athletes represent the university on and off the court. The chemistry he has created is something every coach strives to achieve but seldom does.

Despite the huge demands on his time, he makes community involvement a top priority. For example, he will get in the car very early in the morning and drive two hours to make an appearance for someone and drive back to work to see a donor or player after an early morning workout. Then, he will take on his other daily challenges and it really humanizes his special role as teacher and coach.

The list of the causes Kelvin Sampson supports is long indeed ...the American Lung Association, American Cancer Society, Boys and Girls Club, Boy Scouts of America, Children's Miracle Network, Citizens Caring for Children, Food and Shelter for Friends, Oklahoma Blood Institute, Oklahoma Christian Academy, Coaches vs. Cancer, Oklahoma Committee to Prevent Child Abuse, Special Olympics, NABC Dream to Read, Drug Free Youth and Kids, We Care. In addition, Coach Sampson formed the Sooner Reading Program, which energizes the Norman area elementary schools. OU players and coaches interact with young students and emphasize the importance of reading.

Further proof of the Sampsons' dedication to reading is his and Karen's donation of $200,000 to OU's Libraries and OU Athletic Department's Academic Center in 1998. He deeply cares about his friends and his profession. At a moment's notice, if one of his friends in the coaching fraternity needs help, Kelvin Sampson is there. He is very involved in the National Association of Basketball Coaches (NABC), numerous coaching clinics, and he has coached several teams for USA Basketball.

Former and current coaches come to his practices and watch him in his "classroom." They marvel at the organization, attention to detail, intensity, and player development. I have heard many people remark about the quality of his practices, calling them "textbook." I have also watched him mesmerize the media at the NCAA Tournament. The room is always full when he speaks. The reason? He articulates the story of his team's journey to the NCAA Tournament in a way that leaves you feeling good about the value of the game of basketball, the people who play and coach it, and its relativity to life in general. He is the son of a coach, and he understands the value of hard work and commitment to a goal that is greater than any individual. He communicates that message every time he speaks, sharing the lessons he learned while playing for his father. It is truly something to behold and probably one of many examples as to why his family is so important.

Upon reading this book, you will understand so much about this incredibly bright and talented coach. You will appreciate his passion for fundamentals, his tough-minded competitiveness, his perspective, and his innate ability to virtually will his team to victory while insisting his student-athletes keep their focus on the bigger picture—succeeding in life after basketball.

We have the best possible person to lead the University of Oklahoma. *Kelvin Sampson: The OU Basketball Story* is a must read for Oklahoma fans and alumni everywhere. More than anything, I believe his passion will help lead Oklahoma back to college basketball's spotlight—The Final Four—again and again. Like a lot of people, I would love to be the one holding the ladder as he and the rest of the Sooners cut down the nets after winning the national title.

Joe Castiglione
May 1, 2002

Acknowledgments

To complete a book of more than 70,000 words in less than three months is a daunting task. But with excellent cooperation from Kelvin Sampson, his wife Karen, his entire basketball staff, and the Oklahoma Athletic Department, it was a very enjoyable job.

How appropriate it was for Kelvin Sampson to spend more than eighteen hours taping his biography. Books obviously are an important part of his life. Since Kelvin Sampson arrived in Norman in 1994, he has developed the Sooner Reading Program, which emphasizes the importance of reading to area elementary school children. This is a book that definitely should be on the shelf of every Norman school!

Kelvin Sampson: The OU Basketball Story would not have been possible without Coach Sampson's ability to reminisce about his childhood and reveal the long journey from Pembroke, N.C., through Michigan State, Montana Tech, and Washington State to Norman. In the same careful way he coaches his team, Kelvin Sampson combed through the years of his life and revealed the details of his coaching experiences and methods and relationships with coaches and players.

Karen Sampson was an invaluable asset in developing the book. Nobody knows Kelvin Sampson better than Karen. She added many of the nice little touches that completed the picture of the long journey. Karen opened her home on several occasions and helped gather pictures from Kelvin's early days. And for that, the author is most appreciative.

Special thanks also goes to Renee Forney, Coach Sampson's office manager. She lined up interviews and found time in Coach Sampson's busy summer for tapings. She tracked down phone numbers for former players and associates. Mike Houck, Oklahoma's associate director of media relations, was superb in providing background information, player interviews and pictures. No request was ever too much for Karen, Renee, or Mike.

Appreciation goes to all the former and current players who were interviewed and a cast of literally dozens of people who have touched Kelvin Sampson's life over the years. UTEP head coach Jason Rabedeaux gave up nearly a day of his time to talk about his eleven years with Kelvin Sampson as an assistant coach.

A deep debt of gratitude must be extended to the University of Oklahoma athletic director Joe Castiglione who made this project possible. A long-time friend, Joe Castiglione has the vision, talent, work ethic, and people skills to make Oklahoma truly one of the greatest athletic departments in the country.

And, of course, without the cooperation of the subject himself, this book would not have been possible. Kelvin Sampson is one of those rare coaches in any sport who seems to be able to relate to players from all different kinds of backgrounds and mold them into a team. He does this with a sometimes-stern and always no-nonsense approach that is directly linked to his background. Writing this book with Kelvin Sampson's input was a pleasure.

I hope Oklahoma basketball fans everywhere enjoy this story on one of college basketball's most successful coaches.

Steve Richardson
June 20, 2001

Introduction

Kelvin Sampson was destined to be a coach. That desire ran deep in his blood. Sports were at the center of Sampson's life while he grew up as part of a working-class family in rural southeast North Carolina.

Kelvin's father, Mr. Ned, was his high school basketball coach. But long before the two forged a bond on the court, Kelvin was intrigued by the coaching profession. When Kelvin was old enough, each summer he would accompany Mr. Ned to the North Carolina High School Coaches Association Clinic in Greensboro, North Carolina.

They would rise at 5 a.m. on a Friday each July and travel several hours from Pembroke to Greensboro in the Piedmont region of the state. Friday was the day the father and son didn't work at the tobacco warehouse on those relentlessly hot and sultry summer days in North Carolina.

Young Kelvin, eleven or twelve, was too young to attend the actual coaching clinic. He would remain in the car in the parking lot while anywhere from 1,500-2,000 high school coaches, including his father, would listen to the speeches of the legendary North Carolina coaches.

"The highlight was the All-Star game that night," Sampson remembers. "And I remember one year Bob McAdoo and Bobby Jones, who later played at North Carolina, were the stars of the game."

It was at one of those All-Star games when Sampson first saw North Carolina coach Dean Smith, who three decades later would become college basketball's all-time victory leader. Sampson took notice of Smith, who coached North Carolina to the 1967 Final Four and started one of the most successful runs in college sports history.

Dean Smith's Blue-White game and clinic each fall in Chapel Hill also drew Kelvin's attention. The speakers at Smith's clinic were the four coaches of the previous spring's North Carolina state basketball champions.

"I always wanted my dad to be a speaker in that clinic," Sampson remembered recently. "I always thought that would be the biggest thing. It wasn't so much to win the state title, but I thought he was a better coach than any of those guys."

Ned Sampson never won a state title. But Kelvin still looked up to his dad. Kelvin Sampson grew up on Atlantic Coast Conference basketball as well. The names of the league's coaches during that 1960s still excite him...Bones McKinney at Wake Forest, Everett Case at North Carolina State, and Vic Bubas at Duke.

"And the favorite team from where I was from was North Carolina," Sampson said. "Dean Smith was the man. Everything they did was class. The kinds of kids he had. The way they played. My hero was Charlie Scott. And he was the first African-American player to play in the ACC. And Charlie Scott was my hero because of that. I remember when Dean Smith lost a recruiting battle, I was depressed. I knew their starters. I knew their bench guys. I wanted to be Dean Smith. If I ever coached, I would coach like my father. And I would coach like Dean Smith."

Sampson's current OU teams are as disciplined as his father's were at Pembroke High School when Kelvin was playing there in the early 1970s. And there are definitely some resemblances between Sampson's teams at Oklahoma and North Carolina's current squads, which still bear Smith's trademark.

"For instance, our bench and how enthusiastic it is," Sampson said. "The players stand up and clap. I got that from Dean Smith. I think every coach's players point to a teammate who scores a basket. But we practice that, making sure we acknowledge where the pass came from for the basket. We got that from Dean Smith. Making the extra pass. How many times do you see our kids have an open shot and make a pass for a better shot? I think any kid or coach growing up in that era would be influenced by Coach Smith and North Carolina. Just like anyone now would be influenced by Coach Krzyzewski at Duke. In my era it was Dean Smith."

Years later his father would go from his coach to his advisor and confidante. Mr. Ned has never left his side in spirit despite the distances between the two in Kelvin's eighteen-year head coaching career.

"I don't think he has missed a game calling," Ned Sampson said. "When he was coaching in Montana and Washington State, there was sometimes a three-hour time difference. I used to get calls at 2 and 3 o'clock in the morning. I always knew who it was."

And it was Smith's strong endorsement of OU that convinced Sampson to become the Sooners' coach in 1994. When Sampson was coach at Washington State from 1987-94, he became acquainted with Smith on a professional level. They both had shoe contracts with Converse at the time.

"At the time I was considering staying at Washington State," Sampson said. "Coach Smith didn't beat around the bush. He said Oklahoma was a better job than Washington State. He was real cut and dried about it. He said, 'You are in the part of the country in Oklahoma where you have a chance to get better players and you have a chance to get to the NCAA Tournament every year. Four years from now how good can you be at Washington State? You can be good every year at Oklahoma.' Obviously, that went a long way."

Sampson took on former Michigan State coach Jud Heathcote as a mentor after serving as a graduate assistant coach for him in 1979-80. Heathcote taught Sampson discipline, how to handle assistant coaches, and how to run camps and practices.

"He has always been kind of special, as one of my friends and protégés," Heathcote said. "I am exceedingly pleased with his success."

Heathcote has always been able to make Kelvin laugh.

"I remember one year at Oklahoma we had just played Texas A&M," Sampson said. "He had just retired at Michigan State and he said, 'Hey, Kel, I have good news and I have bad news.' I told him to give me the good news first.

"'I've got a satellite, so I can watch all of your games,' Heathcote said. "'The bad news is I saw your game last night and it was the worst game I have ever seen. Tell your assistants to get you some players.'

"I told Jud we had won," Sampson said. "But Jud always wants you to be better."

CHAPTER 1

The Early Years

Kelvin Sampson grew up in a sports family. Kelvin's father was his baseball coach when he was a youngster and his basketball coach in high school. One of Kelvin Sampson's greatest thrills was his induction into Pembroke State's (now UNC-Pembroke) Hall of Fame in 1998. But the first person in the Sampson family inducted into Pembroke State's Hall was his father, Mr. Ned, in 1980.

"I was inducted more for what I have accomplished after I left there," Kelvin Sampson said. "He was inducted for what he accomplished there. He was a great, great athlete. I remember from one of the school's annuals there was a picture of my father and a quote from Dick Groat, who played at Duke, talking about one of the greatest shooters he had ever seen, 'Ned Sampson, Pembroke State.'"

It was from these origins that Sampson evolved. He always has looked up to his father, who probably never got to exercise his full potential as an athlete.

As a guard-forward at a small Indian college, Ned Samson indeed had shocked the great Groat in a rare meeting between those players.

Groat and Duke's other seniors, after their college eligibility had been exhausted, barnstormed around the region playing small-college teams like Pembroke, Elon, High Point, and Lenior-Rhyne before packed city gymnasiums. Groat, the 1952 National College Player of the Year and also a star on the Duke baseball team, later played shortstop in the major leagues and in the NBA.

And the athlete Groat faced in the early 1950s still was beating Kelvin into his early teens years later.

"I remember playing horse with him all the time, but I couldn't beat him," Kelvin said of Mr. Ned. "And I was one of the better shooters in my class. We would go to baseball games, and he would race me to the car. I couldn't beat him. I must have been eleven to fourteen and he was thirty-six to thirty-nine. But I couldn't outrun him."

Ned, seventy-two, laughs about his former athletic prowess. He starred in basketball, baseball, and football at Pembroke State nearly a half century ago.

"I was probably still beating Kelvin running well into my thirties and early forties," Mr. Ned said. "I played on a summer baseball team until I was close to forty. So I stayed in pretty good shape."

Kelvin grew up with three sisters, including his twin, Karen. Until eighth grade, Kelvin shared a bedroom with his sisters. Then he moved to the den, which was converted into his bedroom. Ironically, years later Kelvin would marry a woman named Karen, who had a brother named Kelvin.

"I grew up with a ball," Sampson said. "I was one of those babies with a ball in his crib. I remember as a small kid climbing up the stairs to a room where my father kept all the baseball equipment. He was coaching summer league teams. My parents were gone a lot. My mother was working different shifts as a nurse. We spent a lot of time by ourselves in the summer. My father was either selling *World Book Encyclopedia* or insurance, teaching Driver's Ed, or working in the tobacco market."

Kelvin would sneak up to the equipment room. From a green army duffel bag, Kelvin would find bats and other equipment. Kelvin would dress in the old uniforms that were six sizes too big for him and don the catcher's mask. The shin guards would clang against the floor. He would grab a catcher's mitt and bat and play. Karen, younger by a minute, was Kelvin's playmate.

When Kelvin was eight years old, his father started a Little League in Pembroke. Kelvin's team was the Phillies, which wore green jerseys. The other teams were the Yankees, Cardinals, and Dodgers. Practices were always on Saturday. Kelvin was a catcher and outfielder.

"I loved putting that equipment on," Kelvin said. "I loved wearing the mask and the chest protector. At the time I didn't understand it, but in high school I didn't want to play any other position. I wanted to be the catcher, who was involved in every play."

His mother, Eva, tried to diversify Kelvin's interests. She lined him up with piano lessons and tap dance. But Kelvin decided enough was enough when it came to tap dance. His mother would drop him off for the dance lessons, but Kelvin had other ideas about how to spend his time.

"He would go shoot baskets instead," wife Karen related recently. "When Kelvin showed up for the dance recital, the teacher didn't know who he was."

Kelvin wasn't much better at singing. "I was the worst singer of all time," Sampson said, laughing about his family in the pew on Sundays at the Southern Baptist church they attended. The only person in his family who could carry a tune was his twin sister, Karen. Karen played the clarinet and drums. Sampson also played the trombone. But sports were his thing.

During the early 1960s in Pembroke, North Carolina, the only organized sport for children was baseball. Kelvin didn't play basketball until the seventh grade. He stayed in Pembroke through junior high before attending a military school, Carolina Military Academy (CMA), for two years. It was less than twenty miles away in Maxton, North Carolina. Kelvin would commute daily with the help of family friends.

"I repeated the eighth grade at the military academy," said Sampson, who was born in October and was one of the youngest kids in his class. "I always look at that as a redshirt year.

"The academic standards were really high there. The discipline toughened me up. I always had good friends in Pembroke, which was a Native American community. One of the first things people think of when they think of Native Americans is reservations. We didn't have any idea what that was. We were just young kids growing up in normal blue-collar America."

In Maxton, Kelvin, a full-blooded Lumbee Indian, first experienced racial prejudice directed toward him. In Pembroke's Robeson County, Kelvin grew up with Native Americans, along with a few whites and blacks. "At military school was when I noticed my skin color was different from other people's," Sampson said. "Not that I noticed it. I was made to notice it. Just the taunts and making fun. I didn't know how to handle it at first."

He was one of only two Native Americans at the military school. Most of the cadets were from affluent white families. There were a few black cadets. Kelvin got into fights. And it was the combination of those fights that landed him with enough demerits that he had to walk them off one day in the hot North Carolina sun. He had a fifty-pound pack on his back. He was carrying an M30-caliber carbine

Left: Twin sister Karen and Kelvin – 6 months. *Below left:* Kelvin, age 5, at a graduation ceremony. *Below right:* First grade. *Bottom right:* Eighth grade Carolina Military Academy. Family file photos.

rifle. And he was taking laps with an older military student screaming in his ear.

"I look over and there is this Driver's Ed car, riding through the trees on this side street. And it was my father," Kelvin said. "He saw his son at about 4 o'clock walking around the track."

By the time he left military school after the ninth grade though, Kelvin was the highest-ranking ninth grader in the school. But in his first year, Sampson said he wasn't sure he wanted to be at CMA.

"That was kids being kids," Kelvin said of the racial taunts. "But that was part of my growing up. You don't forget it. You gain respect by playing on the baseball and basketball team. But that first month was tough. I was from a public school where I had known everybody. Now, I was put in a military school. It was a totally different way of life. Taking you out of your comfort zone, it teaches you discipline and growing up. I never, at first, understood why I had to do that.

"My father had this saying: Nothing has ever been taught until it has been learned, and nothing has been learned until it has been taught. I have always lived by that."

He asked his father why he was at CMA.

"This is good for you," Mr. Ned said.

"The main reason I think is he wanted to separate me from some influential kids in my class at the time," Kelvin said. "He didn't want me to be led astray. And athletics had something to do with it. And it put me in an age group I should be in. I was actually young for my class. I was on schedule to graduate early."

But Mr. Ned even had another reason for sending Kelvin to CMA.

"Kelvin was a twin," Mr. Ned said. "When they were young like that, Karen was a lot more mature. She was a factor for him. She always made sure he got all the assignments. She made sure everything was easier for Kelvin. When I sent him to CMA, he was on his own. And I think that was good for him."

Kelvin returned to Pembroke more of a man. He was a tenth grader, who was the varsity basketball team's backup point guard. And Mr. Ned was the coach. Kelvin also would star in baseball and as Pembroke High School's quarterback.

But there were other lessons Kelvin was learning that would shape his coaching career.

Mr. Ned didn't make a lot of money coaching and teaching high school. Thus, Mr. Ned needed summer jobs to support his four children. Kelvin's mother also worked as supervisor for the health services department at Pembroke State University.

"So, I grew up appreciating the value of a dollar," Sampson said years later. "I grew up appreciating what an honest day's work was all about. I appreciate that my mother and father gave me good values. And I have tried to pass that along to my teams."

Kelvin worked summers, starting at about age twelve, at the tobacco market in nearby Lumberton. His father was a foreman of a crew in the market where tobacco companies would come and purchase the product at auction...R.J. Reynolds, Phillip Morris, Imperial, Export.

"It was pretty tough work," Mr. Ned said. "But around here jobs were not that plentiful. Most of the Indian people in Robeson County went into farming. But I got that job before I finished college. And I worked down there until 1983. My job changed there over the years. But when I started working there, I got just 50 cents an hour.

"Then when I got to be a foreman I would hire different workers. I used to take Kelvin down there just to be with me, and he would pick up leaves of tobacco. Then he became a foreman. People who worked down there got minimum wage. It was tough work, but it made him tougher. He would even come home and help me in the summers when he was coaching basketball at Montana Tech."

Young Kelvin's job began once the sale of a pile of tobacco was completed. At first Kelvin was working on one of his father's crews, which would tie the 300-pound sheets of tobacco together and transport them to the market door of the proper buyer. If a sheet fell out or didn't weigh out properly, there was hell to pay from the rich, white buyers.

"It was hard work," Kelvin said. "It was work kids our age probably shouldn't have been doing. But that is what we did. I would have much rather been cutting grass, selling lemonade, or working at a basketball camp. I think working at that tobacco market helped form what my definition of work is."

When he was fifteen Sampson became a foreman of one of the crews. And that created even more adversity.

"I can't tell you how many times I got my butt chewed out for leaving tobacco laying around," Kelvin said. "But the toughest thing was you never knew who would show up to work. The people who worked this job couldn't get other jobs. This was not a job that you sought. They either were alcoholics or uneducated and poor."

Kelvin was developing leadership skills he later would take to the basketball floor.

"I tried to figure who were the smartest ones," Kelvin said of the workers. "The smartest ones I would have them match up the color with the corresponding door of the buyer. We could do two houses in the morning and three in the afternoon. The sale always ended at 11:30 a.m. But that didn't mean our work ended. We had to finish that house. The next sale would start at 1:30. So there was a two-hour gap there where we tried to catch up. I had to give them time off for lunch. But I didn't get a lunch break."

When Sampson let the workers off for their lunch break, sometimes their drug and alcohol habits would take hold. The workers had little money. But they would make do. Sampson said they would go buy a coke for 15 cents and drink half of it. Then some would mix it with a 69-cent bottle of Aqua Velva aftershave, which sometimes was eight percent alcohol. Ripple wine cost $2, which was too expensive for workers' minimum wage.

"They would get a quick buzz," Sampson said. "Then, in the middle of the afternoon, you would walk behind them and all you would smell was that Aqua Velva because they were sweating like crazy. That's when I found out what they were doing. It was amazing how those guys would work. I developed a bond with them. I would bring them water just to keep them going."

The air was thick with tobacco dust in buildings topped by aluminum roofs. If it was 95-100 degrees outside, it was 120 degrees inside.

"Here I am fifteen or sixteen years old and I am working in a group of guys averaging in ages from eighteen to forty and some of them are grandfathers," Sampson said. "Minimum wage back then was $1.35-$1.65 an hour. And we worked Monday through Thursday. A lot of times we worked on Friday to catch up."

Later Mr. Ned got a contract to actually load trucks and made more than minimum wage. "He actually did pretty well," Kelvin said. "But that was even harder work. That was in the sun."

From mid-July until school started, Kelvin would work at the tobacco market. In high school he would hustle over to football practice after work.

"The people skills I learned were great," Sampson said. "I was dealing with the buyers, who were mostly unfriendly. You found out who to be friends with, the people who swept up for the next day's sale, the truck drivers, the farmers. You learned to be friends with everybody, how to treat people and get what you wanted."

But Sampson, as a youth, wasn't always treated well in rural North Carolina because of the color of his skin. Racial prejudice was rampant in those days. Whites, blacks, and others, which included the Lumbees, had separate public rest rooms and water fountains, especially at the tobacco market. Sampson remembers when he and his father were not served in a restaurant because they were Native American.

"The blacks and Indians were treated the same way," Kelvin said.

He remembered years later being called "boy." At the tobacco market Sampson remembers three different water fountains were marked: "White, Colored, Other." Sampson always drank out of the "Colored" fountain because he didn't want to be known as the "other."

There also were incidents of Klu Klux Klan activity in North Carolina, which Sampson observed.

When Kelvin was eight or nine during the early 1960s, the family was driving through Cumberland County, North Carolina, where Fayetteville was located. The Sampsons had gone shopping. The four Sampson children were in the back seat. Traffic halted, and Kelvin's mother told the children to get down in the bed of the car.

"They were looking for non-whites," Kelvin said. "I am not sure what they were going to do to us. But I just remembered a huge cross on the side of the road burning and these people wearing hoods. That was just something I remembered like the bathrooms at the tobacco market. That was 1960s in the South. Race was part of the deal."

So it was in the mid-1950s. Mr. Ned had been a part of a group of Lumbees who had broken up a Klu Klux Klan rally near Pembroke. The Lumbees, who are believed to be descendants of the Algonquian-speaking tribes who lived along Cape Hatteras, had been aggressive in the past, rebelling during the later stages of the Civil War for full United States citizenship.

"The Klan leader was from South Carolina, and he was going to have this meeting," Mr. Ned recalled. "He said things that disturbed our people. It was being held eleven miles from Pembroke beside this pond in a large field. I really didn't think anything would happen. The Klan had guards at the edge of the field. Several Lumbees started gathering in the road about dark. Everybody had guns. The Klan members had circled their cars, and there was a light and podium in the middle of the cars where the speaker would be."

A Lumbee shot the light out, and it was pitch black. And Mr. Ned related years later how fast he was running for his life. Chaos reigned; gunfire was ricocheting everywhere. The cars sped away, and the meeting broke up.

"I was wondering, 'How fast were you running?'" Kelvin asked his father. "I always thought he could fly. He was talking about running and diving under trucks and cars and behind trees and bushes. And the police came and broke up the rally."

That was the last rally the Klan had near Pembroke.

There were no color lines at Kelvin Sampson's Pembroke High School, which was composed mostly of Lumbees. Sampson was a three-sport high school star at the Class 3A school, the second largest classification of high schools in North Carolina.

He was an option quarterback and outside linebacker, and he kicked off and kicked field goals for the football team, which had its best season (7-3) his junior year. He was the Gordie Lockbaum of Pembroke High School. "I just could move the chains," said Sampson. "I wasn't really great at anything. I could move our offense. I did a little bit of everything."

Sampson's best boyhood friend was the center on the football team, Ricky Locklear. Oddly, Locklear always wanted to be a coach. Sampson always wanted to be a lawyer. Now they have reversed roles. Locklear is the lawyer, and Sampson is the coach.

"We live through each other," Sampson said.

But after Sampson threw a touchdown pass with under a minute remaining to beat Wallace Rose Hill in the Homecoming Game his junior year, he met the most special person in his life. That night Kelvin and Karen, his future wife, had their first date. They had several classes together as well as the same history teacher, Kelvin's father.

"I think I was supposed to meet someone else that night and it didn't work out," Kelvin said. "We started dancing."

It was love on the first date. A couple of days later, Karen Lowery got a call from a sheepish Kelvin asking what the history assignment was. He could have just asked his father. He had shown his hand in a big way.

"Of all the assignments," Karen, also a junior, said with an amused tone. "Why would he ask about history? We had all of our

Kelvin as a high school quarterback.
Family file photo.

classes together. He was interested and nervous. Why not ask about the chemistry assignment?"

He never stopped dating Karen after that. But sports were his second love. After finishing football in the fall, Sampson switched gears and played guard for his father on the basketball team. Then, in the spring, he was a catcher and later an outfielder on the baseball team.

"I was a good basketball player, but I wasn't quite ready for the varsity my tenth-grade year," Sampson said. "My father was harder on me than anybody else. I remember him pinching my leg and telling me I wasn't tough enough.

"He said, 'You are playing too soft. You are playing too sissy.' It wasn't easy playing for your father as a sophomore. I was the point guard. And I wasn't even the best point guard on the team. But I learned a lot. And once I got past the tenth grade, I really wanted to play. I got serious about working out. But my father pushed me. God, he pushed me."

Mr. Ned would take Kelvin to the gym all by himself. Kelvin learned about discipline from his father and how hard he had to practice. Mr. Ned would get on Kelvin because he could take it. And Kelvin made all-conference in basketball his junior and senior years.

"I would say I was probably a little harder on Kelvin," Mr. Ned said. "When you are coaching your own son, everybody is watching and thinking the coach will let him have everything a little bit easier. I didn't want that said. So, I probably was a little harder on Kelvin. He had it tough. I think that is how it is with most father-son, coach-player relationships.

"I don't remember pinching him," Mr. Ned added. "I may have slapped him on the back. We didn't have a great big, strong talented team. We had to play tough. And we had to play hard to have any success."

And Kelvin Sampson was a tough high school player, remembers Joe Gallagher, a high school coach at Carolina Military Academy at the time and later Sampson's basketball coach at Pembroke State.

"We played them his senior year in high school in this old barn," Gallagher said in describing the gymnasium. "At the far end of the gym under one basket, there was a board that went across the door. Kelvin went in hard for a layup. Our kid bumped him, and Kelvin's foot went though the door. And he couldn't get loose. It was a 5-on-4 situation and we scored a layup. They came back down and his foot

Kelvin was a basketball player in high school and college.
Family file photo.

was still stuck in the door. We only beat them by a couple of points. But I have never let him forget that his foot was stuck in the door."

Sampson probably would have been a better high school baseball player if he had not played football and basketball.

"I could hit pitchers who were getting drafted by the pros," Sampson said. "My senior year in high school I hit over .440. I went to some pro tryout camps. The Mets had one I attended. They wanted you to be a four-tool guy. I could run. I could hit. I could play defense. But I had a very average arm. They wanted me to go to college. And if I did well, they felt I would get drafted."

Sampson moved from catcher to the outfield his senior year in high school when 6-foot-5 Dwight Lowery, later a back-up catcher for the Detroit Tigers, joined the Pembroke High School team.

"Without any hesitation at all," remembers Ronnie Chavis, Kelvin's high school baseball coach. "He knew this kid was a better player. And he knew that would make us a better baseball team. You could tell early on he was going to be a leader in something.

"As far as being a natural born hitter, if this kid [Kelvin] woke up at three in morning and you put a bat in his hand, he could hit," Chavis said. "He was a much better baseball player than basketball player. His dad didn't like me to say that because he was a basketball coach. But I saw him as probably having a chance at playing pro baseball. He was a good enough athlete. Most catchers have to be good athletes."

Sampson talked to his father about going to another pro tryout camp. But that was to be the only one he would attend. Mr. Ned told Kelvin he was going to go to college. So Kelvin signed a scholarship to Pembroke State with a major in political science. College basketball eventually became the focal point, although Kelvin started three years for the Pembroke State baseball team.

"I wound up being very average in both," Sampson said of his two-sport college career. "In baseball, I had one year where I hit close to .300 in college. Baseball in North Carolina always started in February. And I never got there until March when basketball was over.

"My greatest contribution in basketball was my consistency. I was a good shooter. And I would have been a better college player if they had had the three-point shot back then. I was a good point guard. I started a lot of games my freshman year and sporadically throughout my career. I felt my greatest contribution was I found ways to help our team win."

His junior year Sampson made a steal with two seconds remaining to preserve Pembroke State's 76-75 victory over Pfeiffer in the first round of the Carolinas Conference playoffs. Sampson called that "one of his greatest thrills" through his junior season.

Sampson usually came off the bench later in his college career for the Braves. Pembroke State was a member of the National Association of Intercollegiate Athletics in those days. And it was a tough level of college basketball in the 1970s because many of the great black players in the South were still going to NAIA schools. Players such as Lloyd Free and John Drew.

Sampson's path also crossed Rick Barnes, later to become the University of Texas coach. Both were North Carolina NAIA players. Barnes played at Lenoir-Rhyne College in Hickory, North Carolina. Tubby Smith, the Tulsa, Georgia, and Kentucky coach, played college basketball at High Point a few years earlier.

Barnes and Sampson were North Carolina contemporaries and remain close to this day despite being fierce competitors in the Big 12 Conference.

"When I was growing up back in North Carolina, coaches back then were friends with each other," Barnes said. "It was much friendlier then. And I think Kelvin and I are somewhat like that. I love the guy. When we compete I want to beat him as much as he wants to beat me. I think it's different in the relationships you have with somebody you grew up with."

"Our schools played in a scrimmage once," Sampson said of Barnes. "Rick was a better college player than I was. They called him 'Rifle Rick.' He had long hair and was a good shooter. We were probably very similar players. He was just a little better. Our backgrounds are similar, blue-collar. Our paths were very similar." Barnes agrees: "I know one thing, if we played today, I would kick Kelvin's butt. I would take him down low."

Faced with the better college competition, Sampson knew his future wasn't going to be as a player. He was already starting to think and talk like a coach. In the 1977-78 Pembroke State press guide, Sampson was quoted as saying about the Braves: "We will lack a proven center, but our experience from last year as well as some talented freshmen could give us a good team."

"He was a great kid to coach," said Joe Gallagher, who became the Pembroke State basketball coach Sampson's sophomore year. "He was raised in a coaching environment. He was very intuitive.

Kelvin Sampson's best sport in high school and college was probably baseball.

Defensively, he could have used some work. He had the respect of peers. He could really shoot it. I thought he was too smart to be a coach. He was an intelligent kid and a very good baseball player. He was always heady. What he lacked in ability, he made up with his head. So, I am not surprised with the success he has had."

Kelvin initially played for the late Pembroke State basketball coach Lacey Gane. Gane, who ran Adolph Rupp's old Kentucky offense (two guards, high post and two wings), may have best summed up Sampson's induction into the school's Hall of Fame three years ago.

"With Kelvin, he started as a man," said Gane, who passed away a few months after the induction. "He never was a boy. He could fight like hell."

And that's the way he eventually would coach.

CHAPTER 2

The Journey Begins

Kelvin Sampson was facing a career decision as he prepared to graduate from Pembroke State in the spring of 1978. What next? He always had wanted to be a lawyer. His father was a history teacher. He had majored in political science. And one of Sampson's greatest heroes was not in the sports arena, but at the center of one of the landmark civil rights cases in American history when the U.S. Supreme Court declared segregated public schooling unconstitutional in 1954.

"I would always say one of my heroes was Thurgood Marshall," Sampson said. "He was one of the NAACP attorneys who handled the *Brown vs. Board of Education* case."

But after his sophomore year in college, Sampson's mother, Eva, had a hunch neither history nor political science nor law nor any combination of the three would be in Sampson's future.

"My mother took me aside and she told me it would be a good idea if I took some physical education classes," Kelvin said. "I went to summer school and started taking some of the harder classes, physiology and exercise kinesiology. I got into teaching certification. Years later she said, 'I always knew you wanted to coach.' I always thought it was amazing she knew that."

Eva had wanted Kelvin to be a dentist. And that's one of the reasons she enrolled him in piano lessons as a youngster—to prepare his hands for the nimble work of filling and pulling teeth. But by this time she was resigned to the fact that young Kelvin would probably follow in his father's other profession, coaching. So he was going to need a teaching certificate.

And Sampson was warned the life of a coach-teacher could test one's pocketbook. But he already should have known that.

"I told Kelvin, if you are going to coach, you are not going to make much money," Mr. Ned said. "He almost went to law school. But I knew he loved coaching. Even after high school, if he wasn't practicing, had a game, or was tied up, he would come over and help me coach. I could tell then he would be a good coach because of his good relationships with the players."

Years later Chicago Bulls coach Tim Floyd, who was a college coach at Idaho and Iowa State when Sampson was at Washington State and Oklahoma, believes that is one of the main reasons Sampson has been so successful.

"He went into coaching not to make a lot of money," Floyd said. "He chose the profession because that's all he wanted to do. Some of the guys view it as an opportunity to become wealthy. I have always valued that part of him."

In the fall of his senior year at Pembroke State, Kelvin did his student teaching at Hoke County High School in Raeford, North Carolina.

"To show you how small the world is, you know who the basketball coach was at the high school? Tubby Smith," Sampson said. "Tubby played at High Point College and is a few years older than I am. We didn't interact much at that time."

Smith, the sixth of seventeen children, was raised on a farm in Southern Maryland. He graduated from High Point in 1973 and then coached four seasons at a Maryland high school before his two-year stint at Raeford where he had a 28-18 coaching record in two seasons. After six years in the high school ranks, Smith became an assistant coach on the Division I level at Virginia Commonwealth. It took Sampson basically the same length of time to become a full-time Division I assistant at Washington State.

Smith's presence at the high school underscored the tough road he, Barnes, and Sampson would have to travel to get to the Division I level as basketball coaches. They all came up the hard way. Sampson just didn't know how hard it was going to be the next few years.

"I admired Kelvin and Tubby as much as anyone because they were not born with silver spoons in their mouths," Barnes said. "It was not like they had head coaches who told them when they got done playing, 'We will make you a full-time assistant coach on the Division I level.' That wasn't the way it happened. I am proud of them because I know where they came from."

North Carolina was a hotbed for basketball, although Sampson, Barnes, and Smith were not the marquee players during those days. There was an incredible array of North Carolina high school stars who went on to star in college and in the NBA during the era Sampson was growing up. A sampling: Michael Jordan, James Worthy, Dominique Wilkins, Sleepy Floyd, Bobby Jones, David Thompson, Phil Ford, and Pete Maravich. But it would be a star player in the Midwest, from the state of Michigan, who would catch Sampson's eye and shape the course of his career: Michigan State's Earvin "Magic" Johnson.

Toward the end of his senior year at Pembroke State, Sampson was taking the LSAT (Law School Aptitude Test) test for law school and still was applying to several law schools. He was accepted to the Wake Forest University law school. His twin sister, Karen, was taking the GRE to get into graduate school. Kelvin decided to take the GRE test mainly to go see his sister in Chapel Hill. He tested high. And because he was a minority student, he checked the minority locator code on the exam.

That started a flood of schools contacting Sampson about attending graduate school. He received letters back from Cal, Cornell, Tennessee, North Carolina, UNC Charlotte...and Michigan State. But Michigan State's letter wouldn't have caught Sampson's eye if it hadn't been for the NCAA Tournament that March.

In the 1978 NCAA Tournament, Sampson fell in love with the dazzling play of Michigan State star Johnson, a 6-foot-9 guard. The Spartans lost to eventual NCAA champion Kentucky, 52-49, in the region finals. But the Spartans returned Johnson and would be national title contenders in 1979.

"I was amazed by him," Sampson said. "I remember watching him on television. And not very long after that I got a letter from Michigan State. I applied. They had an academic scholarship, and they told me I could keep it as long as I maintained a 3.25 GPA. So I said, 'Okay, I think I can do that.' I graduated from Pembroke in June and left that September for East Lansing."

Kelvin was dating his future wife, Karen, at the time. The two were engaged that summer before Sampson left for Michigan State. stayed behind in North Carolina and continued to teach first grade at the same school where she had student taught in nearby Lumberton, North Carolina.

Kelvin marveled at Magic Johnson's skills for a big man. MSU file photo.

"I loaded everything I had up in a Jeep," Sampson said. "I drove from North Carolina to East Lansing, 900 miles. That was the furthest north or west I had ever been."

Sampson taught a freshman-level anatomy class for three credits as part of his graduate assistantship in physical education and took fifteen credits his first semester. From his grandfather, Kelvin heeded this advice and demonstrated it at Michigan State: "There's two kinds of people in the world: the ones who do the work and the ones who take credit for doing the work. You're better off in the first group; there's a lot less competition."

"I was on a crazy schedule," Sampson said. "I always believed the harder you worked and the more you worked, the better you would be. I was getting my master's degree in exercise physiology. I was taking motor learning classes and physiology classes. I even took a kinesiology class with Mike Marshall, who played baseball for Michigan State and later was the reliever for the Los Angeles Dodgers."

During that first year in East Lansing, Sampson coached an intramural team that lost to future major league star Kirk Gibson's team. Gibson played baseball and football for the Spartans.

"But I was miserable," Sampson said of yearning to be close to a *real* basketball team. "The first thing I did when I got there, I went over to Jenison Field House. And they were on a foreign trip. They had gone to Brazil. I went in when those guys got back. I asked Jud Heathcote if there was anything I could do. I wasn't offering help. I wanted a job. But there were already three assistants."

Sampson remembered being very nervous in front of Heathcote. The only time Sampson had seen Heathcote was on television. There was an intimidation factor.

"To this day, Jud says, 'Once a Grad-Ass, always a Grad-Ass,'" Sampson recalls years later.

Sheepishly, Sampson went to Heathcote's office.

"I asked if I could make an appointment to see Jud," Sampson said of approaching Heathcote's secretary. "She said, 'For what?' I said, 'I wanted to talk to him about a job.' She said 'Good luck.' She made me an appointment for the next day." Sampson didn't sleep well that night.

"I was twenty-three years old," Sampson said. "And this guy doesn't know me from Adam. And I am getting ready to ask him for a job. So, when I get in he's sitting there with his green Michigan State coaching shirt and I just ask him real hesitantly if there is anything I can do, sweep the floors. Everything I offered to do, he said we have managers who do that."

"You want to be a manager?" Heathcote asked.

Kelvin's mentor, Jud Heathcote.
MSU file photo.

"I'd say I'd like to coach," Sampson answered

Heathcote said, "Good luck to you. No."

So Sampson regrouped and cultivated the assistant coaches to get them in his corner.

"It wasn't like he was going to have to pay me," Sampson said. "I already had the scholarship."

But the second time Sampson went in to talk to Heathcote, he also got shut out.

"He was warming up a little bit," Sampson said. "He could relate. I was a young guy who played and my father was a coach. And I just wanted to be around it. I told him I loved coaching and wanted to be involved somehow. But he still said no. I wanted to be a part of that basketball program. I would have washed his car. I would have shined his shoes. I would have baby-sat the assistant coaches' kids. It didn't matter to me. I was twenty-three years old, and I was finishing up my master's degree."

Heathcote didn't like hangers-on. But Sampson huddled with the assistants one more time. Michigan State had a junior varsity team. And that's where Sampson would land during the 1979-80 season.

"I went into Jud with that idea and he finally said yes," said Sampson, who merely hung around the program during the Spartans' national championship season in 1978-79. Sampson sat behind the bench during that year and was an errand boy.

Heathcote figured a guy that persistent deserved a try. Sampson received a coaching shirt from assistant coach Dave Harshman that said: "Michigan State Basketball."

"We needed another guy around like we needed a hole in the head," Heathcote said. "But I thought, maybe if he can't help us, we can help him. He was like a sponge."

Sampson and Karen got married in the summer of 1979 and moved to East Lansing. And that summer he also worked Heathcote's basketball camps. Money was not plentiful. Kelvin and Karen lived in married student housing.

Previously back in North Carolina they had picked cucumbers for a month starting at 5 a.m. just to pay for their honeymoon to Myrtle Beach, South Carolina.

"We planted a half-acre of cucumbers near where Karen's parents lived when we went back there," Kelvin remembers. "We would pick them and sell them and use the money for the honeymoon. I think we got $700 out of it. That was hard work. You wanted to start early because the sun was hot. You knew I must love Karen, because she would come out some days to pick cucumbers her hair would be in these big old rollers. I thought, 'What am I doing?' I had never seen her in her rollers before."

Finally married, Sampson then turned to his other love: coaching basketball.

"They made me one of the commissioners at Jud's basketball camp," Sampson said. "And I thought that was a good sign. I wanted to be one of the best commissioners they had ever had. They had three leagues. And I didn't want Jud to come in and see my league being slack. To this day I still have coaches meetings at 7:30 in the morning at camp. To this day, I still do bed checks every day at our camps. You know why? Because that is the way Jud did it. He ran the camp. I could never do it any other way. I could never just show up and make an appearance at camp. I run my camps very much like Jud did."

Once practice started in the fall, Sampson reported to Fred Paulsen, Heathcote's assistant who was coach of Michigan State's junior varsity team. The Spartans would play many of the junior college teams in the state of Michigan and would make road trips in school-owned station wagons. Sampson never had a desk in the Michigan State basketball office. He merely had a stool he would pull up to Paulsen's desk.

"We played a twenty-game schedule with about ten of those games at home," Paulsen remembered. "We played before the varsity the first year, and by half time there were 10,000 people at home games. It was a great training ground."

Sampson finished his master's degree in a year and the second year worked on doctoral classes while serving as a graduate assistant coach.

Heathcote remembers Sampson running the junior varsity practices with Paulsen, then coming up to watch Heathcote coach the varsity and sit in on the coaches' meetings. "He was satisfied to stay in the background and learn," Heathcote said. Sampson learned about Heathcote's 2-3 matchup zone defense and how to coach half-court offense.

"I think one of the things the assistant coaches learned from Jud was to respect the game," Paulsen said. "The biggest thing I learned, Jud by far was the best bench coach I had been around. And I learned you can make your team competitive no matter who your players are. First of all you can do that defensively. And offensively you need to know what your strengths are and somebody else's weaknesses are.

"People liked to talk about running teams, but Jud said he never had seen a great game when it didn't come down to execution in the half court," Paulsen said. "If you can't execute in the half court, you can't be a big-time winning team. That means having the right people with the ball at the right time and knowing what to do."

"Jud was just very professional," Sampson said. "He never forgot where he came from. And he really influenced me in the discipline aspect of the game and how to treat assistant coaches in giving them responsibilities. Jud was demanding. I think we are very similar, but I do things in my own way."

Sampson remembered Heathcote dressing down another assistant coach one day because he forgot the number of a kid on an opposing team. "That was so important to Jud," Sampson recalled. "'How could you not know the number of the other team's best player?' Heathcote asked the assistant."

Sampson took another Heathcote coaching principle to heart.

"He was hardest on his best players," Sampson said. "His hardest workers in practice were Earvin and Greg Kelser. And they were his best players. To this day, I don't think you can have a great team unless your best players are your hardest workers."

By the end of that season, Sampson was faced with another decision. Should he stay at Michigan State another year and continue to work on his doctorate on a $7,000 fellowship? He could continue to serve as a graduate assistant for the Michigan State team. Sampson also had an opportunity to return to North Carolina and coach high school basketball. In the latter scenario, wife Karen would get her old teaching job back.

The Sampsons didn't make the conventional choice.

"The third option was to go to Montana Tech with Fred Paulsen as an assistant coach for $1,100 (for a year) and no benefits," Karen said. "But it was college coaching. Once you are associated with the national championship team, Big Ten, Division I, I think it is hard to leave that. It was his passion. It was the only college opportunity. We were young and had no children. What was the worst thing to happen? It would not work out."

Sampson had applied for assistant jobs at UNC-Wilmington, Columbia, and East Carolina. But he didn't get a sniff. Nothing. So Sampson went back to sage Heathcote.

"What are you going to do with the degree?" Heathcote asked. "Do you want to be a teacher or a coach?"

"A coach," Sampson said.

"You don't need a doctorate to coach," Heathcote said. "But you could get a coaching job on the college level with a master's degree."

Sampson's dilemma was solved. He was heading to Montana, except he didn't even know how to get to Butte, Montana, where Montana Tech was located. Karen paged through her atlas and found Montana.

"I don't know anything about Butte," Karen said. "But they do have a U-Haul drop."

Kelvin and Karen took that as a good omen. They were going to need a U-Haul. They had little money to have their belongings shipped cross-country from East Lansing. But the Sampson's trek from East Lansing to Butte was just like an episode out of "The Beverly Hillbillies."

A Montana Tech player drove Karen's Toyota. And the Sampsons headed out in a twenty-foot-long U-Haul truck with Kelvin's Jeep hitched to the back with a tow bar. They made it fine through Chicago and then through Minneapolis.

"We get right outside of Minnesota, and I couldn't see the Toyota," Sampson said. "We get off at the next exit and we double back. We finally see the Toyota, and he's there with the hood up and the car smoking. The engine was running hot and there was an oil leak. I thought, 'What are we doing going to Montana?' I am going out here for a job that pays $1,100 a year. We don't even have a place to stay. But they said they have a bar on every street corner. I thought well, I guess I could be a bartender."

The immediate problem was to get the car fixed. A mechanic told them the motor was cracked and would cost $800 to $900 to fix. That was money the Sampsons didn't have. So they put the broken-down Toyota on the back of the U-Haul. And they let the Montana Tech player drive the Jeep on the interstate. As the caravan headed west and the sun was setting, the safety clamp came loose from the tow bar.

"I kind of see this car coming along the side of us and give it the one look, and I look back," Sampson said.

"...That's our car! I know that's our car! It had broken loose from the tow bar (and was supported by only a thin safety chain) as we had gone down a hill. Luckily there was not all that much traffic, but here goes our car. It slowly came to a stop.

"This was a trip from hell. We planned to stop two or three times at night. But the only hotels we could stop at had 1 as one of their first numbers like $19.99."

The Sampsons and the future Montana Tech player finally arrived in eastern Montana at Miles City. It was still another several hours to Butte, located in the southwestern part of the state. But Karen took pictures as the couple crossed into their new state.

They finally arrived in Butte, which was already chilly. Fred Paulsen took the Sampsons to his house the first night. But the next day they moved into their new home.

"It was an old, old house," Kelvin said. "The place was scary. And one of the ladies helping us move in dropped a piece of crystal. I looked at Karen and said, 'What are we doing here? If you want to go back, we will go back.'

"We move in. One night we are lying in bed and this guy cranks up a chain saw. All I could think of was *The Texas Chain Saw Massacre*. He was cutting firewood. There was also a public alley between the two houses, and cars were driving through there at all hours of the day and night. It sounded like cars were coming into our bedroom."

There was a dirt floor in the basement, which had no light. The Sampsons had to use a flashlight to hang up their clothes in the basement because there was only a broom closet in the living area. The bathroom in the apartment leaned to one side. The hot water heater for the entire house was on the ledge over the bathtub.

"If you were taking a bath and washing clothes, the water would spill into the tub," Karen said. "I thought, 'Are you kidding me?' We were in a shotgun house between two mansions. I said to Kelvin, 'This is where the paid help lived.'"

Kelvin told Karen they could turn right around and head back to East Lansing. But there was no way she was going to spend three days in the car again.

It was a long way from North Carolina, and winter hadn't even arrived.

But there was some hope. It came in the form of Vic Burt, Montana Tech's director of fiscal affairs. In order for the Sampsons to make ends meet, Kelvin was offered and accepted the manager's position of the Green Apartments for an extra $10,000 a year. The Sampsons, trying to add some class to their managed dwellings, referred to them simply as "The Greens."

After two weeks in the house from hell, they believed they had hit heaven when they got to move into their new apartment. It was just nice by comparison.

The Anaconda Mining Co. had sold the Green Apartments to Montana Tech for $1. But the apartments were so poorly insulated that one-inch thick ice would form during the winters. The insulation was basically newspapers. If one apartment caught on fire, the rest would go up like a tinderbox. One Christmas season the Sampsons were without heat for one night and had to huddle with their young daughter Lauren in their waterbed because of a –70-degree wind chill outside.

The Sampsons still believed they were in paradise compared to their initial shotgun house with the chain saw wielding neighbor. They could live in a three-bedroom apartment rent free if Kelvin would manage the apartments. The couple would also make $40 for cleaning up vacated apartments and turning them over to new tenants. Kelvin would clean the bathrooms and floors. Karen got the kitchen duty and would clean ovens with Mr. Muscle. She still has small scars on her arms from where the gloves ended.

Every weekend Kelvin would have to break up fights. He also received calls from married tenants complaining their single counterparts were making too much noise. Kelvin could usually count on four or five calls a weekend at 2:30 or 3 in the morning. There were four bars within walking distance of the Green Apartments.

"I was the best friend of every policeman in town," Kelvin said. "They knew when I was calling on the weekend, I was calling them to break up a fight."

And weird smells often would circulate in the apartments, he remembers. One day he got a call from Karen complaining about the smell coming from the next door kitchen of a Portuguese family. "You're not going to believe how horrible it smells," said Karen, who was eight months pregnant at the time.

CHAPTER 3

Montana Tech Success Leads to Pullman

By the time Kelvin Sampson left Montana Tech following the 1984-85 season, his team's games were a hot commodity in Butte. In order to watch the perennial Frontier League champion Orediggers, a fan would have to be at the preliminary women's game by half time in order to get a seat for the men's game in the nightcap.

But in the middle of the 1980-81 season when Sampson took over a floundering men's team, he was down to only a handful of scholarship players because of defections during the brief Fred Paulsen regime. Crowds ranged from 200 to 300 for the Orediggers' home games in Butte. Watching ore mining was more fun than watching the men's basketball team play.

Paulsen didn't even make it halfway through the first season after asking Sampson to pick up and move halfway across the country from East Lansing to Butte.

"I wasn't there long enough for anybody to remember me," Paulsen said.

"His wife really hated it," Sampson said. "They were both from Michigan. And I think there may have been problems with one of their families. He left before Christmas. They asked me to be the head coach. I had just turned twenty-five on October 5. There were two or three players who were about as old as I was.

"I was their sixth head coach in three years," Sampson said. "No one had even come close to winning. It was such a bad job they hired me. This had all happened so fast. I was two years out of college and here I was a head coach."

Paulsen and Sampson still are good friends. Paulsen later went on to become a successful NAIA coach at Huron College (South Dakota) and took the team to the national tournament four times.

"I wanted a head job so bad, I took a bad job for me," Paulsen said of leaving Michigan State for Montana Tech. "I got there in April, and they didn't want me by December. I was too hard on the kids. The program hadn't won any games. I just regret not doing a very good job. Kelvin did a great job, but he got to experience some of the same things I went through."

Paulsen does remember going to Calgary to play in an early bird tournament that year. "We had to strap all the luggage to the top of the roof of the bus, and he and I had to drive," Paulsen said. "It was a people mover. We didn't have anything. I got my eyes open."

Once Paulsen left, Sampson finished out the first season with a ragtag bunch of players. He was technically the interim coach when the team won five games. But he was retained as head coach by school officials.

"The president talked him into being the head coach that first year," said Mike Carle, one of Sampson's assistant coaches at Montana Tech. "He had a couple of rough seasons. Then he brought in his players. Tech had very high academic standards. It was difficult to get players into Tech."

Sampson was trying to carve out a basketball program in a tough academic environment where basketball was low on the list of the priorities of many of the players he inherited.

"I remember he called me from Montana Tech when kids left the program," said Joe Gallagher, Kelvin's college basketball coach at Pembroke State. "He asked me to call the athletic director for him. Timing is everything. He is the man who has taken advantage fully of the opportunities presented to him. When it happened, I think he always was well prepared in everything. I have known guys who were assistant coaches, when the head coach gets sick and those fifteen to sixteen inches they move over, they are just not ready. He always has been. He is very, very well prepared."

Don Petritz, "Moose," the team's trainer, remembers the long bus rides, "you [Sampson] being depressed and yet motivated and determined to make the program a success."

That December 1980, Karen and Kelvin would enjoy their last New Year's Eve together without any children. Even if the team was bad, it was Sampson's to coach in the wilds of Montana officially in January 1981. And the two celebrated.

There was a huge mountain where the school was located. And at the top of the mountain there was a big flashing "M." When Montana won, a V within the M would flash at night. Sampson would walk across the mountain to get to his office right under the M.

The Sampsons had the run of the athletic facilities at Montana Tech. The couple would have kayak races in the pool area. There was a sauna and racquet ball and basketball courts. "Instead of going to the movies we would go work out. We didn't have the money to go to the movies," Kelvin said.

"I remember that first New Year's Eve," Karen Sampson said. "We thought life was good. We bundled up. It may have been –40 degrees. And we walked over there."

By the next year reality had set in. The honeymoon was over in more ways than one.

In the fall of 1981 Karen was pregnant with Lauren. Kelvin was having back problems. On Halloween evening, 1981, Kelvin was laid up with his back. Karen was in the latter stages of her pregnancy. Neither of them could bend over. So when a trick-or-treater came by and accidentally spilled all of their candy on the floor, they couldn't prevent the youngster from escaping with all of the candy they had. They had to turn off their lights at the Green Apartments as if they weren't home so kids would quit coming up to their door.

Sampson's first full year, in 1981-82, the team finished with a 7-20 record, but that included three victories by forfeit because fellow Frontier League member Western Montana had played an ineligible player in three victories over Montana Tech. During Kelvin's previous interim season the Orediggers were 5-22.

"So my first full year there we go 4-23. We hadn't gotten the three forfeits yet. This was the day after the season ended. And we were 4-23. The phone rang and it's six in the morning. It was Jud Heathcote. It was eight o'clock in East Lansing.

"Hey, Kel! I just wanted to call and say congratulations. You are the only coach in captivity that could take Montana Tech from obscurity to oblivion."

Montana Tech University. Karen and Kelvin enjoyed the lighted "M".

"'Thanks, Jud, appreciate it.' That was Jud's way of saying I had had a poor year. He told me to keep my head up and go recruit better players."

Heathcote had actually attended Montana Tech his freshman year. So, while Sampson was the head coach of the Orediggers, Heathcote would donate $1,000 each year to the booster club. Heathcote graduated from Washington State. "So Jud's had a little to do with my career," Sampson said.

But Sampson admitted he was learning on the fly. His apprenticeship in East Lansing had been very short.

"I was calling my father mostly because I was having a lot of discipline problems. I was asking him, 'How would you handle this?' It was apparent I was a stickler for detail. I couldn't understand why they couldn't jump rope for five minutes without stopping. I could. Running suicides, why they didn't touch the line. When we ran sprints in college, I touched the line. Kids cut corners. I didn't have any patience. As the year progressed we got better in so many areas. And I convinced the kids it was because we touched every line."

Sampson learned that year not to focus on winning and losing, but improving. And his first season the Orediggers beat College of Great Falls by holding the ball for 30 minutes, 33-31, in February 1982. That's when Sampson started to get a reputation for doing more with less. The Montana Tech players put the young Sampson on their shoulders and carried him into the showers.

"I will tell you how bad that team was, they almost dropped me," Sampson said. "That was a game we had no business winning. And that was when we were getting 200 to 300 people to a game. A lot of the kids didn't want to play basketball the first year. They were OK basketball players. They just weren't good enough to win games."

Loyola Marymount coach Steve Aggers was the College of Great Falls coach during those days.

"The team was also in shambles when I first got to Great Falls," Aggers said. "We came into similar situations. And just being in Butte was a story in itself. There were miners and loggers. It was a tough, tough town. Kelvin did a great job. He did an outstanding job of bringing in a higher talent level than they had. And like anybody when you are rebuilding a program, you are changing attitudes. You change work ethic and work habits. He brought the pride back. He improved the fan base and got the fans interested.

"A lot of these assistants today, they see Rick Pitino and John Calipari and Tom Izzo, and they think you just start right there," Aggers added. "We have such respect for the game and started the hard way at remote locations. We treasure those experiences."

Sampson had had very little experience in recruiting because he did none at Michigan State. "You had to be resourceful," Paulsen said.

"I know there were projects," Carle said. "He took chances on kids. But he developed them into players."

"I started calling everybody I knew," Sampson said. "That's how I found Steve Seaman. He was an unsigned kid. But NAIA recruiting didn't start until May or June. I didn't know that. I was trying to recruit all the best players out there. It was like the Masters in golf. NAIA recruiting doesn't start until the back nine on Sunday. When you get your players is when they find out they are not going to Division I schools."

Sampson recruited by phone basically. He would make three recruiting trips a year—to the Bay Area, to the California junior college tournament in Santa Clara, and to the Junior College Region IX

Tournament in Scottsbluff (Nebraska). He tried to recruit Montana high school players. But the school had a very difficult curriculum.

"It required thirty credits of math [for graduation]," Sampson said. "It was not a liberal arts college. Most kids had engineering majors. I realized I could be good at this when we won championships at Montana Tech. Academically, it was a tough sell; athletically, there were no expectations."

1982-1983 Montana Tech.

Seaman was one of those petroleum engineering majors. He also was a good basketball player. At 6-foot-7, 205 pounds, Seaman came from Yorktown, Virginia. Sampson recruited him by phone. Seaman stayed only two years at Montana Tech because he wanted to change his major when the petroleum field bottomed out. He latter transferred to Old Dominion and played sparingly two seasons for the Monarchs.

"The reason I went into Montana Tech was to get into petroleum engineering," said Seaman, who had inquiries from about 200 schools, mostly mid-Division I and lower. "Coach Sampson contacted me sight unseen. But the first impression you ever get from him is the utmost truthfulness and honesty. I could tell he wasn't going to make this a glamorous thing."

And Montana was anything but glamorous. When Seaman stepped off the plane in Butte, he realized he was in a different world. He had shorts and a dress shirt on because it was August. It was in the thirties in Montana. And it would get a lot colder during the long bus rides.

"These were brown bag and van leagues," Aggers says. "You had sack lunches and were riding in vans."

In the Orediggers' case, it was usually a bus.

Montana Tech's team took its long road trips in an old 1969 Trailways. A minor league baseball team, the Butte Copper Kings, an affiliate of the Milwaukee Brewers, shared the bus with Montana Tech. The baseball team used it in the summer. And Montana Tech took road trips on the forty-passenger bus during the winter.

Because of the stringent academic demands, Sampson's Montana Tech team would have to leave after classes the day before the game. Plane trips where unheard of during those NAIA days when the budgets were razor-thin.

The closest schools in the Frontier League were sixty miles away. That was to Helena (Carroll College) in one direction and in the other direction sixty miles to Dillon (Western Montana). And the College of Great Falls was 190 miles by bus. Rocky Mountain College was 240 miles from Butte. Nonconference games were usually even longer treks. The trip to the College of Idaho in Caldwell took nine hours by bus, if the weather was good and the road was clear.

"Snow equipment was high-tech in Montana," Sampson remembers. "A road plow? You would see one every twenty feet in Montana. The rule on the road trip was what was going to happen first, the blizzard or the bus breakdown. Usually one of those two things happened."

On one trip to Canada, the wind kicked up so hard, remembers former player Joe McClafferty, the door of the bus blew off. And they had to use athletic tape in the trainer's kit to tape the door shut.

Seaman remembers one of those trips all too well during the 1982-83 season, Sampson's second full year at Montana Tech. It turned out to be a defining moment of Sampson's coaching career and set the bar high for what true adversity was on a road trip.

"The bus had little heat," Seaman said. "It would blow cold air. We were all huddled together in the bus in our winter coats to make the trip, our teeth chattering. It was one of those bonding things so vital to team success."

That experience Sampson calls the greatest three-game road trip in his coaching career. And his assistants still hear countless stories about it years later.

"In the NAIA the talent level was never as good as it is here, but the atmosphere, the intensity, the coaching, the road trips...that's what I remember," said Sampson's current OU assistant Ray Lopes, who played at College of Idaho, now Albertson College. "That was an unbelievable road trip. He compares that to winning at UCLA and Arizona or beating both KU and Missouri on the road."

The three-game trip started off ominously. The old Trailways broke down one November night about 100 miles out of Caldwell on the way to College of Idaho for a game the next day. The only thing Sampson's traveling party could see was snow-covered mountains. There were no lights or structures.

"This was the road trip from hell, but also the greatest road trip I have ever been on," Sampson said. "We don't get into our hotel until six a.m. the day of the game after leaving at four o'clock in the afternoon the day before. We get stranded for four and a half hours on the road when the bus broke down. My assistant coach and manager took off walking in the snow. There was no heat in the bus. It was twenty below zero. It was about midnight or one o'clock in the morning when they found a bar."

The entire party jumped out of the bus and started walking to the bar while a wrecker service came out to fix the bus. Sampson's team ate potato chips and drank Mountain Dew in the bar. Then about four o'clock in the morning the team trudged back to the repaired bus.

The Orediggers finally arrived at the hotel a couple of hours later. There was no walk-through for the game later in the day against College of Idaho, which had a fifty-six-game home-court winning streak.

"I remember saying if we played good we could lose all three games on this road trip," Sampson remembers. "If we somehow could keep this game close. . . . Before the shot clock, my buzz words were compete and patience. We had to outcompete them on the defensive end and outpatient them on the offensive end. And I had our kids convinced.

"My analogy for that College of Idaho game was the Revolutionary War. I wanted them to think about how the British fought. They were called the Redcoats. They had wave after wave of men. The first row would bend down and they would fire. The line behind them would fire. And then they would leave. And another line would fire. They were better than us. They outnumbered us. I wanted our players to think how the Indians and the settlers had to fight. They had to get behind every rock and every tree. They had bows and arrows and muskets. I said fellows we're not the British. We are the settlers and the Indians. We have to hide behind rocks and get in the grass, jump out of the water, and hide in trees. That's the only way we can win. That's who we are. That's our identity. I got our kids to buy into that."

It was an us against them mentality. He convinced the Orediggers the other squad was eating steak and baked potatoes and had all the comforts. And his team was eating toast and hamburgers. Montana Tech won that game, 64-63, in a huge upset. Guard Mark Owen, now the school's head coach, was a star guard on that College of Idaho team. He was drafted later by the Portland Trail Blazers.

"Mark was a little kid from Ohio," said Marty Holly, the College of Idaho coach at the time. "And he turned out to be a great player. They held him down. They had a tough guy who did a great job of defending Mark. They were so well prepared for us. We were a very good shooting team. But we didn't put the ball on the floor very well and didn't get to the basket. They put such pressure on the ball, they took away our shooting. He really outcoached me. Having won fifty-six in a row, we thought we would win every game.

"He was one of the few guys I feared. I was a young, arrogant coach and thought I would beat everybody. But I feared him. He can really inspire his team. His teams had no fear of us. I was wary of playing him. His kids play as hard or harder than you do. And when his kids are as prepared or better prepared than your kids, that's a lethal combination for a coach.

"I think Kelvin night in and night out did a better job mentally, physically, and emotionally getting his team ready to play. Some teams are not emotionally ready to play. His kids were mentally tougher. He exudes that toughness. That is something you have or you don't. A lot of guys are good at Xs and Os, but their teams do not play tough. He has the whole package."

The next night, Montana Tech played Northwest Nazarene in nearby Nampa, Idaho. The bus had been fixed.

"We had just beaten one of the top teams in the district on the road by one," Sampson said. "We were playing Northwest Nazarene in their homecoming. Who do you schedule in your homecoming? OK. That became my battle cry. We are not anybody's homecoming bait. They scheduled us because they think we are an easy win. Could a team that just beat College of Idaho on the road be an easy win? I am twenty-six years old and I am in their face. We are not anybody's homecoming game."

Sampson's team was tired. And once again they faced a packed house of more than 5,000 people and another strong team. The game was tight the entire way. The Orediggers trailed at half time, and the score was in the forties, which was bad for Montana Tech, which was less talented and liked a slower pace. It was 68-68 at end of regulation. But Montana Tech won game two on the road trip, 73-72 in overtime.

"It was kind of like winning on the road at Oklahoma State on Senior Night," Sampson said. "The quiet was deafening because we were so loud. There are fifteen people from Montana Tech in that gym. We don't have fans yet. Four people from Montana Tech were basketball fans. The fans from Montana Tech are engineering people."

With two upsets in two days, Sampson said he wasn't going to celebrate. He knew Montana Tech was one game away from a sweep the next day. But it was a two p.m. game. And the Orediggers had to travel 230 miles on their rickety bus to LeGrande, Oregon, to play Eastern Oregon. The Orediggers arrived in their hotel rooms at three a.m.

"Nobody would come to Butte to play us, even though we were no good," Sampson said. "And it was hard to get to nonconference games."

The game on Sunday against Eastern Oregon University went three overtimes, and Montana Tech won, 78-75, again to go 3-0. There were about fifty people in the gym. There was a ten-and-a-half-hour ride back to Butte. And Sampson remembers when he watched his players study on the bus. That was the first time he felt like a college basketball coach. Others already knew he was a great one in the making.

"Kelvin is always a guy who has gotten his players to play extremely hard, extremely physical, controlled the tempo and managed the game well," Aggers said. "I learned a great deal in those areas from him. You knew going into the game it would be forty minutes of war. It was so much fun."

College of Great Falls won the Frontier League regular-season championship that year, but Montana Tech finished with a 22-9 overall record and third place in the league with a 10-5 mark.

And Montana Tech won the league tournament championship by winning at the College of Great Falls.

The Orediggers received extra motivation for the latter game when they arrived at the gym and balloons already were in a net above the floor ready to drop after Great Falls' expected victory. A hint of College of Idaho's cockiness was detected by Sampson earlier in the day.

"I love having causes," Sampson said. "At the hotel that day, we saw on one of the message boards they had reserved a room for CGF (College of Great Falls) victory party at 9:30 p.m. I got our guys out of their rooms. And I brought them downstairs and showed them that. You could tell motivation was high. There was a lot of purpose.

"Every year we led the league in free-throw shooting. That was our deal. If we ever got a lead on you at the six-minute mark on the road, we were probably going to make you foul us. And this got to be a possession game. Montana Tech was hard to play in a possession game. We didn't turn it over. And we could make free throws. Our shot selection was really good. You could tell we were frustrating them. Their shots came a little quicker."

The Orediggers won their first-round NAIA district game, pummeling Jamestown College, North Dakota, and then played Northern State (South Dakota) in the NAIA district championship game in Aberdeen, South Dakota, at the Corn Palace. Sampson was twenty-six years old and competing against the opposing coach, Bob Wachs. Wachs was sixty-six years old.

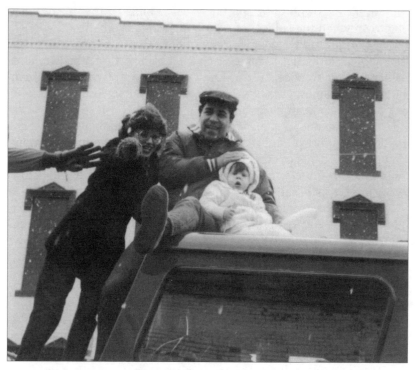

Kelvin, Karen, and little Lauren celebrate Frontier League Tournament title in 1983.

"We were one game away from Kansas City and the national tournament," Sampson said. "You sit back and you are amazed at how far you have come," Sampson said. "We lost to Northern State one game shy of making the national tournament. I had to sign nine guys in one year; I had had to go and get a brand new team because the year before we had ended with four guys on scholarship (1980-81).

"I don't really think a team can be truly your team until you walk in that locker room and every kid is there because you recruited him and he wanted you to be his coach. But academics had to be part of our mission. You had to have kids who were motivated in the classroom and wanted to get a degree or they would not make it at Montana Tech."

After that 1982-83 season, there was a buzz around the old mining town when the subject of Montana Tech basketball came up.

"More and more people were coming to our games," Sampson said. "I was a regular speaker at civic clubs. I started a booster club, which I talked to once a week. And I was doing motivational talks for energy companies. I was having so much fun now. And I was planning two years ahead in recruiting.

"There was not a game we didn't think we could win. But we still had to play most of our nonconference games on the road. Now, we couldn't get teams to come to Butte for a different reason. They not only didn't want to travel nine to ten hours to get there, they didn't want to play us because we were pretty good."

Sampson was charming the community and winning. The city had a parade for Sampson after the team won the Frontier League Tournament championship, which was custom in the Irish town laced with pubs.

"What they always gave you was fire truck rides," Sampson said. "If you won the championship, you got to get on the fire truck and they had a parade in your honor. It is a big deal. This was a town of 30,000 to 35,000 people at the time. They would come out of their businesses. They would have bands on either side."

"He brought his personality," said Vic Burt, Montana Tech's director of fiscal affairs. "He was a dynamic personality. He brought a lot to the game. He was very dedicated. He got the booster thing going after the games. The little old ladies thought he was God. He had quite a following among the little old ladies."

Montana Tech fans had been longsuffering, and they were enjoying winning. Before the team had started his string of winning seasons, the program had won just seventeen games in the previous three seasons.

To resurrect Montana State's program from the dead, Sampson had recruited a bunch of gym rats, who were good students, and molded them into a team. And he started laying the blueprints for future teams at Washington State and at Oklahoma.

He wasn't easy on the players.

"He was a fanatic on conditioning," Seaman said. "We ran, sprinted, did road work, and went to the football stadium and ran the steps. Kelvin could build a player. At the Division I level, they recruit talent. They don't build talent like Kelvin did with us."

Sampson said he had to develop a stern coaching approach early in his career because of his background.

"When I look at my background, coming from Pembroke vs. the guys who coached under Mike Krzyzewski, like Mike Brey, Tommy Amaker, Quin Snyder, they have day-to-day experience being a full-time assistant," Sampson said. "They saw up close and personal how to handle almost any situation. Roy Williams had that with Dean Smith when he was at North Carolina. Look at anybody's tree. I never had that tree. I was kind of a lone wolf. I learned everything on the fly.

"I was a grad assistant. I didn't get to go on the road and recruit. I got to watch Jud in practice. I wasn't privy to the intimate details of handling adversity. And being twenty-three to twenty-four years old at Michigan State, I am not sure I would have known if I had seen it. I didn't have a pulse on it.

"I think not having that, it even drove me harder. I have always coached out of fear. That caused me to want to make our kids touch every line, not ever miss a jump rope turn, having conditioning at six in the morning. The fear to me was a positive fear. I had to work harder because I might be missing something."

McClafferty remembers running up those Montana hills in minus thirty-degree weather, jumping rope in English Comp, jumping benches on trips in the bus, and sliding around with bricks in his hands in pregame meals.

If players missed dunks, they ran the line-to-line drills. They did the bench jump (leaping back and forth over a bench for one minute). And then there was the tip drill in which players had to keep the ball alive on the backboard by racing from one basket to the other for their spot in the tip line.

"He would have those kids run those hills," Carle said. "Butte was a mile high, and he would calculate how fast those kids should run."

"But he didn't just come out shouting orders," Seaman said. "He led by example. There wasn't one thing he would ask us to do that he wouldn't get down and do himself. That is the best teacher—by example."

And the players at Montana Tech he recruited basically took to Sampson's tough hand.

"Anytime we had a free minute we would go to the gym," Seaman said. "Many times the lights would be off. And we would call him up and ask to turn them on and the heat on. Sometimes when we would practice in the morning on the weekends, you could see your breath. I am not talking the forties and fifties, I am talking the thirties."

On his fortieth birthday in 1995, Sampson received this letter from a former Montana Tech player:

"One of the things, I remember about you...is that you soaked every ounce of ability I had out of me and you made me a better player," wrote Joe Puckett, a 5-foot-10 guard from Peerless, Montana. "I was fortunate that you like players who play with heart, because some coaches don't care about your heart, they care about your physical ability. You knew exactly what you needed to do to get me to play hard and you did it. Thank you for making me a better player and for teaching me discipline."

During his third season in Butte, Sampson faced one of his toughest disciplinary decisions.

Montana Tech was getting ready to travel to Mary College (North Dakota) for a tournament. But there was one last practice before the team left on the long trip. During pre-practice stretching Sampson always has talked to his team about what he hopes to accomplish during the day's practice.

"All of a sudden I smelled alcohol," Sampson remembers. "I didn't want to smell it. When it is your worst player, it is an easy decision. When it is your best player, it becomes a more difficult decision. Because if you smell it, the other players smell it. And I am a disciplinarian."

Sampson sent two players to each of the six baskets to shoot free throws. He would find out who the offenders were. He went and stood around each basket as they shot free throws. "Then I look at my best player, the hardest player on that team to guard, first team All-District was Cevin Johnson. He was from Saginaw, Michigan, and another kid on that team, his friend, was Glenn Anderson, a kid we would use off the bench. I was hoping it was Glenn, not Cevin. A lot of times players fail because they can't handle successes."

Both of them had been drinking. Sampson went from being sick to his stomach to getting mad. He believed the act was a betrayal to the team.

"Cevin was gregarious, a great personality," Sampson said "He was a monster inside. He probably could have run for mayor in Butte. Everybody loved him. But I was brought up in a house that had no alcohol. Pembroke was a dry county. So alcohol to me was taboo. You certainly didn't do it on the basketball team when one of the rules was no alcohol. That was early in my career. As the years have gone on, I have learned you don't want to have rules you don't want to enforce. But that was a rule then."

Butte was a big drinking community. It was nothing for kids to drink beer in the frontier town, let alone Sampson's players. Within walking distance of the campus there were several bars. Carle remembers one famous Butte bar in particular, the M&M Bar and Grill. "It's a place that had great food," Carle said. "But you would go in there, and some of the people you would see there would be passed out in their food."

Sampson made both players get on the bus and go to the games, but neither would play. The fuming Sampson didn't speak to anybody. And the rickety bus cranked up and drove from Butte to Billings to stay overnight on the way to North Dakota. Sampson was so mad, the team didn't stop to eat. He gathered the team in a cramped room at the Motel 6.

"I told the team we have a problem with loyalty, discipline, sincerity, and caring," Sampson said. He had Cevin and Glenn tell the team what they did. They said they each had two beers. Sampson believed it was more like three or four apiece.

"I said, 'Do you realize how important these two games are?' All of sudden we have come from nowhere to getting votes in the NAIA poll. Back then Dennis Rodman was at Southwestern Oklahoma and Terry Porter was at Wisconsin-Stevens Point. This was when the NAIA was strong."

Sampson suspended Cevin and Glenn for both games and made them sit beside him on the bench and keep statistics. Montana Tech won the tournament. A 6-foot-7 freshman Brian Vaughns stepped up and became a star. When Sampson left Montana Tech to become an assistant coach at Washington State, Vaughns transferred to Cal-Santa Barbara and played for Jerry Pimm. Vaughns would later be a fourth-round draft pick by the Milwaukee Bucks.

That Montana Tech team eventually won both the Frontier League 1984 regular-season and tournament championships. And in the first round of the NAIA district playoffs, Montana Tech beat Valley City State (North Dakota) before falling again to Northern State in the district final for the right to go to Kansas City.

Sampson already had developed a highly intense courtside manner, even as a young coach. He started his tradition of first taking off his coat, then his tie. He hit one of his players in the head one night with his coat when he threw it down on the bench. And in one game in Calgary, Sampson's sports coat somehow wound up in the stands. Fans tore it up and stole $5 out of one of the pockets.

"I remember playing against him in Butte," former College of Idaho coach Marty Holly said. "We had a real good team. I don't know if it was a planned coaching move or not. We were up by one point with ten seconds to go. And they were going for a last-second shot to win. We stole it and were going the other way to go up by three. He accosted the official, who instinctively gave him a technical."

College of Idaho's lay-up was wiped out because the ball was dead. And College of Idaho missed the one free throw for the technical. Montana Tech stole the ball on the bounds pass and scored at the buzzer to beat College of Idaho by one.

"It was an incredible game," Holly said. "That was the only way for them to win the game. There was no three-point shot then. It was a brilliant move. But I didn't feel that way at the time."

Sampson basically had his players buying into his teachings, and it was showing up on the court. In two seasons Montana Tech had put together back-to-back twenty-two-victory seasons.

"We knew how to win," Sampson said. "We had that team convinced we were going to win by not giving up easy baskets in transition. If somebody goes for an easy basket, club the hell out of him. If it is a breakaway, you go get them. You don't hurt them. You don't do anything intentional. But you send a message they are not going to get any easy baskets.

"That translates to your half-court defense. You start contesting every shot. You start taking pride in putting your butt in somebody's lap when a shot is taken. That way they don't get offensive rebounds. If they make a basket it is going to be with a hand in their face and off a great play. And in reality, how many teams are good enough to beat you that way? Teams will beat you because they will out-tough you. Well, we were not going to get out-toughed. We were the settlers and the Indians behind the rocks. Because we wanted to win the war, we were going to fight longer and harder. That was Montana Tech."

Sampson also was developing roles on the team. One of his first recruits was Kevin Hennessy, a 6-foot-5 forward from Cypress, California. Sampson would bring Hennessy into his office and coach him on being the team's Mr. Enthusiasm. Said Hennessy: "I had four of the greatest years of my life playing for [Coach Sampson]. If I had a chance to do it again, I would not change a thing."

"We'd be on the road and have a big lead," Sampson said. "And he'd be on the bench. He was from California. This kid was a little bit eccentric. He would stand up and start clapping and yelling, 'D-E-F-ense,' clap, clap, 'D-E-F-ense' and pretty soon he would have everybody on the bench doing it. They are stomping their feet in unison. And Kevin was a big, tough guy. He and Steve Seamen got into a fight one day, and that's when I developed a philosophy of never breaking up a fight. Hennessy stayed four years with me."

In the meantime, Sampson was still communicating closely with his father, who actually kept up with Sampson's players through these late night conversations. And they were late because of the two-hour time difference between Montana and North Carolina.

"I looked at him sometimes and wished my father, who was a coach, had been alive and I could have included him in my successes along the way, the way Kelvin included his father," said Kelvin's friend Chicago Bull's coach Tim Floyd, whose father died when he was nineteen. "I think that is special."

"I always call my father after every game," Sampson said. "In those days I would have to stop alongside the road at a phone booth. He knew all of our players, and he had never seen them. He always asked me about certain guys. He would figure out who our keys were.

"How did Terran play?" Mr. Ned would ask about a guard who played for Sampson for two seasons at Montana Tech.

"Terran Carter was our point guard from Texas," Sampson said. "And he was a little bit militant. He didn't handle authority well early because he didn't trust me. Terran had to warm up to me. He didn't want to be in Butte. I didn't recruit him until the first of August. We were the only offer he had. But I thought if I can get him to trust me and believe we care about him, people will have trouble with his quickness. Joe Puckett was the ultimate basketball player. I am not sure Joe could touch the rim. But if I told Joe to run through a brick wall, all he would say is, 'Coach, can I get a running start?'"

Despite the successes on the floor, Montana Tech was still traveling by bus and getting by on a skimpy budget. Sampson ran sort of a one-man show as did other coaches in the Frontier League. But that only tended to toughen up Sampson and prepare him for when he did get a job on the Division I level.

"You were always driving a long ways," Aggers said of the van and bus trips. "You also were washing the uniforms, doing the stats, raising the money, running the booster club, and recruiting. You were doing scouting yourself. A lot of nights scouting you might drive for hours, go through a drive-thru at McDonald's, go to the game, and then go back home at 9:30. A lot of younger coaches don't understand that or appreciate in recruiting you might be sleeping in the backseat of your car and staying with friends. Neither Kelvin nor I were born with a silver spoon in our mouths."

Carle added: "Kelvin has paid his dues to get where he is today. He knows what it is to take a 500-mile bus trip and stay in motels that are not very nice. But one thing he always said, 'If it doesn't kill you, it will make you better.' He already had such a great attitude about everything. He has the ability as a coach to make people feel great and bring out the most in them."

To that end, Sampson would fight for everything he could get for his team. He was at his best bartering for meals for his team and trying to get room discounts on the road.

Sampson always roomed with an assistant coach. He got seven rooms for fifteen people. And in one room there had to be three people. Three of the lesser players would be in a room. The team would often stay at Motel 6.

"Let me just say this: every hotel we stayed at the door opened outside," Sampson said. "We didn't have any inside doors."

And there was an art for negotiating meals as an NAIA coach.

His business manager, called the bursar, would give Sampson $11 meal money per day for each player. The players would get $3 for breakfast and $3 for lunch. One of the other meals had to be Montana Tech's pregame meal. The big restaurant Montana Tech could afford in those days was Sirloin Stockade. Sampson had a spiel he went through to get his team a steak dinner at a reduced price.

"Hey, I am the basketball coach at Montana Tech, in town to play a game tonight," Sampson would tell the manager of the steak house. "I have fifteen people in my party. I have eleven players, one assistant coach, myself, a trainer, and a manager. And I have $5 for each kid. So what can you give me for each player?

"Not much," the manager would say.

"Hmm," Sampson said, noting that negotiations had begun. "Is there any way we can get a 10-ounce rib eye, a baked potato, a roll, and a salad if I bring in fifteen people?"

"No, I just can't do that," the manager said.

"Well, how much would it cost?" Sampson asked.

"I can't do that for less than $6," he said.

Sampson wanted his players to have a steak for their pregame meal. It would be the only decent meal they had all day. And a nice meal would make it seem like a big-time basketball program to the players.

"I say I have the $5, what if we take away the drink and have water?" Sampson asked. "Is there any way?"

I wasn't too proud to beg. I wanted our kids to have a steak. Sometimes I had to go to an 8-ounce steak. Sometimes we had to get a cubed steak or chopped steak. But my deal was a 10-ounce rib eye and more often than not I got it for $5. That gave them $3 for meals on either side.

"A little later I had $6 for the pregame meal. When I had $6 to work with, I felt like we could get a T-bone."

By the time Sampson reached his final season at Montana Tech in 1984-85, the Orediggers were packing their 1,500-seat on-campus gym, getting big crowds downtown at the Civic Center, and had replaced College of Great Falls as the top team in the Frontier League. Beat writers on the local paper were following the team. And four-year-old Lauren was the queen of the home games when she would arrive in a pink party dress with white tights.

"This was her party," Karen said. "Fans would baby-sit next to the stands during the games while Kelvin coached."

Karen also was very involved in the program. She would tutor players and make them feel they were part of a family atmosphere despite the fact some of them were in culture shock. Players from New Hampshire, New York, New Jersey, and California were introduced to the Wild West.

"She was tremendously active in support of everything he did," Seaman said. "She tried to get help for the program from professors' wives at the college. From what little I know of Karen, I honestly don't think he would be half of what he is without her. She was his emotional heartbeat."

The bottom line, in four short years Montana Tech had gone from the outhouse to the penthouse. A last-place team in the Frontier League was now a first-place team.

"Everybody was gunning for us," Sampson said. "We had the bull's-eye on our back. I told our players there was a responsibility to uphold your expectations of yourself. We are supposed to be good. We played off that. Now I was starting to be more demanding of administration. And I wanted a new wood floor. We played on a polyurethane floor that had cracks in it the size of your finger. I was afraid I was going to lose some kids in transition if they fell into those holes. So I went to Vic Burt, our vice president.

"I said, 'Vic, we have to have a wood floor.' And Vic loved to play basketball. He was an old Montana boy who loved basketball. I think that is one of the reasons we hit it off so well. I think he appreciated how we built the program from the ground up. We gave him something to cheer for. If it weren't for Vic, I wouldn't have been there. He is the one who took me from $1,100 to the full-time job. I had such admiration for him and his wife, Peggy. But when we started winning, I said, 'Vic we can do better. We need a new wood floor.' I never saw it. They had started construction of that floor when I left and went to Washington State."

During Sampson's final season, the Orediggers once again would get a fire truck ride. Montana swept the league's regular-season and post-season titles and finished the season with a 22-9 record.

"My last year there were about three teams in our league all about the same," Sampson said. "One of them was Rocky Mountain College coached by Mark Adams. We beat Rocky Mountain three times and played them a fourth time in the district championship at Montana Tech. They had a seven-footer who got drafted by the Utah Jazz—Dale Breeding. They beat us in the district final. This one we should have won. We were the best team. And this one stayed with you. That was the last game I ever coached there. We had all five starters back for the next year. Our program was here to stay. It was getting better. For the first time we were going to have more home games than road games."

And the new floor would be in place as well. Vic Burt would lament to Kelvin: "You never did get to play on the $80,000 floor we put down in there for you."

Burt added: "A lot of us would like to take credit. But his success was basically his own doing. We were just happy he stopped by our place for four years."

In his final three seasons at Montana Tech, Sampson compiled a 66-25 overall record and was 33-12 in Frontier League games. That was after his first team finished 7-20 and 1-14 in the league.

"How do I go back over the years working with an individual who took over a program that had been given a self-induced death penalty of player loss and departure as well as coaching dismissal, and brought it to the pinnacle of success?" asked Montana Tech trainer Petritz.

People in the Montana region were starting to take a little notice of this young coach who had dusted off the Montana Tech program and lifted it off the mat. But it wasn't like North Carolina coach Dean Smith was calling to ask him to join the Tar Heel staff.

"I was twenty-seven and I was starting to get feelers for jobs," Sampson said. "I got a call from Idaho State. I called Jud. Jud has a way of putting things in perspective real quick."

"I don't think you can get that job," Heathcote told Sampson.

"Why?" Sampson asked.

"You are at an NAIA school. Division I schools hardly ever hire NAIA coaches," Heathcote said. "Outside of Butte and your conference, no one cares what you have done at Montana Tech."

Sampson said he didn't take that as cruel or negative, but just as fact.

"In the NAIA you are the king of your community, your area, but outside of that, it is not as important as you think it is," Sampson said. "And the company answer Idaho State gave me was I was too young. They didn't want to hire a coach as young as I was, even with what I had accomplished, what the program had accomplished at Montana Tech. Anybody they hired would have been proud about what we had done at Montana Tech. That was not easy. I was thinking I could go coach anywhere now."

Then the call came from Len Stevens at Washington State.

"The year when I took over the Montana Tech program during mid-season, our first road trip was to Western Washington," Sampson said. "We played Western Washington, Saint Martin's College in Lacey, Washington, and then Whitworth College. And when we played Saint Martin's, the head coach was Len Stevens. Then the next year he left and became George Raveling's assistant at Washington State. That's how I got to know Len.

"Len said he was looking for a minority assistant and had called around and gotten my name. I had never thought about that. I had a hard time leaving Montana Tech. I was making $16,500 a year. The guy I was replacing was Stu Jackson. He had gone to Providence as

Rick Pitino's assistant. I called Jud. And remember, Jud is good at asking questions."

"Do you want to be a head coach in Division I?" Heathcote asked. Sampson: "Yes."

Heathcote told Sampson if he was going to be head coach in Division I, he should be in Division I.

"That was twice he had told me that. And I heard him loud and clear this time."

Heathcote said recently: "Sometimes they live and die there [NAIA schools] and they can't get out of there."

Stevens sent a plane to fly Karen and Kelvin from Butte to Pullman. Karen was eight months pregnant with Kellen in the spring of 1985.

"I thought this is big time, a plane!" Sampson said. "But the plane they sent, I think, during the week they rented out to spray weeds. This was scary. The guy who flew the plane had the worst emphysema you'd ever see. The throttle on the airplane, it was like he was priming a pump to get the propeller to go. He'd wheeze every time he would push it. I was scared to death. The weather was bad in Butte. I was so disappointed in the plane. I wanted it to be a bigger plane. There are four seats and there is only one pilot. And this guy is about sixty-five years old. My first thought is what happens if something happens to him. The wings start to ice and all of sudden he is starting to take the plane lower."

"Why are we getting so low?" Sampson yelled above the roar of the propellers.

"What's that?" Chick Lange, the pilot, yelled to the backseat.

"Why are we getting so low?" Sampson repeated.

"If we don't get this ice off the wings, we are going to have an emergency landing. And I am looking to see if I can find an open highway."

"This is not like the bus tearing up; I can deal with the bus."

Sampson and Karen finally got to Pullman. They went to lunch with Stevens. When they returned to the basketball offices, the first person Sampson saw was PGA Tour pro Fred Couples, who is from Seattle. Sampson was impressed. He started talking to the other assistants, including Prescott Smith, who ended up being his roommate on road trips.

Sampson took the job in June. It would be Len Stevens' third year at the school.

"That team had a lot of individual talent, but it just didn't click," Sampson said. "Len Stevens was a good basketball coach. We were competitive. But I just felt I wanted to go back and coach NAIA. I wanted to be a head coach. I would rather be a head coach than an assistant in Division I. You are cut out for certain things. And I was never cut out to be an assistant. I don't think I did a good job as an assistant coach. My thought process was way too much like a head coach. I wasn't happy."

Sampson had a chance to move during the 1985-86 season at Washington State. Alaska-Anchorage, an NCAA Division II school, called and offered him the head job there. The athletic director at Alaska-Anchorage had previously been athletic director at Montana Tech. An excited Sampson went home to tell Karen the news.

"I followed you from Pembroke to Michigan," Karen said. "Michigan to Montana and Montana to Washington. I am not going any further west. If we move again, we are going that way [east]. We are going back toward North Carolina."

At twenty-eight, Kelvin just wanted to be a head coach. And he looked at Alaska-Anchorage as a step up from Montana Tech. But he turned down the offer, saying it was bad timing and he had made a commitment to Stevens. And he suffered through two losing seasons as an assistant coach. Sampson's first season in Pullman, the Cougars finished 15-16 overall.

"We were up and down that year," Sampson said. "We could just as easily have won eighteen to nineteen games. The following year was a tough year. There were some personnel decisions. But Len was the head coach, and he did things he believed were best. I think it is tough to go from being a head coach to an assistant coach when you know you want to be a head coach. I was internalizing a lot of things then, but I was still very loyal to Len. Losing got to the players, and when you are losing, little things become big things. The Pacific 10 that season was tough. Kevin Johnson was at Cal. Reggie Miller was at UCLA, and Lute Olson was starting to turn around Arizona. When you are losing and you have immature kids, it is a bad combination."

Sampson remembers getting to head up practice before he became a head coach.

"Coach Stevens would get so upset sometimes, he'd go to the sidelines and let Coach Sampson take over the practice,"

Washington State guard David Sanders told *The Seattle Post-Intelligencer.* "Sampson took the whistle and players were at attention."

Even before the end of Stevens' fourth season in Pullman—all losing ones—alumni were calling for his head and players were revolting.

"I remember when I was coaching Montana Tech and Len was coaching Saint Martin's, I thought his teams were the best defensive teams I had coached against," Sampson said. "When he called me to be one of his assistants, that's one of the reasons I wanted to go. I said this would be a good opportunity to learn from a great defensive coach.

"But Lynn didn't coach at Washington State like he did at Saint Martin's. Some guys are cut out to be coaches at different levels. I think Lynn was much more effective at Saint Martin's than he was at Washington State, for whatever reasons. Being able to find the buttons to push. It is almost like an art being able to push kids to the limit, yet get them to chew and spit it out."

Sampson's second season as Stevens' assistant was even worse on the floor. The Cougars finished 10-18 overall, ending with a 76-60 loss to Arizona State in the first Pac-10 Tournament in Los Angeles.

"Len Stevens was a great teacher," said Prescott Smith, a Stevens' assistant at Washington State and now the head coach at Cal State-Chico. "I think at times, if he had a fault, he tried to do too many things. But I don't know if I have been around a better pure teacher. He could really be something when he wanted to teach. He was really exceptional.

"Kelvin and I had a good time together. Anytime you spend as much time around someone recruiting, scouting, and all that kind of stuff, you develop a unique relationship. We had a lot of laughs together and solved all the world's problems during those times and, I am sure, made the world safe for democracy."

Even then Smith saw Sampson as a great communicator with the Washington State players.

"He [Sampson] is really an outstanding communicator," Smith said. "When he wants somebody to understand something, he has the ability to convey the meaning. There is absolutely no doubt what he has in mind. In coaching one of the problems is players become a little confused and don't know what you want them to do. He does an excellent job of making sure they know exactly what he wants them to do."

After the season, Sampson was looking for a job as were Stevens and Smith. Sampson was in Dallas recruiting when he got a call from Stevens about three one early April morning. He told Sampson he was going to be named the head basketball coach at Nevada-Reno in the Big Sky later that day. Stevens believed he could get into the NCAA Tournament easier from Reno than Washington State. Sampson told Stevens he understood.

"But I am in limbo now," Sampson said. "I didn't want to go to Reno, and I didn't necessarily want to stay at Washington State. Tom Davis was talking to me about an assistant's job at Iowa, and Steve Patterson was talking to me about an assistant's job at Arizona State. I didn't know if I wanted to go from being an assistant at a Pac-10 school to becoming one at a Big Sky school."

When Sampson got the call from Stevens, he actually was in a hotel room in Dallas. Next door was a Washington State recruit, Danny Hughes, a junior college guard. Sampson was bringing Hughes to Washington State for a scheduled visit. And Sampson still didn't know the next day if Stevens had been named the head coach at Reno, until he landed at the Spokane airport with Hughes.

Sampson went down to the baggage claim, and two TV crews were walking toward him. He knew Stevens had gotten the job. They were going to ask him about Stevens leaving. Sampson pulled Hughes aside and told him what had happened. Hughes still visited Washington State, but he wound up signing with TCU.

"When I got to the offices I had a message from Sam Smith, the president at Washington State," Sampson said. "A million things are racing through my mind. I am thinking about my family. And will this all work out? I still was thinking about Reno and assistants jobs at Iowa and Arizona State.

"But I had never thought about the head job at Washington State. This is where Jud Heathcote, a Washington State graduate, helped me out. He had been an assistant coach seven years at Washington State under Marv Harshman. Sam Smith had done some background checks on me. The three people he interviewed were Dan Fitzgerald, the head coach at Gonzaga; Tim Floyd, who was at Idaho; and me. The president's words were, 'Would you be interested in applying for this job,' and my response to him was, 'Would you have an interest in me applying for this job.' He said, 'We have an interest.' 'Then I have interest.' This was a Friday.

"On Sunday, I interviewed. I thought the way the program was they probably needed to go out and hire a bigger name. I didn't feel my chances were good."

But Sampson got the job.

CHAPTER 4

Taking Over at Washington State

The stress and strain of becoming Washington State's head coach took its toll on the thirty-one-year-old Kelvin Sampson. He slid over into the hot seat in early April. And for the first time Sampson would find out he was an asthmatic.

"By Monday night after he got the Washington State job, Kelvin was in the hospital," Karen remembers of April 12, 1987. "Stress and fatigue play a factor. Kelvin didn't have asthma as a kid. It was an adult onset."

Both Lauren and Kellen, Kelvin's then small children, already had been diagnosed as asthmatics. Lauren's asthma was induced by allergies; Kellen's, by viruses. And Kelvin's asthma, he would learn, was caused by the high levels of stress and fatigue associated with being a big-time college basketball coach.

And since Washington State had suffered through four straight losing seasons under Len Stevens, it wasn't a very good place for Sampson to de-stress himself. But he took his health news in stride and started his career as the youngest basketball coach in the Pac-10. His beginning base salary was $42,500—the lowest salary of any Pac-10 men's basketball coach.

"It was a total building process," said Donnie Newman, one of Sampson's assistants at Washington State. "He was a guy who was very serious, very intelligent, emotional, with pride and principle in what he does. He was a very dedicated individual. But I remember it was a program having a very long ways to go, trying to compete with Arizona, UCLA, and later Stanford. Gary Payton was at Oregon State then.

"Here's the Washington State Cougars trying to compete," Newman added. "I remember a lot of lonely nights on the road talking and a lot of long meetings on Sunday afternoons. We were trying to get those kids to Pullman and believe in what we were selling."

There was not a lot of Cougar tradition to sell.

"It's an outpost like Penn State or Fayetteville [Arkansas]," said Dennis DeYoung, one of the Cougars' most ardent basketball supporters during the Sampson era. "You have to be able to recruit the good athletes. It is a place that is not near a metropolitan area. Kelvin's greatest strength was he was like a father to all the recruits. He must have checked their grades and conduct on campus on a daily basis. If anybody was not going to class or embarrassing themselves or the program, he knew it...I had a daughter over there and he monitored her. I think he was somebody all of the players looked up to and feared for their life if they crossed him. And George Raveling was much the same way."

Prior to Sampson taking the job, only two coaches in Washington State history had taken the Cougars to the NCAA Tournament—George Raveling (1980, 1983) and Jack Friel (1941). And the Cougars' home court was named after the latter coach. Through the 2000-01 season, Washington State still had not won a Pac-10 title since 1941 when the Cougars finished second in the NCAA Tournament.

"It is one of the toughest jobs in America for a school in an elite conference," said Raveling, who coached in Pullman for eleven seasons and had seven winning seasons from 1973-83. "It is in a very isolated area. It is a rural community. It's a school that doesn't have a rich basketball tradition. And the state doesn't produce a lot of Division I prospects. And Seattle is a six-hour drive. What did I do for entertainment? I went out and watched the wheat grow. It was an area of wheat, barley, and soybeans.

"I recruited all over the country," Raveling added. "Somewhere in America there were twelve kids good enough for us to win. We needed to find those twelve kids and get them to come to Pullman."

Bud Withers, the well-respected writer for both the *Seattle Post-Intelligencer* and now the *Seattle Times*, is a Washington State graduate. So he knows the territory.

"You have just about everything stacked against you," Withers said. "For in-state recruits, Washington State had a better building for awhile, now Washington has equalized that and modernized its facilities. If Washington really wants a recruit, and Washington State is involved, the edge probably goes to Washington. So you automatically have a problem in state. Beyond in state you had the whole West Coast.... A Los Angeles kid wanted to go to UCLA, Arizona, Arizona State, and if he had good grades to Stanford or Cal."

Sampson, that first season in Pullman, also had the added chore of making sure the returning players saw him as the head coach, not as an assistant. At his first team meeting, he told the team to forget that assistant's tag. And he embarked on a preseason conditioning program that made Stevens' preseason drills seem like a country club.

Sampson had a 3.5-mile uphill running course in Pullman. It was Sampson's Camp Nightmare for unsuspecting freshmen.

"The biggest challenge for me was for them to see me as the head coach," Sampson said. "That's always difficult. The year before I was the supporting guy. I felt like I was prepared to be a head coach. A lot of people made a big deal about my age. I was only thirty-one, the youngest head coach in the Pac-10. I didn't see that as a detriment. I had been a head coach at maybe the toughest job in America at Montana Tech.

"Washington State was a tough job. But it was all relative. Look what I had to compare it to. Look at the road I had traveled to get there. I had already seen hard. My ultimate simplification of coaching is this. You take yours and get them ready to play. You let me take mine and let me get mine ready to go play. And now, let's go play and see who can win. I always felt that was my strength. I could get my kids to play. A lot of the mentality we had at Montana Tech, we brought to Washington State."

Sampson was hired by Washington State Athletic Director Dick Young, but before Sampson coached midway through his first season, Jim Livengood became the school's athletic director.

"That first year, 1987-88. I will never forget this," Livengood said. "We were playing a football game in December. This was Dennis Erickson's first year as our head football coach, and we were at the Tokyo Bowl. I heard that perhaps our best basketball player, Brian Quinnett, broke his foot. We go on and have a not bad year. I thought we might have been too good that first year."

Quinnett, a forward, had been the team's leading scorer the previous season under Stevens. And even with Quinnett, Washington State was picked to finish near the bottom of the Pac-10 in Sampson's inaugural campaign in the Palouse. There was little reason to think things would change. The coach may have changed, but the players remained the same. And Stevens' four Washington State teams had finished 10th, 8th, 5th (four-way tie), and 8th (two-way tie).

Sampson won his first game on November 27, 1987, as a Division I head coach, 68-46 over Eastern Washington at a tournament in Spokane. Then, in the second game of the tournament, Sampson faced Coach Tim Floyd and Idaho. The Vandals, whose school was located only nine miles away from Pullman in Moscow, Idaho, defeated Washington, 53-49, in the title game of the Northwest Classic.

"I think he was trying to hold the ball and nullify the great talent we had," Floyd said sheepishly of the low score.

"I had just finished my first year at Idaho when Kelvin got the job at Washington State," Floyd continued. "We felt like we were out on an island, not secure within who we were as coaches in the profession at that time. We spent a lot of time together. We'd go to dinner and have a beer. Our families would have dinner together. And we would talk basketball. We developed a bond as a result of those days.

"Our campuses were nine miles apart. We basically shopped in the same grocery store and got our hair cut in the same places because there were not a lot of options. There were not a lot of options on players in that part of the world, either. And there were an awful lot of colleges and universities in between Moscow and Pullman; we wound up getting players in Alabama, Louisiana, Oklahoma, and Texas."

And more often than not, Washington State and Idaho would be recruiting the same players.

"It always bothered me that he would beat us in recruiting," Floyd said with a laugh. Floyd and Sampson had a close relationship because their coaching styles were quite similar. They both were defensive-minded coaches.

Later, during that 1987-88 season, Sampson's Cougars defeated Idaho, 56-43, in Pullman. Floyd and Sampson officially ended their Washington State-Idaho series, 1-1, because Floyd left before the next season to take the University of New Orleans head basketball coaching job. Years later the two coaches would renew the rivalry when they both landed in the old Big Eight.

But Sampson first had to make his mark in the Pac-10. He started fast during the conference season, when the Cougars swept a three-game road trip to go 3-2 in league play. The Cougars won four more league games to finish with a 7-11 league record, good for sixth place.

"My first season at Washington State was the year we beat Stanford, Cal, and Washington on the road," Sampson said. "It was a tremendous road trip. They asked me if that was the best road trip of my career. And I said no, the trip to Idaho-Oregon when I was at Montana Tech was. But we played everybody tough that year. The team we couldn't beat was Arizona. We won at Arizona State, beat UCLA, and lost in double overtime to Oregon State and Gary Payton to end our season.

"We got so much better as the year progressed," Sampson said. "Todd Anderson was a success story that year, because he had very rarely gotten to play in his career before that season. He had low self-esteem and very little confidence."

Anderson, a senior center, wound up being the only Cougar who started every game that season. He averaged 11.9 points per game for a team that had to win at Arizona State, 70-66, the last game of the regular season to qualify for the Pac-10 Tournament.

"Then we played UCLA in the first round of the tournament and beat them 73-71," Sampson recalled. "That game was in Tucson. And I got back to my hotel room and I had two messages on my phone. Don Monson [at Oregon] and George Raveling [USC] had left them. They both said, 'You beat UCLA. They are going to fire Walt Hazzard. And UCLA is going to go out and hire somebody, and we will never beat them again.' They were calling to congratulate me. But they were right; UCLA fired Hazzard and hired Jim Harrick."

Even during that first year as head coach of the Cougars, Sampson already had begun to build a platform for winning seasons at Washington State. He determined he was going to use a three-guard offense and eventually run the 1-4 offense.

"The guy who influenced me the most was Ralph Miller at Oregon State," Sampson said. "I couldn't be like Arizona or like UCLA. But Oregon State was in Corvallis. We could be as good as them. And they were winning the league then. I can't remember one post player at Oregon State, but I remembered every one of their guards. And Ralph Miller ran the 1-4 offense. It was damnedest thing I had ever seen. I was completely fascinated with the 1-4 offense. When people today in this part of the country think about the 1-4 offense, they think about Oklahoma. It wasn't my idea. I stole it from Ralph Miller. I just modified it for us.

"Jud Heathcote was my mentor. He got me started. It was in my genes to coach, with my father. But in those years I was losing, I was searching for something that worked. Recruiting good players wasn't good enough. If that was the case, then why doesn't the team that has the best recruiting year every year win the national championship? It is having a plan, something strategic. How are we going to win this game?

"My feeling was three guards. I knew at Washington State we couldn't get great post players. If we did, we got projects and had to develop them. We could get good 6-foot-6, 6-foot-8, 6-foot-9 types who were athletic, who could run the offense. There are so many great players in this country who are 6-foot-5 and under. There are so very few who are 6-foot-6 and over. There's a list of about twenty schools who are going to get the bigger kids who can play. And Washington State is not one of them, unless one of those tall players grew up in my best friend's house or was from Pullman. And I didn't see any of those."

The 1-4 offense put a premium on having good wing players who could shoot well off the dribble and take passes from the forwards and slash to the basket for short jump shots or stay outside for three-pointers. With only average big men who could pass, a team could win consistently without having to have an overpowering low-post scoring presence.

Still a healthy Brian Quinnett returning was a plus. And Sampson had hopes of improving on the 13-16 overall record of 1987-88. Quinnett held up his end, leading all Washington State scorers with 18.4 points a game. But injuries wrecked Washington State's player rotation. Guard David Sanders and forward Neil Evans, two starters from Sampson's first team, were both hurt.

"That was a tough, long, long year," Newman said of Sampson's second season. "We were going to battle with bayonets, and they were shooting big-time bazookas at us. We were trying to do a lot of it with spirit, motivation, and mirrors. We had some very, very competitive games. Shots rimming out to beat UCLA there. We had some heartbreakers."

The season started on a bad note when Washington State lost to Gonzaga, 64-63. The Cougars dropped three Pac-10 games by one point on the way to a 10-19 season and 4-14 league record.

Washington State finished in eighth place ahead of only Oregon and last-place USC and won only one league road game all season at Arizona State.

In early January 1989, the day after Washington State dropped a 69-63 decision to Washington, Kelvin received a letter from his father, Mr. Ned. Years later he still keeps it tucked inside his desk at Lloyd Noble Arena in Norman.

Jan. 8, 1989

Hello, Kelvin,

I just wanted to write you a note of encouragement and tell you games like the Washington game will make you a better coach. I know your first two years in Montana were tough and made you tougher. Coaches who are coaches learn from their losses. And I know you are a coach. Kelvin, you can't lose unless you quit, so keep on keeping on. Work hard and good things will happen to you. You will get some big wins. Your mother is fine. We love you and pray for you each day. Tell Karen hello and give Lauren and Kellen some sugar for me.

Love,
Daddy

Sampson needed the encouragement. But there was some light beginning to shine through the dreary basketball clouds in Pullman. Sampson was about to land a guard, Bennie Seltzer, from Birmingham, Alabama. He would be the first in a series of standout guards who would make Washington State a force in the Pac-10.

"The first thing is you kind of doubt yourself as a coach," Sampson said of the two losing seasons. "What could I have done better? You don't realize this when you are young. This is a players' game. And our turnaround started with Bennie Seltzer. I could sell Bennie Seltzer on a dream."

Seltzer was talented and would develop into a tough player. As a four-year starter for Sampson, Seltzer would become one of the best three-point shooters in Pac-10 history and also demonstrate the strong will that became the trademark of Sampson's teams.

"I have two new teeth," Seltzer said years later in his OU assistant coach's office. "I went diving for a loose ball against Cal my junior year. I spit them out and went back playing.... Taking charges and diving for loose balls are the two most important things a kid can do for the program that require no talent."

Sampson looked at the 1989-90 season as a turnaround year. But it would be anything but that on the floor. While recruiting was going well, it didn't translate in the win-loss column during Seltzer's freshman season.

Bennie Seltzer, Kelvin's prized Cougar point guard. WSU SID file photo.

The season started innocently enough. Washington State won its first Pac-10 game on November 30 over USC, 68-67. But that would be Washington State's only league victory of the season (1-17). On December 29, Washington State stood 7-4 after beating Ohio by three points. The next night the Cougars dropped an 83-82 decision to Tennessee in the Volunteer Classic championship game in Knoxville, Tennessee. That began a string of nineteen straight losses, seventeen straight in regular-season league play, and then an 85-68 loss to USC in the first round of the Pac-10 Tournament.

"But there was never a doubt in my mind that he would not be a good, but a great coach," Livengood said. "There were three reasons. No. 1, he was a great human being. And I know that is not necessarily synonymous with being a good coach. No. 2, recruiting was getting better. And No. 3, I watched the Cougars practice after they had lost eight, nine, ten games in a row. And you wouldn't be able to tell they had lost nine or ten in row or had won nine or ten in row by the intensity and enthusiasm of the kids. He got those kids to play so hard during losing streaks."

Seltzer remembers a light moment during that season.

"After a hard practice, he came out in a hard hat and boots," Seltzer said. "He coached just as hard when we had lost seventeen or eighteen in a row as when we were 6-4. We just had to work harder and get better. When we won my sophomore year, we just had better players. We played the same exact style of basketball. In many of those twenty-two losses my freshman year we were right there. We were just not good enough to win those games. We could not get over the hump."

Sampson was going to ride Seltzer, win or lose, his freshman season. He had no choice. And there were some severe growing pains. During the losing streak in February, Seltzer was matched up against Oregon State's All-American guard Gary Payton, a senior that season. Payton would be drafted No. 2 in the first round of the 1990 NBA Draft by Seattle.

"I remember Gary Payton backing Bennie over toward me," Sampson said. "I was sitting on the bench. And Donnie Newman, my assistant, was chirping at Payton. Payton was dribbling in front of our bench. And Payton said, 'You better take this freshman off me. I am getting ready to kill his confidence.' Then he spun...Newman was talking smack to him. I said, 'Donnie don't get him mad. He is a handful even when he is not mad.'"

"It was funny, it all started at a shoot around," Newman said. "Gary Payton walked into the shoot around. I was talking to him in Seattle about this recently. He came in there and said, 'Hey, Coach Sampson, why are you shooting around and even bothering?' He messed with me and Kelvin. Kelvin said, 'All right, Gary, get out of here.' That night, Gary beat our brains out."

Oregon State won easily, 79-64. Washington State was on the way to a record-tying number of losses for a Pac-10 team during a league season.

"We didn't get many fans," Seltzer said. "I remember one game when we were going to tie for the most losses in the conference. And I remember a couple of fans came to the game with bags over their faces."

Sampson was trying to sell to Washington State fans, players, and media he knew how to fix the problem. It was tough as the losses mounted. Kelvin tried to look ahead.

"No matter how bad that season got, we had signed an outstanding class early," Sampson said. "We had a great mixture of junior college kids and high school kids. We had signed nine players. That's when I felt like we were on our way. I wanted to make sure our media, our players, and our fans knew that better days were ahead.

"In our last game of the season in the Pac-10 tournament we were ahead of USC 22-2 and lost by 17," Sampson said. "I remember when I went into the locker room after that game. We had lost all those games in a row. And Bennie Seltzer was a freshman. It had been a long year for him. He had had the mental strain and anguish of being a freshman. It was not the most ideal situation for him, especially that year with all the great guards in the Pac-10...Terrell Brandon [Oregon], Gary Payton [Oregon State]. But what I remember about that year is the effort those kids gave."

There was at least some comic relief from little three-year-old Kellen, the coach's son, after each loss that season.

"Oh well, lost again, where's the pizza?" Kellen would say in the home locker room.

Or, during one phone conversation Kelvin had with Kellen during a road trip: "Where are you, Daddy?" Kellen asked.

"I am in Corvallis trying to get these Cougars a win," Kelvin said.

"Well, you better do it there, because you haven't here," Kellen answered.

Sampson was convinced that would soon change. The 1990-91 season would be better because of the recruited class coming to Pullman in the fall.

Washington State had landed three of the top high school players in the state of Washington. Six-foot-eight Rob Corkrum had picked the Cougars over BYU and Washington. Sampson looked at that as a big recruiting coup. Sampson also signed David Vik, a 6-foot-11 center from Everett, one of the best players from the west side of the state, and 6-foot-6 guard Joey Warmenhoven from Grandview in the middle of the state. The other good catch was Eddie Hill, a high school guard from California.

Sampson also struck a vein of gold when he mined some of the best junior college talent out of Texas. Sampson signed four players there: guard Neil Derrick (Trinity Valley), forward Ken Critton

(Western Texas), guard Terrence Lewis (Howard College), and guard Tyrone Maxey (Tyler). Sampson signed Maxey late because he believed he needed another backup point guard.

"I felt like this was my team," Sampson said. "I knew how good Terrence Lewis was. And I knew Bennie's greatest improvement would come between his freshman and sophomore years. We went to the junior college ranks and got the best 6-4, 6-5 guard there. And that's how we came up with our system. We got the best guards we could and made sure that shooting was not an equal opportunity position."

Lewis, originally from Alabama, averaged more than 30 points a game in junior college. And he would be the perfect off guard complement to the point guard, Seltzer, who actually helped recruit Lewis.

"Bennie was a great, great recruiter and a great, great program guy," said Jason Rabedeaux, Sampson's Washington State assistant and later an aide at OU. "He and Terrence Lewis grew up together in Birmingham. Bennie could deal with white kids, black kids, Birmingham, Spokane, Seattle. It didn't matter. Bennie could deal with people. He was a pilgrim for Coach in that respect. Bennie was so good with recruits when we brought them on campus."

Lewis had signed with Pick Pitino at Providence. But after his freshman season he transferred to Howard College in Texas. The third guard in the starting lineup would be Derrick, another slasher-scorer type.

"We signed Dwight Stewart (a big man), but he didn't make his grades and he wound up going to South Plains and then later signed with Arkansas," Sampson said. "That was another kid I got real close to. He came close to making it. Another kid we had on was campus Oliver Miller, but he went to Arkansas. We knew we were on the right track. We knew we were going to get better. I was still counting on Bennie, this being his sophomore year and the fact he had been there through a losing streak. It was almost like Montana Tech all over again. I could see our future."

At a Junior College All-Star game in Texas that spring, Washington State was well represented.

"Bob Huggins from Cincinnati and all the coaches in the Southeastern Conference were there," Newman said. "They all had players represented in the game. And here is Washington State, which had four guys in the game. Everybody spoke about those guys. We were humping in recruiting. It was a lot of phone calls on the road, driving up and down, stopping in pouring rain because there was no cell phone back then."

There was one big unknown in the recruiting class.

Sampson was taking a chance on Derrick, a 6-foot-2 guard from Garland, Texas, a suburb of Dallas. He was one of four basketball-playing brothers. One of the Derrick brothers, John, had been shot to death in Oklahoma City in 1983 after a disagreement with two men in a motel parking lot. And another brother, Richard, was in and out of problems with the law. Neil Derrick averaged twenty-seven points, five rebounds, and four assists in a game for Trinity Valley his sophomore year. Texas A&M, TCU, Auburn, Cincinnati, and Arkansas-Little Rock were also trying to sign Derrick. And he would have had more suitors had it not been for his shaky past, which threatened also to end his potentially good college basketball career.

Derrick, whose father died when he was in ten, was in constant fights as he grew up. He didn't even play basketball his senior year of high school because he was kicked out of school for blowing up at school officials at the beginning of that year. He had been expelled for fighting the last day of his junior year but was reinstated with help from the NAACP, only to slide again.

In his last high school game, as a junior, Neil, a lefty, scored forty-two points in a 96-83 loss to Skyline, before he was kicked out of school. Derrick had to earn a high school equivalency diploma before going to Trinity Valley.

"You don't want to walk that road again," Neil Derrick told *The Dallas Morning News* the week he signed with Washington State.

Earlier, Sampson had gone to Neil's old Garland neighborhood and met with Neil's mother, Mary. He told her he wanted Neil to succeed and graduate from college. Sampson described Neil Derrick as a "poor man's Stacey Augmon" in reference to the UNLV star. Sampson liked the way Neil played defense. One question persisted: could Neil keep his life in order? Sampson and other recruiters wondered.

"He [Sampson] was very candid about taking a chance [on Derrick]," Livengood said. "I encouraged it every bit. What happened was good. It was a good chance to take. Kelvin can make a difference. That is one of his strengths. He made a difference in that young man's life."

"At that time I had so much confidence in my ability to rehabilitate kids," Sampson said. "All coaches think they are big-time psychologists. And at Washington State, I thought I had to take gambles. I could gamble on Neil because I knew the investment I would put in with Neil off the court. The most important thing coaches have is their reputation. And if a coach takes a bad kid, he can ruin your reputation. I had a tremendous support group of players around Neil. But I also told him that I had a permanent bus ticket in my desk for him."

Sampson believes everybody should be given more than one chance.

"The first time you have a problem, it may be an accident," Sampson said. "The second time it may be a coincidence. The third time it is a habit. You have a habit, I told Neil. But every kid deserves to get to three in terms of chances, as long as one of them is not a felony. It was a great gamble. He later came back and got his degree at Washington State after playing professionally. Your rewards don't always come when you have more points on the scoreboard."

"Neil was a guy who brought that edge to Washington State," Newman said. "Of all the guys we recruited, he was a competitor. He was borderline mean and nasty. He was a super athlete. Neil was so physical and so focused. He would just as soon hurt you as beat you. Neil raised the bar. He gave us energy. His competitiveness and Kelvin's matched. They were the same kind of fighters. That's when we started getting our own identity."

During the summer of 1989, Sampson had an opening for a graduate assistant coach on his staff. That's when Jason Rabedeaux, a former non-scholarship player at NCAA Division II Cal-Davis and an assistant coach at Division III North Adams State, applied for the spot on Sampson's staff at Washington State.

"To me Washington State was UCLA, it didn't matter," said Rabedeaux, who was twenty-two and hungry to coach on the Division I level.

Sampson asked Rabedeaux to work the Washington State basketball camp. Rabedeaux was already working a camp at Santa Barbara, California, on a Saturday afternoon. Sampson wanted him to be at Washington State the next afternoon for a coaches' meeting. Rabedeaux drove nearly nonstop from Santa Barbara to Pullman. He arrived at two p.m. Sampson was so impressed that someone would drive that far in such a short period of time, he hired Rabedeaux a few days later.

"I didn't know much about him," Rabedeaux. "But I knew what I was. And that was hustle all over the place. I was going to make a favorable impression. I would get there early. I would sweep the floor. I would stay after and sweep the floor. If he said, 'Get over here.' I would sprint to him.

"He sold us on work ethic. He is so big on want-to and try-to. 'Jason, this is what I expect from you, and what I expect from you is everything. You have to be the first one here in the morning and the last one to leave every day. You can't ever have a bad day. But this is a great opportunity for you.' It was like I had been named head coach at UCLA."

After getting the job, Rabedeaux went out to Wal-Mart and bought a little partition desk and set it up behind the door leading into the Washington State basketball offices. "Every morning when coach opened the door, I would be sitting right behind there, with a little stool," Rabedeaux said. "I had a little cubby hole there."

That was the beginning of Sampson's eleven-year association with Rabedeaux which ended when "Coach Rab" became the head coach at Texas-El Paso in September 1999.

With the enthusiastic Rabedeaux aboard and the new recruited class, Sampson was ready to post his first winning season in Pullman.

"In our fourth year, it was the first time I had ever felt pressure as a head coach because we had three straight losing seasons," Sampson said. "And I know Len chose to leave after he had had four straight losing seasons at Washington State. I was creeping up on the fourth year and really hadn't made a dent. But I felt good about recruiting. I was only thirty-five, so I didn't feel career pressure. But I thought we needed to win this year."

And Washington State did it with a gritty defense, the 1-4 offense, and players with well-defined roles.

"Kelvin sort of turned it around with junior college kids," Withers said. "That was to Kelvin's credit. They were not all-world students. But they were not bad-apple kids. They were rough-edged kids. They were not bandits. But they got things going. He recruited hardscrabble guys. I think he loved to get hard-nosed kids who would get down and battle. That's the way he came up as well."

At one point during the 1990-91 season Washington State was 16-8. But after a big 80-76 victory at Washington, the Cougars lost their last four games, twice to ranked UCLA teams and twice to good USC teams. Lewis, Derrick, and Seltzer combined to average more than forty points a game in the three-guard offense that season.

"We had talked about getting into post-season play," Sampson said. "I kind of thought we might get to the National Invitation Tournament (NIT), but we didn't. For the first time since I had been there as an assistant or head coach, we had a winning season, and the Pac-10 was extremely tough that season."

Four Pac-10 teams went to the NCAA Tournament. Five teams finished tied for fifth place with 8-10 records, including Sampson's Cougars. Oregon and California had the worst overall records at 13-15.

Sampson was named Pac-10 Conference Coach of the Year after taking Washington State to a 16-12 overall mark and a fifth-place finish in the Pac-10. It was Washington State's first winning season since 1982-83 when Raveling was head coach. That was an indication of the appreciation the media and other coaches had for the job he was doing.

Sampson had developed a fiery style on the sidelines, causing some of the other Pac-10 coaches to gawk at his in-game stripping routine. "I was always afraid you would keep tearing your clothes off until you were down to your skivvies," wrote Stanford coach Mike Montgomery on Sampson's fortieth birthday in 1995. "And once you hit forty, it is not a pretty sight."

"At the two-and-a-half-minute mark, seventeen and a half minutes left in the first half, Kelvin's coat was coming off," Livengood remembers. "There were some times the coat and the tie came off then. Now, he wears a collar and no tie, the mock turtleneck. Karen would say, 'We are paying good money for the ties; why are you taking them off and throwing them away?'"

His players' fire matched his fire, particularly the guards.

"Kelvin believed in playing the guards forty minutes," Newman said. "We could take away things teams did by pressuring full court. We kept three guards in there for forty minutes. Kelvin still has great guards."

One of those guards coming off the bench in the early 1990s was Dale Reed, who was the son of a high school basketball coach. Reed, from Wyoming, was one of the leading high school scorers in the country when he signed with Iowa in 1989, turning down an offer to go to Washington State among other schools. But he reconsidered and transferred to Washington State and sat out in Pullman during the 1990-91 season.

"As far as coaching he was very intense," Reed said. "He was hard on everybody. But there was a lot of responsibility on the point guards. He expected us to win. He taught us pressure man-to-man defense. And he made us very physical, which, on the West Coast was a little different. Our bread and butter was our aggressive scrappy defense. We would make our own breaks and make up for not having as much talent."

Sampson had also developed a way of recruiting players to Washington State, which only Raveling had been able to master.

"You had to get a read on people in recruiting," said Prescott Smith, who had been an assistant at Washington State when Sampson was an assistant under Len Stevens. "If you got involved with good players, were they a fit for Pullman and Washington State? There was a real kinship at Washington State...All the coaches had the same problems recruiting. We couldn't go out recruiting with the same approach as Arizona and UCLA had."

"One day I was talking to him. I said, 'Kelvin, you get kids to come in, and you don't have a lot to sell in the Pac-10,'" said his former Pembroke State coach Joe Gallagher. "He said, 'On the Sunday morning of a visit, I would sit them on the couch, and they say yea or nay; if they don't want to come we move on. I can tell. I say here are the cold, hard facts. Here's the situation. I have assistant coaches who can evaluate who we can get at Washington State.'"

Sampson added: "I would always take them [the recruits] to my house to our team room in the basement. It was a recruiting room. There was a wood-burning stove down there. And there was Washington State stuff plastered all over the wall. I wanted recruits to see how close knit we were. My family is a big part of our program."

The Sampsons had created a family atmosphere for the Washington State program as well. The team came to dinner on weekends during recruiting season. Karen also would prepare Thanksgiving and Christmas dinners for the players, especially those who were thousands of miles away from home.

"I hope when my kids go away, and if they can't make it home, someone would take care of them like that and not leave them alone," Karen said.

Washington State forward Mark Hendrickson counted those dinners and frequent film sessions at the Sampson house among his fondest memories. His mother remembers. "The thing Mark liked about Kelvin was he had a family unit, which he was so used to," said Barb Hendrickson. "Going to Kelvin's house to review films—they need to see a coach has a family."

"Karen Sampson is a lot like Bobbi Olson," Livengood said of the late Lute Olson's wife. "Kelvin and Karen made a great team. Kelvin would get out and do any type of club thing. He got his players out in the community. He was very supportive of other programs. At Washington State it was essential. It was amazing what he created there in a relatively short period of time. Karen is, and was, a huge part of that."

Karen, a former elementary school teacher, once helped tutor two Montana Tech players seven straight days so they could pass their exams and stay eligible. Kelvin once called her the "glue to everything we do off the court."

"I don't think every coach's wife is as involved as she is," DeYoung said. "Sometimes she knows more than he does or as much as he does. They are her children."

Sampson created an environment where the players he recruited could talk to him freely. The family unit. The father figure. He could be compassionate, yet stern.

"I get the feeling his players love him," said Chicago Bulls coach Tim Floyd. "And with as much as he asks, I think that makes him an incredible communicator."

"I have been around some really good ones," Livengood added. "And I have seen a lot of coaches and coaches practices. I don't know that anybody gets his kids to play harder. And this is not necessarily a day and age when everybody plays hard. He is hard on kids, in a positive way. As hard as he is, he is fair and they know that."

CHAPTER 5

The Soviet Union Experience

Sampson wanted to take the Cougars on a foreign trip during the summer of 1991 so they could bond. The upcoming 1991-92 season could be a big year for Washington State basketball. And a foreign trip could give the team that little extra edge.

Sampson didn't want the foreign trip to be a vacation. So he eliminated the thought of going to a comfortable country like Australia where his players could lie on the beaches and play volleyball. He wanted a boot camp. So, he lined up a seven-game tour of the Soviet Union.

"I wanted us to go where it would be a little bit tough," Sampson said. "I think when you are roughing it in a foreign country you do bond. The housing was poor and the food was poor. The only hot water we could get was at three or four in the morning. If you wanted a shower, that's when you took it. There weren't a lot of the conveniences, 7-Elevens, or drive-thrus.

"I didn't want it to be easy. It was important for us to grow and get tighter. I think when you go through adversity you have better respect for people on your right and left. They could complain all they wanted during the trip, but everyone around them was going through the same thing."

Washington State players packed candy bars, granola bars, and cans of soup and prepared for a seven-game war of attrition with their communist brethren. A Washington State instructor, who had been to the Soviet Union numerous times and was a big basketball fanatic, organized the trip.

"It turned out to be the trip from hell," said Sampson. "I have never had a worse experience. It was almost a life-changing experience. We talk about it now and laugh about it. But at the time, there was nothing funny about it. It wasn't good for an American team, a regular college team, to go over there and win. But that was what we did. When we were leaving, that is when the revolution came. The tanks were literally rolling up to the American Embassy as we were leaving."

In August 1991 the last of the vestiges of the hard-line Soviet Union Communist power were shattered when the coup against Boris Yeltsin failed. Communism was dead. And the Soviet Union would continue to break up into individual states.

The Washington State players and coaches were shocked at the poor conditions in the Soviet Union.

"We played good teams and good athletes," remembers assistant coach Jason Rabedeaux. "But outside of the military and their natural resources, it was really a third-world country. The facilities were terrible and the food was terrible. I remember eating tongue and having hot dogs and eggs for breakfast. Another thing I remember is that a lot of places we went to they didn't have any condiments like ketchup and mustard. The players wanted to drown out the taste of the food. So we went to this pizza place where they did have condiments, and the players took the ketchup bottles and mustard. The owner of the place said he had to have them back."

So back on the bus, Coach Sampson passed the hat and the players returned the condiments.

Under these sometimes tough and barren circumstances, Washington State still won four of the first six games on the tour.

On August 8 the Cougars lost to Central Army, 81-71, despite thirty-two points by Terrence Lewis. The Cougars then won the next three games: 98-92 over Dynamo, 77-54 over Moscow Select, and 76-69 over Svetlana. Svetlana won a rematch, 89-71, before Washington State knocked off powerful Spartak, 86-68.

"Bennie Seltzer was clicking," Sampson said. "Terrence that next year was going to be a Pac-10 all-conference guard. And Neil Derrick was not quite as good as Nolan Johnson here at Oklahoma, but he was a lot like Nolan. He was a slasher. And Ken Critton was a Dennis Rodman-type rebounder who went after everything. And I had another big 6-foot-10 kid, Brian Paine. Everybody called him the 'House of Paine.'"

Washington State's victory over Spartak was a rough, physical game and tempers flared. Sampson remembers that after the game the handshakes from the opponent were like handling cold fish. There was one last game on the tour, and it would honor Aleksandr Belov, who made the winning basket in the Soviet Union's controversial 1972 Olympic Games upset of the U.S. in Munich.

Russian officials substituted Spartak for the scheduled team much to Sampson's chagrin. Washington State was 4-2 on the trip. And Sampson would just as soon have gotten on the plane and headed back to the United States without playing Spartak again.

"Our kids were tired," Sampson said. "These were men, twenty-four to twenty-nine years old. And they were professionals. It started in the first half. Ken Critton grabbed a rebound and ripped it away from one of the Russian players. The guy came back with his fist and hit Ken in the mouth. Ken was bleeding. Ken is from Homer, Louisiana. You hit Ken, Ken will hit you. It doesn't matter whether you are from Russia or Yugoslavia or from Shreveport. Ken hit him back. The international trade agreement was just about busted there. This was bad blood. These guys didn't like us."

Sampson started to worry. Neil Derrick was a street scrapper from east Garland. Sampson cautioned Derrick not to provoke a fight. Sampson also had an assistant coach from the streets of New Orleans, Donnie Newman. He knew he had some tough hombres on his team.

"We were ready to go home, but we had one more half of basketball," Sampson said. "Little did I know it would be one of the most eventful, historic halves of basketball I would ever see.

"At this point, I didn't care about winning or losing. There was fifty some seconds remaining in the game. We were still trying to win the game. A lot of elbows were being thrown. Our kids would come back to the bench and say, 'They are hitting us after the whistle.' I would say an hour and a half from now we will be out of here; take it, swallow your ego, and just get out of here.

"Our kids are taught to dive on the floor to go after loose balls. This guy fell on Neil. Neil pushed him off and scrambled up. And while Neil was scrambling up, the kid was on the floor and grabbed Neil's ankle. Neil turned around and stomped the kid's head. Not a crushing blow. The kid hit the floor and rolled over like he was dead."

The Russian crowd was throwing bottles and lighting coins with cigarette lighters. The game was over. This was the ultimate road game for Sampson before about 8,000 fans. Washington State had ten to fifteen fans who made the trip. Many of them were in their sixties and seventies.

"The assistant coach from the Russian team comes after me swinging and hits me in the shoulder," Sampson said. "That's the worst thing because Donnie Newman is like a mother bear, seeing someone attacking his cub. Donnie comes across me and his fist just collides with this guy's jaw. Bennie Seltzer and Terrence Lewis are fighting with one or two of their players. Neil was visibly shaken about what happened. His teammates knew what was going on in the game with the cheap shots. I don't think Neil deliberately did that. But he was wrong."

Spartak had won the game, 70-57. Washington State had finished the tour with a respectable 4-3 record. Now, it was time to get out of the arena alive!

"All mayhem broke loose," Newman said. "They were throwing bottles on the floor and hot coins. They were yelling, 'Kill the Americans.' I will never forget it. I was having to fight off guys to make my way to the tunnel. There were a few guys on my shoulder. I was trying to hold my guys and tackle a few Russians myself. You take a few blows and you throw a few. But you ran for cover when those bottles started hitting the floor. The coke bottles were very thick. They would hit and explode."

Sampson finally got his players headed to the locker room as fans chased them. The team went up the tunnel where a man had previously been passing out pamphlets. This time he had a tennis racket and was swinging at the Cougars. When the Cougars finally got to the entrance to the locker room, the door was locked. Sampson had to find the person with the keys to the locker room as fights broke out behind him. The Cougars finally made it inside the locker room, but the hostile crowd gathered outside the arena and started throwing rocks at the locker room's window.

All the Cougar fans and coaches' wives were stuck in the upper section. Sampson sent the group's Russian interpreter upstairs to get them and bring them to the locker room. Mark Adams, an assistant coach, started to panic, yelling, "Where's Judy [his wife]? Where's Judy?"

Tyrone Maxey, said: "Judy? I lost my wallet."

Adams said: "Your wallet? I lost my wife."

In another corner, Rabedeaux remembers burly Washington State center Ken Critton breaking one of the ketchup bottles he had retained from a Russian restaurant and exclaiming with broken bottle in hand: "Bring those mugs in here!"

The Russian game officials told Sampson the Washington State party was not leaving until the Russian player's condition was determined. The Russians were considering pressing charges and taking Sampson off to jail. Finally, all the Washington State fans and wives were herded into the locker room.

"They told us to get the hell out of there," Karen said. "I got kicked and was bleeding and didn't realize it. Only we could take a team over there and cause an international incident."

Four armed Russian policemen arrived. The leader of the facility wanted to talk with the American coach, Sampson. Sampson told the Russian officials their players had set the mood by throwing elbows and punches. But Sampson apologized for Derrick's action.

"I was at a head table with these armed guards all around me," Sampson said. "They were talking in Russian. I did not know what they were saying. The interpreter whispered back to me that we had to wait for the test results from the hospital. I started thinking, 'What if this guy dies?' The interpreter said from preliminary reports, 'His brains were scrambled.' I thought at the worst he has a concussion. His head hit the floor. And he lay there for a while. Then he was sitting up when we were leaving the floor."

Sampson said he never was told the condition of the injured player. But the Russians made him watch a replay of the game for about an hour and a half. The play in question did not occur until the final minute. "They started yelling and hollering when they saw the play," Sampson said. "And they weren't saying, 'Good hustle play by Derrick.' They were saying American players are dirty."

Finally, five hours after the game had ended, Sampson negotiated a way for the Washington State team to return to its hotel in Leningrad. "I think they found out the kid was OK, but they wanted to call the American Embassy so they would know about the incident," Sampson said. The American consulate was summoned.

The Russian officials also requested that Sampson sign a contract "in case the kid died, to take care of his family because he was a great basketball prospect. It was almost like I was guaranteeing his future earnings." Sampson refused to sign the paper. But the Washington

State party was allowed to return to its hotel, after walking through an angry mob to the bus.

"I remember they were calling me the 'N' word," Sampson said. "They knew what the 'N' word was and they knew what the 'F' word was. They were calling me and all of our black kids the 'N' word. 'F------ Americans.' It was pretty nasty. We put the women and the older people in the middle and the kids on the outside, walking with their hands over their heads and their heads down."

The Washington State players were tired and hungry. And Sampson had concerns about getting out of the country. After returning to the hotel, the Washington State team had to take a train from Leningrad to Moscow. And then, from Moscow, the Cougars were to fly to Copenhagen, Denmark. They would then fly nonstop to Seattle.

It was a sleepless night for the Cougars. On the train, the players weren't saying anything. But the Washington State team made it safely back to Seattle without incident.

"You could tell they were visibly shaken," Sampson said. "I think for the first time Neil was in an athletic family who cared about him. He was an outcast in some ways. He had a temper. But I can honestly say in my two years, I never had an incident with him that was serious. He would get in a scuffle in practice sometimes, and I would have to calm him down. I think that incident helped him understand what could happen if he did not control his emotions."

Sampson hoped the riot at the game with Spartak would not become an international incident. He told the players not to mention it in interviews in the United States. But when the Cougars arrived in Seattle, they were greeted by TV cameras and reporters.

"I am thinking it has already hit the news," Sampson said. "But these people had no idea what had happened to us. They were asking what it felt like to be the last Americans to be in the old Russia. Did we see the revolution? Did we see the tanks roll up on Red Square? We had been there two days before, but we didn't see any tanks. We didn't know what they were talking about. So finally we had to get briefed on Russia. Now that I look back at it, it was almost a surreal experience."

But the bonding had been accomplished.

"I think that trip brought us unbelievably closer together," Sampson said. "If we were to have a reunion twenty years from now with that group of kids, that is something we would talk about. Everybody went through it together. We have a saying in our program. It is not what you accomplish that is important, it is what you overcome. And that is something we all overcame. It helped people grow up. We had some guys go over there as boys and come back as men."

CHAPTER 6

Breaking Through at Washington State

The Russian trip paid off in a big way. Washington State won its first twelve games to start the 1991-92 season.

On December 29, 1991, Washington State beat Hawaii, 63-61, in the semifinals of the Rainbow Classic to extend its season-opening winning streak to twelve games. It was the Cougars' longest winning streak since a thirteen-game winning streak to begin the 1935-36 season.

"And it should have been thirteen," said Sampson of the championship game of the Rainbow Classic. "We lost to Alabama, 71-68, and they had three very good players in Latrell Sprewell, Robert Horry, and James Robinson. We were up nine with five minutes to go. Bennie fouled out. We had beaten Wisconsin by twenty-two in the first round of the Rainbow. And we beat Hawaii in Hawaii. Do you know how hard that was? We were good."

Again, the three guards were leading the way. Bennie Seltzer, now a junior, was running Sampson's offense for a third straight season. And Terrence Lewis and Neil Derrick, the junior college stars, were dynamic on the wings. They had totally surrendered to Sampson's system. That threesome accounted for 42.6 points a game that season.

"They were very athletic junior college players," remembers Dale Reed, a reserve guard. "They really helped turn the corner for our program. Terrence Lewis was a real smooth scorer. Derrick was very athletic. And Tyrone Maxey was a point guard [off the bench] who could shoot it."

Lewis and Derrick became the only Washington State teammates (at the time) to reach the 500-point plateau during the same season. Ken Critton was a moose inside, grabbing 270 rebounds.

Washington State finished the season as the fourth-best free-throw shooting team in Division I (76 percent), breaking the sixteen-year-old Pac-10 mark. The Cougars were also buying into Sampson's defense. They held ten opponents to under 40 percent shooting.

"That team had a chance to be good, but I also knew our conference was going to be brutal," Sampson said. "It was hard to win on the road. Everybody was good. The thing was we had started off 12-0. And I always thought back to those seventeen straight games we lost in Pac-10 play. I think it is important you go through something like that."

Washington State lost its first three Pac-10 games that season, including a 78-65 decision in Pullman to No. 7 Arizona. But the Cougars bounced back and won four straight league games, including a road sweep of the Oregon schools. During the season, Washington State would sweep the four games from the Oregon schools for the first time since 1983.

"We were 16-4. We are the buzz. People are talking about Washington State," Sampson said. "But we have the hardest part of our schedule coming up [four straight road games]. My goal was to win one of them. But we didn't win any of them."

The first three road games were against ranked teams. Washington State lost at No. 16 USC, 75-62; at No. 4 UCLA, 81-62; and at No. 7 Arizona, 94-72; before dropping a 71-70 decision at unranked Arizona State. Then, the Cougars came back and won five of their last seven Pac-10 games.

Seltzer was a key during that stretch. He made 59.1 percent of his shots, an amazing 53.1 percent of his three-point tries. The big victory, which pretty well clinched an NIT berth, was on March 8. Sampson won his twentieth game of the season when the Cougars defeated eighth-ranked USC, 82-68, at Friel Court.

And ten days later Washington State made post-season play for the first time since 1983 when it was invited to the National Invitation Tournament. The Cougars defeated Minnesota, 72-70, in Pullman in the first round. Then the Cougars lost to New Mexico, 79-71, at The Pit, a few days later, when New Mexico put together a 14-4 run in the last 4:21 of the game.

Kelvin celebrates after an 82-68 victory over No. 8 USC at
Washington State during the 1991-92 season. WSU SID file photo.

"I felt we were making great progress," said Sampson, who
became only the fourth WSU coach to win twenty games in a season.
"Even though we were losing Neil and Terrence, we had recruited
those good freshmen. And we still had Bennie. I was realistic at
Washington State. My goal was to be the best team in the Northwest

(Oregon, Oregon State, Washington, Washington State). And we were accomplishing that goal.

"With that eight-man class we won thirty-eight games in two years. I was proud of that. I figured this next class was going to be equally important. But the fact of the matter is at Washington State, you are always going to have a down cycle. You are going to go down before you go up. All of sudden we have gone from seven victories to sixteen victories to twenty-two victories. And I didn't know if we could maintain it."

Sampson's three-guard offense during the 1992-93 season would be Seltzer, Eddie Hill, who moved into the starting lineup, and new recruit Tony Harris, a junior college transfer.

"Eddie Hill moved into the starting lineup, and we signed Tony Harris," Sampson said. "If you look up the word eccentric in the dictionary, you will find Tony Harris. He was quiet. We clashed a lot. He was the high school player of the year his senior year in Washington along with Rob Cockrum. Now we had them both."

But the big recruit in the state of Washington that year was 6-foot-9 Mark Hendrickson, a baseball-basketball star from Mount Vernon. Hendrickson's brother Steve, a soccer player, was already a student at Washington State. And that was a major plus for Sampson in his recruitment of Mark, also a star pitcher.

"Mark's only hang-up at Washington State was could we win and was I going to be the coach," Sampson said. "The rumors were starting to fly that I was going somewhere. That I didn't know where I was going. That's what other coaches were using against us in recruiting. I said, 'Mark, if coaches don't think I am going to be here, I guess that means we will continue to win.' We tried to use that in recruiting.

"I also think it helped our recruiting that high school coaches from all over the state were coming to our basketball camp in the summer. We had a golf tournament. I loved being around those coaches. We would have coaching clinics at 10:30 at night. We got to the point we had dozens and dozens of high school teams waiting to get into the camp.

"But I had to convince Mark we were a program that had established itself. At the same time we were benefiting from all the coaching changes at Washington. They went from Andy Russo to Lynn Nance to Bob Bender as their coaches."

Hendrickson was a thinker, according to Sampson, and would overanalyze almost any situation. And he was one of the early nutritionists in college basketball.

Remembers Karen: "Mark Hendrickson was one of the most mature kids. I remember in the airport when everybody else was getting pan pizzas, he was getting apples, bananas, and maybe a yogurt."

Hendrickson took to Sampson immediately. And Washington was never really in the picture, according to Hendrickson, who said he had received only a typed form letter from the Huskies.

"They were shying away from recruiting me," Hendrickson said. "They had recruited a teammate of mine a couple of years earlier and it didn't work out. I didn't give them the time of day."

So it was easy for Sampson's assistant Jason Rabedeaux to outflank the opposition.

"Coach Rabedeaux made a point to send cards to me every day," Hendrickson said. "He came over to visit me in high school. And I brought him into the cafeteria, and he ate lunch with all of my friends. You don't normally see an assistant coach do that. It was kind of neat to see my friends take to him. It was a good thing."

And Washington State's Rabedeaux won him over.

Mark Hendrickson helped Washington State to the NCAA Tournament in 1994. WSU SID file photo.

"We never had a great back-to-the-basket player at Washington State, but Mark Hendrickson was a big guy who was tailor-made for the 1-4 offense," Rabedeaux said. "He could catch it at the elbow on the floor and shoot or pass."

Hendrickson, however, had to go through the Sampson indoctrination. And he was surprised when preseason conditioning and practice started. He had never been around a coach like the fiery Sampson. September's preseason conditioning was a time when Sampson weeded out the men from the boys.

On the first day at Washington State, unsuspecting recruits such as Hendrickson faced a six a.m. wake-up call. They would then get to run a hilly 3.5-mile course on the first day of conditioning. Sampson would ride around in a van, monitoring the players' run. He would yell, "Pick it up!" Players had to have a better time at the end of the conditioning drills than at the beginning or they would have to keep running the 3.5-mile course until they did.

"One time during practice he kicked a ball into the second level," Hendrickson said about the beginning of drills in October. "I was scared. And the next day I did not want to come to practice. For a young kid it is intimidating. That's his style. It brings out the best in players. Bennie Seltzer was a senior that year and he helped me through it. To see a guy throw up at Coach Sampson's practices was not unusual. It was business. And it fit my practice personality."

His players often swore by, not at, Sampson's methods.

"From you, I learned firsthand the influence that a college coach can have on his players," wrote Eddie Hill in a 1995 letter to Sampson. "You have taught me a great deal about what it takes to succeed. The work ethic that you instill in your players carries on far past their playing days. Your hard work and dedication continue to motivate me as I travel down this coaching road. Thank you for all the help."

Joey Warmenhoven, a forward who twice was the team's co-Student-Athlete of the Year, agreed: "I have an MBA and a great starting job. And I know I will be successful because of the work habits that I picked up while playing for you. A lot of people underestimate the power of hard work, and I hope the other fellas on the team all remember this in whatever they are doing. I just wanted to let you know that you helped me grow up and become a man. And you were right, things do pay off for those who work hard."

Entering his sixth season in Pullman, Sampson was feeling good about the program. *His* hard work was starting to reap dividends.

"We had gotten better each year," Sampson said. "We had an impact freshman in Mark. We had one of the best point guards in the Pac-10 in Bennie Seltzer. And we had an explosive guard in Tony Harris. The three freshmen we recruited when we were 7-22 were now starters. I thought silently to myself and without sharing it with anyone, 'We are coming.' I felt really good about the coming year. We had only one senior starter, Bennie. We had been to the NIT. Now, I wanted to go to the NCAAs. That was the motivation."

Hendrickson was a big key that season on the front line. As a freshman that season he scored 12.6 points and grabbed 8.0 rebounds a game. He would wind up starting four years and would be All-Pac-10 twice before he graduated. He was selected in the second round of the 1996 NBA Draft (31st overall pick) by the Philadelphia 76ers.

But Hendrickson was having confidence problems even before practice started. He was a sensitive kid. And the pickup games, with their helter-skelter style, didn't fit his style of play. Enter Kelvin, the psychologist.

"Structured basketball was my strength," Hendrickson said. "And I was a little frustrated. My confidence was hurting. Coach Sampson looked me straight in the eyes. I was only eighteen years old, and he told me, 'You're my guy. I am going to ride you. We are going to win or lose with you. Don't worry about it right now.' That gave me the world of confidence."

Early in the 1992-93 season, Sampson took the Cougars to Birmingham where they lost to Alabama, 70-68. That was a homecoming game for Seltzer. Sampson remembers having a big ol' Southern-cooked dinner provided by Bennie's relatives before the game.

"They had all this soul food," Sampson said. "They had fried chicken, black-eyed peas, and chitterlings. I remember my kids from the Northwest almost vomiting when they saw the chitterlings. They did not know what chitterlings were. I am from North Carolina. I knew what they were. It was great food for me."

The Cougars were picked to finish last in the Pac-10, but Sampson knew better.

Later that month Sampson faced mentor Jud Heathcote in a game in East Lansing.

"Jud always brought his former assistants back to play in a tournament," Sampson said. "We beat Princeton in the first round and then the next night we played Michigan State. We played them tough. That was the first time we had played against Jud. It was such a weird feeling. And I remembered how intimidated I was when I first went to his office and tried to get involved with his program.

"Now, here I am at the Breslin Center, the brand new arena they have built, and coaching against him. Your career kind of flashes in front of you. And that is when I thought what a good job we had done at Washington State. This is why you coach. I wanted to see our kids compete against Michigan State. We were a fledgling Pac-10 power. I felt like we had a chance to do well in our league. We lost the game, but afterward I talked to Jud and I remember how proud he was of Washington State. That is where he graduated from. And here is one of his guys. That was a little bit of a tender moment. Jud had given his approval."

Michigan State defeated Washington State, 77-61. The Spartans were ranked seventh nationally. And Sampson didn't know how he would have acted if he had beaten his old boss.

Washington State lost its first three conference games: a home game to Washington and road games at Arizona State and Arizona. The Wildcats of Lute Olson blew out the Cougars, 87-63, in Tucson. That loss ran Sampson's record against Arizona to 0-12.

Then Washington State bounced back with six straight conference victories. And a defining moment of Sampson's career and the season occurred at half time of a game at cramped Harmon Gym in Berkeley. Washington State trailed Cal, 44-24, late in the first half and by nineteen at half time.

"They have Jason Kidd, Jerod Haase, and Lamond Murray," Sampson said. "We are down big at half, and we came back and won the game. They were the sexy team. We thought we were an up-and-coming program, but the northern and southern California teams and Arizona schools would get most of the attention. I would use that as motivation. I looked at it like the Christians and the lions. But I was so disappointed at half time. We were better than that. Our program was to the point it shouldn't be going through something like that."

Sampson went into the showers he was so angry. He turned the water on and swiped at it before he entered the closet-like locker room. He was mad at all his players, but he directed his rage at

Seltzer. He called him selfish and soft. And Sampson pointed out that Kidd, only a freshman, was outplaying Seltzer, a senior.

"I have twelve guys in here, all I need is five," Sampson said. "I want someone in here who realizes what Washington State basketball is all about. I told Bennie to pick the five guys. I told them we had come too far for this. But I knew walking out of the locker room this game would be decided in the first four minutes of the second half. We had to either get in or out."

"What I remember about it was that we knew we weren't playing well," Reed said. "But Coach never panicked, and we didn't either. We just fought back, had a chance to win, and took advantage of it."

By the sixteen-minute mark, Washington State had sliced Cal's lead in half. The Cougars got out of their set offense and ran 1-3-1 motion. The Washington State guards freelanced and dominated the second half on the way to an 83-75 victory. It was the Cougars' fourth straight in Pac-10 play.

"Seltzer literally took over that basketball game," Sampson said. "Our kids just followed him. Those are the games you live for."

The Cal victory was part of a six-game Wazzu winning streak, which also included a sweep of USC and UCLA in Pullman. During that two-game set Hendrickson was named Pac-10 Player of the Week. Sampson began to run key plays for him against UCLA.

"But I was disappointed that year we did not make the NIT," Sampson said. "And we should have. The thing that hurt us was road games we lost—by one at Oregon State, by two at Oregon, and by one at UCLA. I felt like we had to win one of those last three road games. And we had the ball and a three-point lead late against UCLA."

With the late lead against the Bruins, Sampson didn't want anybody to touch the ball except his three guards because they shot free throws well. But Eddie Hill threw it into one of the Washington State big men who was fouled and missed a free throw.

"We fouled UCLA's Shon Tarver, who is a 60 percent free-throw shooter," Sampson recalled. "But they send Tyus Edney (who is a much better free throw shooter) to the line. I come out of my box to argue with the official about that. We end up losing the game, 71-70. But I was upset with Eddie Hill. Why did you pass the ball to a 50 percent free throw shooter? That's why we have him up the floor."

Of their last seven games that season, the Cougars won only two. But one of those was an 87-54 victory over Stanford, which was Seltzer's last game in Pullman.

"I always get emotional on Senior Day," Sampson said. "And it was that day Bennie set the Washington State record for most three-pointers made in a game [nine]. This skinny little player from Birmingham, Alabama, had developed into one of the best players at Washington State."

Sampson labeled some players "tuxedo players" because they looked pretty on the outside but had nothing on the inside. "Bennie was not a tuxedo player," Sampson said. "He was really good around the basket. He was one of the great lay-up shooters. He could make it off the glass, in traffic." By the end of his senior year Seltzer set a Pac-10 record for most three-point baskets in a career.

Sampson hoped for an NIT invite, but the phone never rang.

"I wanted to keep playing," Sampson said. "I didn't care if we played at home or on the road. That was disappointing. We went from a high of winning at Washington to not playing. That's when some jobs came up. But I was excited about the next season. We had had one of our best recruiting classes...Nate Erdmann, Isaac Fontaine, Donminic Ellison. We had had so many near misses on the road. This team had a chance to be really good."

It had been a decade since Washington State had made the NCAA Tournament. That would change in 1994.

The Cougars would win their first seven games of the season.

They would post their first winning record in Pac-10 play since Raveling's last season in 1983.

And Kelvin Sampson would become one of college basketball's hottest young head coaches.

By the end of the season Sampson was on the hiring lists of most athletic directors with job openings.

"Our program had gotten better," Sampson said. "I knew we would miss Bennie Seltzer. But that was part of our growth and development. We had to move past that. We had a new set of players. And no one in the program was there when we went 1-17 in the 1990 Pac-10 season."

Sampson's senior class had experienced winning records the last three years. The senior backcourt of Tony Harris and Eddie Hill and senior forward Fred Ferguson were teaching the freshmen. And

NCAA Tournament coaches, left to right: Jack Friel, 1941;
George Raveling, 1980, 1983; Kelvin Sampson, 1994.

winning was expected. The next step was beating the top teams, achieving a national ranking, and making the NCAA Tournament.

Hill predicted at the Tip-Off Banquet that the Cougars could win the Pac-10.

"Coach Sampson kind of looked at me, but I was serious," Hill said. "He just kind of looked at me like 'You're getting me in trouble here.'"

Prior to the 1993-94 season, Sampson also hired Ray Lopes as an assistant coach from Cal-Santa Barbara. Lopes joined Jason Rabedeaux as one of Sampson's top assistants. Rabedeaux had been on Sampson's Washington State staff in some capacity since the 7-22 season of 1989-90.

"It was in the Pac-10 and it was a good step," said Lopes, who played college basketball at the College of Idaho, now Albertson College. "Working for Kelvin Sampson, I thought, he's good and he's going places. I liked him as a person. And he was a big people person. I knew he was good with his players because for his teams to play as hard as they do, they had to buy into that with the coach. I took the job on the phone. I never flew up there.

"And I didn't buy a house in Pullman for a reason. Two years previous to that they had been to the NIT. And I knew they were good. They had good seniors on that team. And they were deep. I knew within a two-year period it was possible we could move."

Lopes made a smart decision not to sink his roots too deeply into the eastern Washington soil.

Washington State opened up the season successfully at the San Juan Shootout in Puerto Rico with a true freshman at point guard, Donminic Ellison. The Cougars defeated Coppin State, 57-55. Sampson, however, had experience with three seniors in his starting lineup: guards Tony Harris and Eddie Hill and forward Fred Ferguson, who played alongside sophomore star Mark Hendrickson.

"Ellison wasn't ready for this starting role," Sampson said. "So I moved Harris to the point and Isaac Fontaine, a freshman, to the wing. I also had Nate Erdmann, but he had hurt his knee, and he didn't even dress out for this tournament. I remember Fontaine had a good game against Coppin State. And I remember saying he was special. He was tough. He was a freshman, but he wasn't nervous."

The next day was another meeting against Michigan State. Sampson was pumped. He had an advantage because he knew the

Isaac Fontaine, one of Kelvin's star recruits at Washington State. WSU SID file photo.

way Jud Heathcote coached. So he could give his team a solid scouting report in the short turnaround. Sampson said there were only three players on that team who Heathcote would let shoot. And one of those was standout Shawn Respert.

"Our guards ate them alive," Sampson said. "The final score of that Michigan State game was 76-71, but we were up by eighteen in the first half. Beating Michigan State and walking down the sideline and shaking Jud's hand, that was hard. He was not only my mentor, he was my idol. I looked up to him so much. Then one thing I learned from Jud was his honesty. I saw him later at the hotel and the only thing he said to me was: 'Don't screw this thing up in the championship game.' I didn't want to let him down."

Heathcote recounted years later: "They just worked harder than we did. They weren't better than we were. I am not sure we weren't outplayed and outcoached. Fontaine had thirty-three points, and Gus Ganakas, our play-by-play man, said that was the greatest game he had seen a freshman play."

Sampson was flying high on the way back to Washington after the Cougars easily dispatched Marquette, 56-46, in the title game of the Puerto Rico Tournament. He beat old friend Kevin O'Neill. After a victory over Pittsburg State (Kansas), Washington State was 4-0. Alabama, which had beaten Washington State in two close games the two previous seasons, was the next opponent in Spokane.

"I wanted to put a whupin' on Alabama," Sampson said. "Everybody said on paper they have all of these pros. I didn't care about that. It is our team vs. their team. But we were two really good teams. It was nip and tuck. The Spokane Coliseum was packed. And I thought back to the year we were 7-22 and you could have shot a shotgun blast in the stands and not hit a soul."

Sampson really had it going now after the 76-70 victory over the Crimson Tide. Sampson's players, particularly Hendrickson, bought into his blue-collar approach. And that was important to Sampson that his star player not be selfish. Sampson started a "Blue-Collar Award" that season.

"I liked to do all the little things," Hendrickson said. "And he was a blue-collar coach. I remember he had a Blue-Collar board. At Washington State he would keep track of everything but points: rebounds, blocked shots, steals, charges taken, and assists. At the end of the year, he gave out the Blue-Collar Award. And I was lucky enough to win it my first two years."

Washington State was unbeaten going into the Indiana Classic in Bloomington, Indiana. The Cougars knocked off Oral Roberts by forty-eight in the first round and then faced twelfth-ranked Indiana in the title game. Sampson was switching man and zone defenses against the Hoosiers' Damon Bailey and Alan Henderson.

"You aren't going to beat Indiana on their home court in the championship game of their tournament with one defense," Sampson reasoned. "You have to mix it up to see which is the most effective. I was hoping our man would be effective, because I was hoping our quickness would be a factor. We lost, 79-64. I was disappointed we didn't win. I thought it was a winnable game, especially since we had beaten Michigan State and Marquette. The fact was Indiana had a very good team and for twenty-five minutes we had competed well with them."

Indiana coach Bob Knight sent a runner over to Washington State's locker room to tell Sampson to meet him for a post-game Italian dinner at Leslie's in Bloomington. Knight was joined by other friends.

"We sat there and ate and talked basketball," Sampson said. "When people do something nice for you and don't have to, I appreciate it. He didn't have to do that. But he was extending a hand to a young coach. He and I have always had a cordial relationship. I don't know the Coach Knight some people write about."

And Knight gave Sampson a ringing endorsement in case any athletic director at another school was listening.

"Kelvin Sampson is about as good as there is out there," Knight told the *Seattle Post-Intelligencer.* "If someone were to call me and ask for a coach they might hire to stay at any basketball program in the country, he's the first one I would recommend."

About that time Sampson was beginning to realize how remote Pullman actually was. A move, indeed, might be necessary.

"We had been 7-0 and we were not ranked," Sampson said. "And that is when reality started to hit me, in terms of where we were and time zones. I wondered how many people who voted in the Top 25 knew this team was 7-0. We had beaten Marquette, Alabama, and Michigan State and had played Indiana very tough. We were barely getting any votes. The teams ranked ahead of us had barely accomplished anything. I wondered if it was the fact we were on the West Coast and when we played most people who voted were already in bed and were missing our scores. Or were we not doing a good job of getting the story out on our program?

"There was a seed planted in the back of my mind. We are 22-11 two years ago and we go to the NIT. The next year we go 9-9 in the Pac-10 and have some great wins and we don't go to the NIT. Now, we were 7-0 and we hardly were getting noticed in the polls. That was something that worried me."

And there were scheduling problems as well at Washington State.

"Whoever is the head coach at Washington State is going to be at a competitive disadvantage because everybody will want to play you home and home," Sampson said. "You don't have enough guarantee budget to bring in buy games. So you are locked into playing as many road games as home games. Look at Iowa State last year. Their only nonconference game on the road was at Iowa. Every other nonconference game they bought. Here at Oklahoma we have a good budget. If I wanted to and I was hard headed about it, I could play every nonconference game at home. But at Washington State you were lucky if you could play four nonconference home games."

And eventually all those thoughts would drive Sampson to take the Oklahoma job.

Washington State started off what turned out to be Sampson's last Pac-10 race, with losses at Cal and Stanford. But Sampson wasn't worried because both teams were strong. Cal had Jason Kidd and Lamond Murray and would make the NCAA Tournament. Stanford was establishing itself as a national power.

Sampson's freshmen guards Fontaine, Erdmann, and Ellison were starting to excel. Fontaine would only play one season for Sampson, but he would wind up as the school's all-time leading scorer the next three seasons under Kevin Eastman.

"Hill and Harris were seniors, but the freshmen were starting to pass them up," Sampson said. "That was not good for team chemistry. That was something I was going to have to deal with. I loved Eddie Hill. But I loved my program more. Harris can get to a certain point as my point guard. But my leading scorer can't be my point guard, not the way my system is set up. Ellison at some point has to be my point guard. And he was not going to learn by sitting next to me."

Four different freshmen would start at one time or another that season, including Fontaine, who was an all-Pac-10 freshman and led the league in three-point shooting. The three seniors along with Hendrickson, though, would all average in double figures.

Washington State's third conference game was against UCLA in Pullman. Sampson labeled an 81-79 loss to the Bruins the most disappointing defeat of the season, despite the fact UCLA was ranked fifth nationally. It was time that the Cougars won one of those games, Sampson believed.

The Washington State practice the next day was a little intense. On Saturday Washington State beat USC by thirty then went on the road and won at Oregon, Oregon State, and Washington. The old Arizona jinx prevailed when the Wildcats, ranked twelfth, defeated the Cougars, 80-68, in Pullman to end the winning streak.

"That was the thing about the Pac-10," Sampson said. "It was almost like you were playing for third place. Arizona and UCLA are going to finish first and second or second and first every year. And they should. Whether it was weather, recruiting, or tradition, there were advantages with the southern schools in our league. That's why I liked that challenge. I was supposed to coach the underdog because I was the underdog. And it was a good fit.

"The great thing about that year is we go 10-8 in the league and we lose three home games. It's hard to win ten league games when you lose three home games. When we had five games left, we felt we had to win four to get into the NCAA Tournament. That's after we had lost to Oregon at home. And I thought that was a critical loss. We had a team meeting after the game, and I said we lost the game but we hadn't lost our season. 'We can still do this' [go to NCAAs]. I never do this, but I looked ahead. I told them if they wanted to get to the NCAA Tournament (and some did more than others), we need to win four of our last five."

The five remaining games were Washington, a road trip to Arizona State and Arizona, and home games to end the season against Stanford and California. Washington State walloped Washington in Pullman, 75-51, and then won a key game at Arizona State, 80-71. It was a game where the Sun Devils later would be investigated for possible point shaving. Arizona State was a three-point favorite in the game.

But given past history, going to play the Arizona schools, a split was about as good as Sampson could hope to get.

The Cougars played Arizona two days later with the predictable result. The eighth-ranked Wildcats won, 85-69 as Sampson's record against the Wildcats dropped to 0-15. The game was close before Ferguson suffered a broken nose and Arizona went on a late run to pull away. That set up the Stanford and Cal games as must victories if Washington State wanted to make the NCAA Tournament.

"It was the most exciting week we had as far as fan support," Hendrickson said. "It was a great crowd on Thursday night when we beat Stanford (77-71). And when we played Cal, when I showed up a couple of hours before the game, there were people all around the arena waiting to get in. I had never seen that before or since." A crowd of 11,019 in Beasley Coliseum, the largest home crowd since 1983, watched Washington State fall behind early.

Kelvin had told Karen she would receive a new diamond ring if Washington State made the NCAA Tournament in 1994. And it didn't look good in the final regular-season game when the Cougars fell behind California, 25-5. "I remember thinking, 'My ring is toast,'" Karen said.

Hendrickson remembers during one of the early time-outs the team was shell-shocked. Sampson thought of Murphy's Law, i.e., what could go wrong would go wrong. But the Cougars were able to fight through the California talent and won 94-82. Washington State's victory knocked Cal out of a share of the Pac-10 title with Arizona.

Washington State flashed up early during the NCAA Tournament Selection Show. The Cougars were a No. 8 seed and would travel across the country to play No. 9-seeded Boston College in Landover, Maryland. The winner would face the region's top seed North Carolina in the second round. Both teams had 20-10 records going into the NCAA Tournament.

And the way it looked early, Washington State would advance. The Cougars led by ten points at half time and during much of the second half. Then Boston College's 6-foot-9, 220-pound senior Bill Curley, who finished with twenty-five points and ten rebounds, began to dominate the game.

With eight seconds remaining, the Cougars' Harris made two free throws to tie the score at 64, but three seconds later Harris fouled Boston College's Gerrod Abram. Only a 48 percent free throw shooter, Abram made both of them for a two-point Boston College lead. A desperation half-court shot by Harris, which could have won the game, was no good. BC tacked on a final free throw for a 67-64 victory.

"We should have beaten Boston College," Reed said. "And Boston College made a great run to the Elite Eight. It was a very tight game. We had to have chips on our shoulders. We had to prove ourselves to get to the NCAAs. We didn't have All-Americans on our team, but we wanted to beat the ones who did."

Karen at least would get her ring.

While attending the Final Four in Charlotte, North Carolina, the couple went to a jeweler in Lumberton because Kelvin's mother had gotten a good deal on the price of a new ring. Kelvin paid cash for the ring. Then he told Karen they were going to drive through the old tobacco market.

"We drove right through the middle of the market in a Lincoln Town Car," Karen said. It was a symbolic gesture. Sampson had come a long way from those summer days under the tin roof.

And now schools from one coast to another were starting to get interested in this one-time tobacco market foreman.

Livengood had taken the Arizona athletics director's job in early December 1993, so he wasn't at Washington State when the Cougars made the NCAA Tournament the following March. But Kelvin leaned on him for advice about the job inquiries he was starting to receive.

"They got beat in the first round, but Arizona went to Charlotte," Livengood said. "On Friday before the Saturday semifinals, Kelvin called up where we were staying and said, 'I need to talk to you. Let me come over.' We go for a walk for a half hour. He said Donnie Duncan had called from Oklahoma and that was really intriguing to him. I said I think that's a great opportunity for you."

After the victory over California, Kelvin never went back into Washington State's Beasley Coliseum. When he had his picture taken with the graduating seniors later that spring, it was outside the building. Sampson wanted the memories of his final victory over Cal to be his last of the building.

"You can get a total appreciation of what he has been then and now," Newman said. "He still has a tremendous work ethic and belief. He hasn't changed. Along with the work ethic is loyalty. I saw guys grow from the program winning hardly any games, jumping into the NIT and then to the NCAAs."

Many of his Washington State players still call him. And a number of them have advanced degrees.

"Just another example of Coach caring about his players: my wife was recently diagnosed with thyroid cancer," Reed said in the spring of 2001. "And I had only mentioned it to a few people, but he had caught word of it and took the time to call me to see how she and I were doing. That is the type of stuff he does that he doesn't have to. And this was during a busy time of recruiting for him. My wife has had her surgery and is on the way to full recovery.

"A comment that Coach really believes and has passed on to me that I totally believe is when he said, 'Good things do happen to good people.' He has taken pride in building programs with good student-athletes because he knows good things will happen."

CHAPTER 7

Becoming a Sooner

Kelvin Sampson was about to embark on a new coaching marriage with the Oklahoma Sooners in April 1994.

Oklahoma was coming off the Billy Tubbs regime, which had been colorful, controversial, and high scoring for the greater part of fourteen years. But in recent seasons, leading up to Sampson's hiring, the Oklahoma program had stumbled.

In three of the previous four seasons, the Sooners had failed to make the NCAA Tournament. The season before Sampson arrived the Sooners finished 15-13 overall and 6-8 in the Big Eight, the second time in four years OU had a losing record in league play.

The high-water mark for the Sooners under Tubbs was making the NCAA final game and losing to Kansas in 1988. Oklahoma had shots to win it all again the next two seasons but lost in the Sweet 16 and the second round of the tournament in 1989 and 1990. In the previous eight seasons before 1990-91, Tubbs' teams had won twenty-four or more games every year.

Tubbs, quick of wit and tongue, sometimes got himself in trouble by what he said and did. But there was never a dull moment in Norman with the Tulsa native calling the shots. The end of his OU tenure basically occurred when TCU, seeking to make a statement with the breakup of the old Southwest Conference looming, hired Tubbs away for more than $300,000 a year over five years. The move probably helped TCU, now a member of Conference USA, become a viable school for the Western Athletic Conference at the time.

"I think for me it was time to get something else," Tubbs said. "It was a good move for OU, a good move for me, and a good move for TCU. So that's kind of the beauty of the deal. I think everybody in the whole deal came out better."

Tubbs was basically right. As the new millennium dawned, Tubbs was still winning games as coach at TCU, and Sampson had entrenched himself in Norman as one of college basketball's top coaches.

John Underwood, an OU associate athletic director and the point man for finding a replacement for Billy Tubbs, was hot on Sampson's trail. Sampson also was getting calls from Iowa State, which wanted to interview him. The Cyclones eventually would wind up landing Tim Floyd from New Orleans. But the Washington State coach was high on their list as well. Clemson, Marquette, Dayton, and Auburn also had shown interest in Sampson. And South Carolina and Washington the season before.

"I called Oklahoma and they didn't call back," Floyd said. "They had their sights set on Kelvin. And he was a great hire. He has proven them right."

Sampson, on a Cougar Booster Club tour of the state, was in Seattle when the OU story was starting to develop. Attending a Seattle Mariners baseball game, Sampson was approached by a television reporter, who asked him about the OU job. But Sampson basically brushed aside the question.

"We were going to be good the following year at Washington State," Sampson said. "We had a great recruiting class. We had gotten Carlos Daniel (one of the top high school players in Colorado) and Chris Griffin (the No. 2-rated high school point guard in California). I was excited. But when I got home the next day, John Underwood had called me again at the office and at home. By then I had three messages. Donnie Duncan, the OU athletic director, had called the office."

Sampson finally returned OU's calls. Underwood, a former basketball assistant coach for Dave Bliss at Oklahoma and SMU, had done his homework. He had called former Washington State coach George Raveling and Kansas coach Roy Williams about Sampson. Sampson, knowing he was going to have a Washington State team that could contend for the Pac-10 title the following season, gave Underwood a half-hearted "yes" he would talk.

"I was attached to these kids at Washington State," Sampson said about his reluctance to pursue the Oklahoma job.

Underwood didn't have much information on Sampson until he called George Raveling about Stu Jackson, who was the Wisconsin coach at the time. OU officials had admired the fact a minority coach, Arkansas' Nolan Richardson, had just won an NCAA title.

"George said, 'Johnny, you can't afford Stu Jackson,'" Underwood recalled. "I don't know if we could or not. But he said the guy you ought to hire is Kelvin Sampson. Raveling told me the best coach out in the West was Kelvin Sampson. I related this to Donnie. He said, 'Do you know how tough it is to recruit to Pullman?' And Dean Smith had called and recommended Kelvin. I didn't know much about Kelvin; I had seen him excitable on the bench. And now I knew the things Coach Raveling had said about Kelvin. He was great with kids, a tireless worker, young, enthusiastic, knowledgeable.

"Donnie and I always used this analogy: when you coached at Navarro Junior College [as Duncan, a football coach did], you have paid your dues. And with Kelvin having coached at Montana Tech for five years, we thought here's a guy who had worked his way up, who had traveled from Pembroke, North Carolina, all the way to Pullman, Washington, for opportunity."

But Underwood knew he had to work quickly or someone else might snatch Sampson away from Pullman before the Sooners could.

Sampson was scheduled to speak at a clinic in Panama City, Florida, but had a long layover in Dallas. Little did Sampson know he would be having the meeting that would change his life.

Washington State assistant coach Jason Rabedeaux was along on the trip. And the two were going to sign forward Ernie Abercrombie, a junior college player at Weatherford (Texas) College, to a letter of intent to Washington State.

This was early April in Texas. It was warm. But Underwood had a heavy coat on when he met Sampson at the DFW Airport gate. Sampson noted this must be a "covert operation." Rabedeaux went to get a rental car for recruiting to be done later, while Sampson went to the Delta Crown Room for an initial two-hour meeting with Underwood. Rabedeaux, ever the loyal assistant, circled the airport for about two hours in the rental car.

"I tell you in about two hours it became very, very clear to me this guy was the one we needed to have involved in our program," Underwood said. "Anytime you talk to Kelvin Sampson, he is very, very deliberate. He knows what he is going to say. He is not going to react to a question with some outlandish response, even though he might want to. I had told him Oklahoma had had great years under Billy

Tubbs and that style of play was very important to our fans. And how would you, Kelvin, describe your style of play?

"I would ask a question and then he would repeat a question to me. I said Oklahoma people are accustomed to a style that is up and down. I asked him how would he describe his style? He then asked me a question. 'John, how would you describe KU's style of play?' I said Kansas has won by scoring in the fifties, sixties, seventies, eighties, and nineties. He told me that's how his teams played. Come to find out, he averaged about eighty points a game."

"Coach Rab" as he is known by the players, then, on his own, drove up to Oklahoma and somehow slipped into Lloyd Noble Center and looked around. He spotted the championship banners.

"John got me excited about Oklahoma, but I had mixed emotions," Sampson said. "I still went on to Weatherford and signed Ernie. I had his national letter of intent. Now, there's a little guilt complex coming over me, because I couldn't talk to him about Oklahoma. I hadn't said in any way I was going to Oklahoma. I was just going to talk to them. But Rab has been with me for a long time and he was excited about Oklahoma. Of course, he was more excited at the time by Iowa State. Rab was pushing Iowa State and Ray Lopes, my other assistant, was pushing Oklahoma. And Karen liked the idea of Oklahoma because it was closer to home [North Carolina]. When she got the atlas down, I knew she was serious. But I am saying we have a chance to win the Pac-10 the next year."

Sampson believed he had an investment at Washington State. He remembered losing seventeen straight Pac-10 regular-season games only four years earlier. But everything had turned around at Washington State, where the home crowds had doubled since his arrival. Recruiting had picked up. And Sampson's basketball camps were among the largest on the West Coast.

Sampson went on to Panama City for the clinic and got another call from the persistent Underwood. Sampson knew he was getting recruited because he was usually the one recruiting players. Underwood wanted to talk to him further on another layover at DFW. But Sampson said it was too short and flew on back to Pullman.

Now OU had the unenviable job of prying Sampson out of Pullman. Sampson had ruled out pursuing Iowa State. He didn't believe it would be that great of a difference from Washington State. Neither school was a major power at the time.

Jason Rabedeaux (right) was Kelvin Sampson's assistant for 11 years.
UTEP SID photo.

"Roy Williams called me and told me he thought the Oklahoma job was a very good job, but he was not so sure he wanted me in his league," Sampson said. "He was being kind of honest about it. I said, 'Roy, if you were ranking the Big Eight, 1-8, which is the best job?' Roy said right away, Kansas. That's what I would have said. I asked him what was the second best job. 'On paper, probably Missouri.' I thought to myself if he went a couple of more names and didn't say Oklahoma that would be it.

"I asked him what's the third best job. He said, 'It can be Oklahoma. Look what Billy Tubbs did there. He has given them an awareness of basketball.' He said 'they may be No. 2.' I asked him if he thought it would be a good move. And he said, 'No question.'" That put a different spin on things.

Underwood had stepped up the recruiting. Sampson committed to a date to come to Norman. Sampson had never gone to a campus for an interview. Schools he had been involved with had just wanted to call a press conference to announce his hiring. The voices were saying go. The timing was right. Oklahoma could be a great job.

"I think the thing that really clinched it was when Dean Smith called," Sampson said. "He didn't beat around the bush. He thought Oklahoma was a better job than Washington State because Oklahoma had an opportunity to consistently make the NCAA Tournament. He thought Washington State was a cyclical job."

Sampson also asked Jud Heathcote his opinion. They played a round of golf in Spokane, where Jud's retirement home is located. Sampson said he couldn't breathe while Jud swung and had to stand in a certain place. He gladly put up with those golfing habits. He wanted advice. Michigan State had played a first-round National Invitation Tournament game in 1993 at Oklahoma and lost, 88-86, before only 5,483 fans.

"Jud said he was really concerned about the Oklahoma attendance in basketball," Sampson said. "He said he believed there were only about 6,000 fans at the game they played there. He said check the attendance. That was his only concern. And it was a football school. Jud was black and white. There was no gray area with Jud. And you were talking about leaving his alma mater, Washington State, too."

Heathcote asked, "Why do you want to go to Oklahoma?"

Sampson told him it was an opportunity to win on a more consistent basis.

Heathcote advised him he needed to get a raise. And he needed to at least go listen to Oklahoma's sales pitch.

Kelvin and Karen drove the eighty-two miles from Spokane to catch a flight headed to Oklahoma. Sampson ranted and raved at Karen during the car ride about all the people he would be letting down if he left Washington State—the players, the fans. Then, when he and Karen arrived at the airport, he felt even more guilty when he saw some Cougar fans. "Great year, Coach," they told him.

The Sampsons finally landed in Oklahoma City and went from temperatures in the fifties in Washington to about eighty-five degrees in Oklahoma. Sampson's asthma started acting up. He started wheezing. He didn't think that was a good sign. He also noticed how flat the land was. He was looking for reasons not to take the job.

His OU escorts, including Oklahoma associate athletic director Larry Naifeh, went to Charleston's for dinner that night in Norman. The first person Sampson saw was Billy Tubbs! Duncan and Underwood were attending another OU function. And OU officials were trying to keep Sampson's arrival in town quiet. That didn't last long.

"Kelvin!" Billy blurted out in the crowded restaurant. "So you are going to be the new coach. I was wondering who they were going to hire, and they are going to get you!"

"Billy was with a guy I later became great friends with, Walter Duncan," Sampson recalled. "Billy and his wife, Pat, were there. I had gotten to know Billy really well from a Converse shoe trip, and I loved Billy. He was one of the most fun guys to be around, whether it was on the golf course or having a beer or just getting together. But the Oklahoma people didn't know he was going to be there."

Sampson didn't feel well during dinner. Because of the pressure and stress of a possible career move, his asthma was acting up. He and Karen went back to their hotel room. He was taking inhalers and was afraid he was going to have to go to the hospital for a treatment, but he got through the night.

To complicate matters, Washington State had called and was going to sweeten Sampson's contract. His entire package at Washington State was worth about $150,000. Sampson said that Washington State was probably going to more than double his package.

Sampson found out from Underwood that then Tulsa coach Tubby Smith, the old North Carolina NAIA player at High Point, had interviewed for the job and nearly been hired, but then dropped out of the running. Smith would take the Georgia job the next year.

Smith liked living in Tulsa and didn't know how the Tulsa fans would react to his moving to Norman.

"I was their second choice, but that didn't bother me so much," Sampson said. "You are talking about a guy from Montana Tech."

The next day Underwood and other OU officials took him to Lloyd Noble Center. One thing Sampson noticed was the absence of a trophy case. And he also noted there was no weight room at the arena. The basketball players used the football weight room about a mile away. He knew that would change if he became OU's head basketball coach. At Washington State an alum had donated $15,000 to build a weight room near the basketball floor so the Cougars could lift around practices.

Sampson visualized a storage room at Lloyd Noble as a new weight room for the OU basketball team. Sampson also noted other facilities were not up to date. It was the same locker room that Wayman Tisdale graced from 1983-85. It was small. And there was no whirlpool in the training room. He also said Tubbs' office reminded him very much of a banker's office. He wanted an office that had a worked-in look to it with a VCR for his game tapes and a white board on the wall to diagram plays.

But he was impressed with the center for academic support for OU athletes. And Sampson felt comfortable around Underwood's wife, Janet, and Duncan's wife, Sally. They made him and Karen laugh. Kelvin began to feel OU was a good place for himself and his family. Duncan actually conducted the interview at lunch with the whole group.

By this time Karen already had looked at houses and wanted to go to OU. And Sampson started thinking about how much travel there was involved in recruiting to Washington State and how much easier it would be at Oklahoma. He remembered what Williams and Smith had told him about going to the NCAA Tournament every year at OU.

But later that night, in the privacy of their hotel room, Kelvin started crying and Karen joined him. Kelvin thought about leaving his players because he knew they had come to Washington State to play for him. But the pressure was on the next day. Duncan no longer was recruiting Sampson. He wanted him to sign on the dotted line.

Sampson told Duncan he needed to fly back to Pullman and speak to his family of assistant coaches and players. Duncan told Kelvin OU needed an answer now.

"We convinced him we needed to get this deal done," Underwood said. "I think anytime during recruiting, when they say they want to come, it becomes an investment on everyone's part to do it as quickly as possible.... If he had gone back, would he have stayed? I think that has happened with a lot of athletic directors. I think that happened with Rick Barnes when he was interviewed at Virginia and then decided to go back to Providence."

OU wasn't going to let Sampson go back to Pullman. Duncan was sitting at a conference table in his office with a yellow pad. He asked Kelvin to write on the pad what it was going to take for OU to hire him.

"I didn't know what to write down," Sampson said. "Money didn't make my decision, although I knew I was going to get more money. I wasn't raised with money. I wasn't a material guy."

Sampson wrote down $400,000 as a total package, country club membership, car deals for himself and Karen, camps, and shoes. Duncan then called the OU attorney. Kelvin called his best friend and attorney, Ricky Locklear, back in North Carolina. Kelvin got his $400,000 a year salary. Sampson asked OU to fly in Lopes and Rabedeaux and his two children, Kellen and Lauren, for the press conference.

The deal was done.

Sampson didn't give Washington State a chance to counter. There would be no bidding war.

"Money wasn't the deal," Sampson said. "It was a great opportunity. I was thirty-eight years old and had been a coach seven years on the Division I level, eleven years total. The NCAA Basketball Tournament was a big thing to me. And maybe you can't get to the NCAA Tournament every year at Washington State. At Oklahoma, you will have a chance to go every year."

Sampson initially signed a five-year contract with Oklahoma, with a $115,000 base salary, but the aforementioned extras brought it to the $400,000 level. And by September 1995 the OU Board of Regents would approve a seven-year contract for Sampson. So Sampson knew he eventually would have the same eight-year commitment he would have had if he had stayed at Washington State.

"This guy is a leader," Duncan said at the news conference announcing Sampson's hiring. "He is a demanding guy and demands a lot of his team. But he's also a guy who cares a great deal about his team. That's one of the reasons he has been so successful."

Sampson's most immediate concern was Ernie Abercrombie. Sampson believed he was caught in a moral and ethical crossfire. If he turned in the letter, then Abercrombie would be bound to Washington State. But he knew Abercrombie was only going halfway across the country to Washington State because Sampson was the coach of the Cougars. Now he was coach of the Sooners.

"I thought I would be doing that kid a serious injustice if I turned in the letter," Sampson said. But he also felt an obligation to Washington State. So Sampson let Ernie and his family decide. Ernie originally was from Houston. And the Abercrombies had a lot of family and friends in the Norman-Oklahoma City area. If Ernie still wanted to go to Washington State, he had a scholarship there. Or if he wanted to go to Oklahoma, he had that option as well.

Ernie's father, John, told Kelvin that Ernie's first priority was to go with Sampson. He had always struggled with the distance to Pullman. Abercrombie just wanted to play for Sampson.

"It was quite a shock because he never talked about leaving," Abercrombie said recently. "The situation at Oklahoma was better than where he was. It was only three hours from the school I was attending at the time. Instead of traveling across the country, it was only three hours for me."

The good-byes to the players at Washington State were tough for Sampson.

When he was driving back from Spokane to Pullman for his farewell press conference, the tire on his car went flat just as he entered Pullman. Sampson then broke down at the beginning of the press conference.

"Some of the players were upset he left," Hendrickson said. "Eventually, we got it all straightened out. He brought me into his office and talked to me. He said there were a lot of jobs he wouldn't leave Washington State for. But this was one he had to pursue. I respected that.

"It was a tough situation for myself. A bunch of us, including Nate Erdmann, didn't know what to do. I thought of following him to Oklahoma. It was something I had to look at. But I thought if I didn't play basketball, would I be happy at Washington State? And the answer was yes. The only reason I was going to Oklahoma was basketball."

"It was tough for me to call Erdmann and tell him I was leaving," Sampson said. "His father used to coach in Oklahoma and he had been recruited by Billy Tubbs, but they didn't recruit him hard enough to Oklahoma. I remember talking to Nate's mother and she took it hard. In the last five games we had to win to make the NCAA Tournament my last year at Washington State, Nate was one of the stars down the stretch."

Sampson told all the kids to stay together. But several of the players wanted to go with Sampson. Donminic Ellison's mother asked if he could transfer. Sampson had no additional scholarships at OU available, and he wasn't going to raid the Washington State roster.

Sampson wanted the new Washington State athletic director, Rick Dickson, to hire Rabedeaux as the Cougars' new head coach. He believed that would help keep the team together. But Dickson opted to hire Kevin Eastman from North Carolina-Wilmington.

Most of the players stayed including the stars, Hendrickson and Isaac Fontaine. And Washington State, with basically Sampson's players, would go to the NIT during Eastman's first two seasons in Pullman. But those would be the Cougars' only post-season appearances during Eastman's five-year regime.

"Both Kelvin and I left good teams with players coming back," Raveling said. "We had three starters back from a team which won its first game in NCAA and then lost to Virginia and Ralph Sampson by five. After I left, they didn't even come close to making the NCAA Tournament [under Len Stevens]. The same thing after Kelvin left. There was a sense both of us experienced leaving in similar circumstances. We thought we had left enough talent for the next guy to win And it didn't happen."

"I look back and in my junior and senior years, if Coach Sampson and Nate Erdmann had been there, we would have had a pretty good team," Hendrickson said. "Nate was my roommate. And his best situation was to follow Coach Sampson. It worked out for Nate and for Coach Sampson."

Erdmann waited until Eastman got to Washington State then decided he wanted to follow Sampson to Oklahoma. But Sampson had no room for him. Erdmann already had used up a red-shirt year because of a wrist injury his first season at Washington State. He had played his second season at Washington State in 1993-94 and averaged 5.8 points a game. So if he transferred to a Division I school such as Oklahoma, he would have had to sit out a year and lose a year, under NCAA transfer rules. Erdmann played his sophomore season eligibility-wise at Hutchinson Community College (Kansas), a junior college. He led Hutchinson in scoring (16.3 points a game), rebounding (6.7), and steals (4.0).

Then Erdmann transferred to Oklahoma for the 1995-96 season and was immediately eligible to play for the Sooners. Erdmann had been sold on Sampson and his style, but he knew he couldn't handle a year without basketball.

"I had red-shirted my first year at Washington State, and it probably was my hardest year," Erdmann said. "I had played ball for all those years. And I could not play that season. All I could do was practice. I didn't want another year like that. The main thing behind that was play games. I took a couple visits to OSU. But it was pretty much a done deal with Coach [Sampson]."

"I told Karen that may be the greatest compliment I have ever had as a coach that a kid would basically give up a year of his life to come play for me at Oklahoma," Sampson said.

Erdmann's picture, along with those of Ryan Minor, Eduardo Najera, and Corey Brewer are dominant on one of Sampson's office walls at Lloyd Noble Center. All four were drafted by NBA teams. And they have been players he has built his team around with the 1-4 offense.

Sampson often thinks of the road Erdmann traveled to Oklahoma.

"He came in here and became first team All-Conference, then he was drafted by the Utah Jazz to now be playing professionally in Italy," Sampson said. "He is a good story."

And years later Underwood, who became director of sports marketing for the Dallas Convention & Visitors Bureau, was satisfied he had made the right choice for the Oklahoma basketball program.

"Kelvin was a guy who got involved in the community and had great outreach," Underwood said. "He would go anywhere, anytime to speak to alumni groups. I remember he started a program like he had at Washington State, called the 'Sooner Little Dribblers.' Three of the players and Coach Sampson would hold a one-hour clinic and then the kids would go to station drills on Saturdays of home games. I watched both the young people who were involved and the players who had to get up early on Saturday morning and be there at Lloyd Noble. It was infectious. You could see he was building camaraderie with his team. It was not just a coach, but with the entire team and assistants.

"I had to drop a bomb on my daughter, who was about eight at the time, to get her up to go to school. But on Saturdays for Little Dribblers, she would be up because Coach Sampson said they had to be there by eight a.m. That's the kind of pied piper syndrome he created."

CHAPTER 8

Instant Success at OU

Sampson was very familiar with OU forward Ryan Minor when he was still coach of Washington State. Minor had been a member of the West team in the 1993 U.S. Olympic Festival in San Antonio, which Sampson coached. But Minor had a separated shoulder and didn't get to compete for Sampson's team, which won the silver medal.

It didn't take Sampson long to figure out Minor was going to be the centerpiece player on his first OU team in the 1-4 offense. The 6-foot-7 junior could make acrobatic shots from all over the floor.

"Our philosophy has always been that shooting is not an equal opportunity position," Sampson said. "I want to get shots for my best shooter and my best scorers. That's one of the reasons I have never liked the passing game and the motion offense because when you play against a good defensive coach, he will always make sure the wrong guy is holding the ball when it is time to shoot.

"My first year at Oklahoma, it didn't take me long to figure out our best player was Ryan Minor," Sampson said. "He didn't know it yet, but he was getting ready to get a lot of shots in this offense."

Sampson, in the early fall of 1994, was itching to get to see his players practice. But in those days, under NCAA rules, there were no individual workouts until practice officially started in mid-October. Word was getting back to Sampson everybody was playing well in the pickup games, but no one ever talked about Minor, who was the leading returning scorer from Tubbs' final OU team. Minor had scored 16.2 points per game as a sophomore, but the team was only 15-13, 6-8 in the old Big Eight.

Forward Jeff Webster had been the team's leading scorer and rebounder, but he was gone. He had been selected by the Miami Heat with the fortieth overall pick in the second round of the NBA Draft.

"I asked the players, 'If you had to play a game right now, who would you start?'" Sampson remembers. "And hardly any of them said Ryan. What about Ryan? Then I found out that if Ryan didn't have the ball in his hands, he didn't look like he was playing. He was one of those guys. He was one of the fiercest competitors I have ever coached. But he was not a great practice player."

Minor was going to give the new coach a chance. "He built up a program that was struggling. So I would think all the guys are willing to stay and stick with him," Minor said.

For a time all the players did stick. But there was a huge difference between Tubbs and Sampson in coaching philosophy. There also was an about-face in regards to how players conducted themselves off the court.

"When coaches say you have study hall, they don't want to be the caretaker of all that...." OU's then associate athletic director John Underwood said. "Kids under Kelvin knew what was expected of them from the very beginning both on and off the floor."

And some of those players like Shon Alexander and Antonio Bobo would wind up leaving the team early because it was a much tighter ship.

"We had a great group of guys coming back," said John Ontjes, Oklahoma's senior point guard that season. "But we did not have much discipline the year before. Coach Sampson gave us the discipline that the group of guys needed. You could tell from his actions it was either his way or the highway."

Abercrombie was actually the only player Sampson had recruited. The rest were strangers to Sampson's ways. And even Abercrombie hadn't gone through Sampson's preseason conditioning rigors.

"We went through a six-week conditioning program early in the morning and ran like a track team basically," Abercrombie said. "He was busting our butts to see if we were determined to make the team. I wondered why these guys didn't quit then. Then, the third or fourth week of practice, some guys were quitting. I didn't understand that. I just remember the coaching relationships I made the first year. I had better relationships with coaches than with any player on the team. I was recruited by Coach Sampson, Coach Rabedeaux, and

The Sooners went unbeaten at home during Sampson's first season (1994-95) at OU.
Photo by Lisa Hall Photography.

Coach Lopes. They were more like my friends than guys on the team. I had no idea who the players were until we met for the first time."

Sampson said as the numbers dropped on the team, the chemistry became better. Sampson said his biggest selling job was to get his new players to buy into their roles. He calls it "surrendering."

Sampson had a team meeting early in the fall and explained Minor would be the center of the offense. He hoped the players would buy into their roles. If they did, the Sooners could win games. "I couldn't keep them happy and win games," Sampson said. "My personal philosophy has always been it is not what you accomplish, but what you overcome. They had to overcome how easy it was to quit."

Sampson kicked the team out of practice very early in the fall. And his rule is, if he kicks the team out of practice, it comes back at 6 a.m. the next day and practices as well as at the regularly scheduled time.

After the initial six a.m. practice, Sampson took his new players up to the team meeting room. On the blackboard he wrote strengths and weaknesses. Some of the players were half asleep and slouched down in their chairs. He made the slouchers sit up and take notice or leave the room. Sampson could tell the attitudes weren't good.

"I am pissed off I have to kick them out of practice," Sampson said. "Now, I am pissed off they are pissed off. This didn't set well with me. I told them we have to determine right now how we are going to win these games. Is winning important to you? What do you think the strengths of our team are? One of them said rebounding. I wrote down everything they said. 'We are fast, we are shooters, we are quick.' Not one time did they say anything about defense. Not one time did they say anything about playing hard as a team.

"I asked Calvin Curry what he thought one of our strengths was and he said, 'my jumper.' We had just practiced three or four days and I hadn't seen him make a jumper yet. I said, 'OK.' I looked at some of the kids and they were rolling their eyes. I asked about weaknesses and they got lockjaw. I went to the board and erased everything."

Under strengths, Sampson wrote one thing: Ryan Minor. That was going to be Oklahoma's plan, get the ball to Minor.

During that same early morning meeting, Sampson had the team members stand up and reach into their front pockets and grab an imaginary object and put it in their back pockets. He was playing an elementary school game with them. He told them they had just put their egos and their me-first attitudes into their back pockets.

"Now you can run down the tunnel and play for Oklahoma," Sampson told the team. "Do you have any idea why your names are on the back of the jerseys and why Oklahoma is on the front? I got a response from Ryan. I could have gotten him to walk backwards tip-toes over a cable wire 100 feet above the ground between two buildings. But I knew I was walking on thin ice with some of these kids because I didn't recruit them. They didn't trust me. There was no loyalty factor."

They had to buy into Sampson's philosophy. And the survivors would by the end of the season.

"He gets his players to play hard," said UNLV coach Charlie Spoonhour, who was on the Sooner Sports Network telecast team for two years. "He is pretty blunt. Kelvin still has guys who really play hard. He has them thinking they ought to do things that way. And that is the way I believe. He does things the way they used to be done. I think Kelvin's guys are taking the old-time approach about team unity and working together. Some of us like that. I try to do that, but I'm not sure I take it to the level that he has."

While there were still some mutineers on ship, Sampson knew the schedule wasn't demanding to begin the season, with teams like Cal-Irvine, Nicholls State, and Jackson State playing in Norman. Winning would cure a lot of problems. And, despite the questionable attitudes, the Sooners would win.

Minor had a blazing start with the new emphasis on getting him the ball. He failed to score less than twenty-three points only once in Oklahoma's first seven games as the Sooners rolled to a 7-0 record.

Sampson had to find out what the other players could do. He found out Prince Fowler was a really good scorer but not a point guard in Sampson's 1-4 offense. Dion Barnes was a player who could develop into a scorer.

"Dion Barnes was a good player, but Billy had told me he didn't think John Ontjes was the answer at point guard," Sampson said. "He said Prince Fowler was a great point guard. He was, but for somebody else. Prince was a talented, talented kid, but he wasn't a 1-4 point guard. He wasn't cut out to run a set, run a play. He was cut out to run. We couldn't run that year because at one point we were down to seven scholarship athletes."

Sampson was trying to define roles.

James Mayden wasn't an effective scorer, but he could rebound and block shots. And he sold Mayden, a 6-foot-10, 230-pound center, on screening for Minor and grabbing offensive rebounds.

And he told Minor he had to be the coach on the floor. Every time Mayden set a screen for him, to acknowledge it. And every time Calvin Curry snared a rebound, to compliment him as well.

"You not only have to be the best player, Ryan," Sampson said. "You have to be the cheerleader. Teams win when their best players are gracious. If the best player is a jerk and he is a me-me-I guy, the team usually does not win. But Ryan was a humble star. He was from a small town in Oklahoma. He didn't have a big ego. He was a shy kid. He was quiet. He didn't say much. But he was a great teammate. And when the lights went on, Ryan Minor came to play."

Minor would wind up as the Associated Press Big Eight Player of the Year and lead the Big Eight in scoring with 23.7 points a game. And he really didn't crave the spotlight. Coming from tiny Hammon,

Oklahoma, a town of 650, three hours west of Norman, he and his fraternal twin, Damon, lived in the gym. If one of them had a girlfriend, she would be the rebounder. There was little else to do in the western Oklahoma town besides play baseball, which ultimately would lead to pro careers for the Minor brothers.

Minor only realized during his senior year in high school he was good enough to play college basketball. Until then, Minor had played basketball only during the winter and never was involved in summer basketball, which gave players national exposure.

But while Minor was fitting nicely into Sampson's system, there still was some run-and-gun in the Sooners. And once it was show time, some of the Sooners reverted to old habits.

"Matter of fact, you can go back to my first game at Oklahoma against Coppin State," Sampson said. "I called a 30-second time out before the first minute was over about shot selection. Calvin launched one from thirty to thirty-five feet out. We had worked and worked on shot selection. Calvin sat about ten minutes before he hoisted another one up there. Then he started pouting [on the bench]. We had some great attitude guys—Ryan, John Ontjes, Dion Barnes. But we had some guys who didn't trust me yet."

The Sooners, though, were unbeaten before playing Arkansas in the first round of the Rainbow Classic in Hawaii in late December.

Oklahoma led Arkansas, the defending national champion, at half time, 46-32. Oklahoma had the advantage until Razorbacks guard Clint McDaniel's basket made it 72-71 Arkansas, with five minutes left in the game. The teams battled into the final minute before OU lost, 86-84. A three-pointer by Barnes with one second left made the score look even closer against the No. 3-ranked Razorbacks.

"It kind of gave us an idea, we are not a bad team," Ontjes said. "That increased our confidence the rest of the year."

Minor showed why he was the Big Eight's best player that season. He had thirty-one points and nine rebounds against the powerful Razorbacks.

"This was probably the first game we played that year against a team we probably shouldn't have beaten," Sampson said. "Here we are playing against Arkansas' Corliss Williamson, Dwight Stewart, Scotty Thurman, Corey Beck. They have all of their kids back. But even though we lost, we won that night. Our heart and hustle showed up."

The OU locker room was somber. And Sampson liked it that way. The next game wasn't much easier. Georgia Tech, led by guard Travis Best, was the opponent. Oklahoma lost another close one, 89-85. But Sampson had no complaints. The team was playing well against top-flight competition.

Oklahoma went into Big Eight Conference play with an 11-2 record after beating Tulsa, 76-61, behind Minor's twenty-three points. In the first thirteen games, Minor was OU's leading scorer in eleven of those games and the top rebounder in ten of those contests.

"Ryan was so talented, it was amazing," Abercrombie said. "He was such a natural athlete. It came so easily for him. His junior year he was getting bored with playing. But I remember the way he carried himself all the time. He would go all out and help the team win. And he would not get carried away with the publicity."

The other big key was Ontjes. During the same thirteen-game nonconference stretch, Ontjes was the leading assist man in all but two games. And he had been in double figure in assists five times. In addition, Ontjes was Sampson's whipping boy.

"Ryan, although he was a great competitor, wasn't a kid I could get on like I could get on some others," Sampson said. "I have always picked on my point guard to be the one to take criticism. All of my point guards have to be tough kids. They have to be able to absorb things that are meant for somebody else. John Ontjes was a great example. John Ontjes could take it. He was secure enough in himself. He was a fifth-year senior. Ryan Minor was our best player. But our most valuable player was John Ontjes that season."

Ontjes said he was more suited for Sampson's system than Tubbs' freewheeling attack.

"Coach Sampson knew how to get the most out of players. And maybe John Ontjes did not have that much talent, but he was a perfect example of that," Abercrombie said. "In pickup games at the beginning of the year, other players were giving him everything he could handle. Once Coach got a hold of him and told him what he wanted run, he had an excellent season."

With Ontjes and Minor leading the way, Oklahoma started the Big Eight season winning a home game against Colorado and losing at Oklahoma State. Before the Sooners got into the teeth of the league season, they had a big nonconference home game remaining against Texas.

Kelvin Sampson gives guard John Ontjes a pointer during the 1994-95 season.
Photo courtesy OU Athletic Media Relations.

"We were just kind of bumping around in the living room with the lights out, trying not to run into the coffee table and knock over the lamp," Sampson said of inheriting a team of which Minor and Ontjes were the captains. "We were holding hands and not quite sure where we are going."

Sampson was always concerned about the confidence level of the players on that team, including Ontjes.

Ontjes didn't get much respect from some opponents. And Sampson used that to his advantage.

Sampson had played in the Red River Shootout golf tournament against UT coach Tom Penders the previous fall in Dallas. They were riding around in the same golf cart as captains of the two teams.

Penders talked about UT's 87-75 victory over Oklahoma in Austin during Tubbs' last season. Penders told Sampson how his guards trapped Ontjes. Penders basically said the weak link on the OU team was point guard—Ontjes.

Sampson waited until the eve of playing Texas in Norman to relay Penders' comments to Ontjes during the pregame film session.

"I took that to heart," Ontjes said. "I had played so badly the year before, and they kicked our butts. Coach Sampson always had something to inspire us, something in the film sessions to get us more fired up for the games."

Sampson needed a motivational edge for what he knew was one of the bigger games of the season, even though in those days Texas was in the Southwest Conference and OU was in the Big Eight.

"By this time I had been in Oklahoma long enough—and had been through an Oklahoma-Texas football game—to realize the Oklahoma-Texas rivalry was real," Sampson said. "I knew that we could lose to certain teams and it didn't cause many ripples in the water. But you didn't want to lose to Texas. I figured that out real quick. Even this little ol' boy from North Carolina figured that an Oklahoma-Texas game was a little bit different from the rest of them."

Sampson had never coached against Penders, but he had watched the tape of the OU-Texas game the previous season. His biggest fear was could Oklahoma guard Texas? He believed the Sooners could score against the Longhorns. And he used Texas's press to OU's advantage.

"I just can't remember a lot of games over the years where presses have really hurt our teams," Sampson said. "They didn't know that from the year before. But John was going to be the key guy."

Ontjes started off badly once again but would make a turnaround in the second half. Sampson started Dion Barnes in place of Fowler at shooting guard because Fowler had been five minutes late for a team meeting earlier. But by half time, OU led by five. In the second half, OU attacked the UT press.

"The coaches' biggest fear should always be pressure," Sampson said. "If you fear pressure, then you are always prepared for it."

And OU was prepared.

Sampson put his scorers, Minor and Abercrombie, in the corners near the basket. And OU attacked the pressure up the middle. The key was Ontjes because he was going to be trapped. But the Sooners threw it into him. And he was able to beat the initial trap and get the ball up to the scorers.

Sampson believed any shot the Sooners took would be a good one because it would be from Minor or Abercrombie, who combined for fifty-one points in the 100-75 OU win. It was the only time during Sampson's rookie campaign in Norman that OU scored 100 points in a game. And the ball-control Sooners held down a Texas team that scored 100 or more points nine times that season.

"We convinced the kids, though, we had won because of our defense," Sampson said. "It had created opportunities for us. I thought that was an important win because it gave us great confidence."

Penders added after the game: "They have been have-nots for a couple of years, so they are hungry. They're going to be a team to beat this year. They're not going to lose many here. I will guarantee you that."

Sampson liked the way the team was developing because the players were getting involved in scoring besides Minor.

"Calvin Curry had twenty-seven points off one play at Baylor called 10," Sampson said. "He had eight three-pointers. I was calling the plays at this time. And John Ontjes would run down the floor and he would look at me and always nod his head. I kept telling him 10 every time down. He would look at me and I would say, 'What do you think, John? Calvin is getting open off the backside of 10. Why don't we run 10 again?' He was so tuned into getting the plays in. He was the only guy I would talk to during the game."

And Abercrombie was developing into an inside force, despite giving up several inches to most players he played against inside.

"I don't think any other coach in the Big Eight would have put a 6-4 post man in the paint and expect something out of it," Abercrombie said. "He allowed me to play and use my quickness and use my strength and play hard. Coach always said my talents were my ability to play hard, taking charges, and diving for loose balls. I had no problems with it."

Sampson recorded his first victory over a ranked team as the OU coach when the Sooners beat No. 11 Iowa State in Norman on February 1. OU had a 4-3 Big Eight record when it went to Kansas on February 11. Sampson found it was about as much fun to play the No. 2-ranked Jayhawks in raucous Allen Field House as it was playing Arizona in McKale Center in Tucson.

Sampson received a technical foul as Kansas shot forty-one free throws to OU's twenty-one in a 93-76 Kansas victory in Lawrence. Sampson believed the officiating in the game was so "ridiculously one-sided and our kids were not getting a fair shake and our kids were not playing as hard as they could. That was the first time all year I felt we didn't come out and kick and claw and scrap all the way to the end."

After the game *The Daily Oklahoman* writer Bob Hersom pointed out to Sampson there was a good chance the Sooners, 17-6 overall and 4-4 in the Big Eight, might not win any more games the rest of the season. Oklahoma had a road game at Colorado coming up next and home games against national powers Missouri and Kansas and in-state rival Oklahoma State. The Sooners finished the regular season with road games at Iowa State and at Missouri. Hersom had a point. The finishing schedule was tough.

But OU would go 5-1 during that stretch and grab OU's first NCAA Tournament berth since the 1991-92 season. And Sampson would garner National Coach of the Year honors by the United States Basketball Writers Association, the Associated Press, and *Basketball Weekly*.

At Colorado, Sampson's superstitious nature played a part in developing a new piece to his game-day wardrobe. Karen usually packed a white shirt in his bag. But Karen didn't have a white shirt ironed when Kelvin was packing to catch the flight to Colorado. Kelvin, remembering he had just lost at Kansas wearing a white shirt, thought "Why not wear a blue dress shirt?" But it turned out to be a blue denim shirt that Kelvin had thrown in his bag.

OU won at Colorado, 82-75, for its first Big Eight road victory under Sampson as Curry hit his first five three-point shots and Minor added twenty-eight points. So Sampson would wear the blue denim against Missouri, which was ranked No. 9 in the country.

"We've been playing hard on the road all year, but we weren't getting anything accomplished," Minor told reporters after the game. "This is definitely a game we had to have. In the first half it seemed like we were playing under Billy Tubbs again, running and gunning. But in the second half we really started to play hard and play good defense again."

Against Missouri, the first of a tough three-game home stand, Minor set an OU record with twenty free throw attempts. It was an OU record that would be broken a couple of years later by Corey Brewer. Oklahoma won 94-89 and ran its home record to 13-0. Oklahoma played with great passion and hit Missouri with a 23-8 scoring run in the second half to win the game.

Sampson wanted to sleep in blue denim now.

There was only about a 48-hour turnaround before Kansas came to Norman for the ESPN Big Monday game. And the powerful Jayhawks, which had knocked off OU by seventeen points only ten days before in Lawrence, had ascended to the No. 1 ranking in college basketball.

Sampson was ill, however. He had a temperature of 104 degrees before the game. He was suffering from a virus and was vomiting and experiencing chills. Nevertheless, he held to his superstition.

Part of Sampson's routine is to get on a treadmill and go five miles before every home game. He usually wears a sweat suit. He sheds pounds, and the exercise also calms his nerves. Sampson felt so bad this night in 1995 before playing the Jayhawks, he hardly felt up to his pregame ritual. Then he was light-headed on the bench because he hadn't eaten all day.

But Sampson just loved the way the Sooners were playing against a very good Kansas team, which included a huge front line of 7-foot-2 Greg Ostertag, 6-foot-11 Raef LaFrentz, and 6-foot-10 Scot Pollard, not to mention guard Jacque Vaughn. All were future NBA players.

The OU fans, who sometimes seemed to be indifferent, were into this game. And the OU players mentioned it after the game. Some of the OU fans in the partisan crowd of 11,385 even got a little too carried away for Kansas coach Roy Williams, who stormed the court when he believed KU guard Jerod Haase had been touched by an OU fan. Williams picked up his first technical of the season when he left the bench to confront an OU student who had taunted Haase near the Sooner basket.

"It bothered me and I reacted," Williams said after the game. "I apologize to the University of Oklahoma. That's not the way I normally act."

Said Ontjes: "I watched Roy Williams get the technical. He had first thought someone in the student sections had touched him [Haase]. I was right in the middle of it."

Oklahoma led by thirteen points twice in the first half, but Kansas came back in the second half and took a six-point lead with 8:45 remaining. KU even led by four with 1:22 remaining.

Ontjes and Abercrombie wouldn't let the Sooners lose. The OU point guard drove the lane with 1:08 remaining and made a short jump shot to get OU within two points. After LaFrentz missed the front end of a 1-and-1 with a minute to go, Abercrombie buried a three-point basket from the left corner to give OU a 74-73 lead with 45 seconds remaining.

"It was a struggle the whole game," Abercrombie said. "They have all these big All-Americans and that whole front line is in the NBA now. Ryan Minor had a great game. I just happened to be sitting in the corner when I took the shot. If I had thought about what I was doing, I would never have hit it. The moment was right. And I took it."

Abercrombie, up until that point, had connected on only three of nine three-point attempts at OU. He hadn't made a three-pointer in nineteen games and hadn't even attempted a three-pointer in the Sooners' previous eleven games.

"All of sudden you can talk about all the loud arenas in the country," Sampson said. "Duke, Allen Field House, Gallagher-Iba, McKale Center. On that night, after Ernie's basket, that was the loudest crowd I had heard anywhere. Our fans willed us to win that game. After Ernie hit that three and we went down and got a stop [a Jayhawk turnover], I motioned for us to go to our spread delay. The only three people who were allowed to touch the ball were Ryan, Dion, and John—the guys who will shoot free throws. I remember how sick I was. Now, I was a live wire."

Minor was fouled and made his final two points on free throws with twelve seconds left. That put him at twenty-eight points for the night. Haase missed a three-point basket as time ran out. Ontjes, who had twelve points and eleven assists, grabbed the rebound and tossed the ball high in the air. OU had pulled off the 76-73 upset. After Sampson and Williams shook hands, Ontjes headed straight for Sampson and jumped on him.

OU had its first victory over a No. 1-ranked team since beating Missouri and Kansas in consecutive games on February 25 and 27, 1990, under Billy Tubbs. It was also Oklahoma's second straight home victory over a Top 25 team.

After the game Sampson went to John Underwood's house for a celebration. And he started thinking about Underwood's covert operation at the Delta Crown Room at DFW Airport a few months earlier. Sampson believed beating KU was a watershed victory. The Sooners were on their way.

"Roy Williams is the guy I want to beat," Sampson said of the KU coach. "I would say that because he has had the best program in our league. When we are recruiting, we try and measure ourselves in our league against Kansas. I think Kansas is the biggest game on our schedule other than our natural rivals. Kansas has been a standard bearer in our league."

Next up in Norman was Big Country Bryant Reeves and Oklahoma State. The Cowboys had won Sampson's first match-up in the Bedlam Series, 72-64, in Stillwater. But the rematch would be different in front of the first OU record crowd under Sampson, 12,671 fans. That record would be broken six times during the next six years as Sampson solidified the Sooners as a national power.

"This was going to be a discipline game," Sampson said. "The key was we couldn't let Big Country [Reeves] get seventeen or eighteen shot attempts. And the way you limit his touches is you control the game with your offense. Oklahoma State is a controlling team. They are like a pit bull. Once you get them on your neck, you can't get them off of you. They control the flow of the game. But I know that's the way we play, too."

There was pressure for Oklahoma to win this game, despite the 25th-ranked Sooners' most recent triumphs over Missouri and Kansas. The Sooners had to hit the road for their final two regular-season league games. And they were 1-4 in Big Eight road games under Sampson.

But the OU fans embraced the team again. The Sooners limited Reeves, the behemoth center, to thirteen shots. After OU led by nine at half time, OSU went ahead by a point with thirteen minutes left. The game went into overtime where the Sooners made all of their shots and free throws and pulled out an 82-74 victory over the Cowboys behind Minor's thirty-two points. He played all 45 minutes of the game.

Three Oklahoma State players fouled out trying to guard Minor, who sank a three-pointer from the corner to ice the victory in the closing minutes of overtime.

"Defensively, you have to play several guys on him and keep a fresh guy on him," said Tom Asbury, Kansas State's former coach. "If you are not toe-to-toe with him, he is going to bury it."

The victory over OSU broke a three-game losing streak against the Cowboys, and it was on Senior Night in Norman for Ontjes, James Mayden, and Calvin Curry.

OU ran its winning streak to five with its second Big Eight road victory under Sampson. The victory at Iowa State was accomplished before a revved up Hilton Coliseum crowd of 14,202 who showed up for senior Fred Hoiberg's final home game. The Sooners, however, clamped on Hoiberg's three-point shooting like a pit bull. He was 0-for-8 from behind the arc in OU's 71-68 victory, which boosted the Sooners' overall record to 22-6.

"They were throwing roses on the floor at Fred Hoiberg, and the referees had tears in their eyes," Sampson said of the pregame ceremony. "This was my first year in the Big Eight. But I knew they called him 'The Mayor.' I caught the end of the ceremony. And I thought we had no shot. I thought we wouldn't throw one fastball. Every pitch we throw tonight is going to be a screwball or a curve ball."

Sampson started off the game running the 1-4 offense. But he ran it wide. And it was harder for Iowa State to guard because the Cyclones had to spread out on the floor to guard the Sooners. Ontjes' dribble penetration worked better. Center James Mayden, the player who usually couldn't shoot straight, remarkably made six of seven shots and scored thirteen points.

OU's defense throttled Iowa State, which connected on only two of fourteen three-point shot attempts.

"When we went on the road those days, I always had our team shoot at the basket in front of our bench in the first half," Sampson said. "I always wanted our defense to be playing in front of our bench in the second half. Most people did the opposite. But then you could do that. Now, there is a new rule you have to shoot at your end [where your bench is] in the second half."

The Sooners' winning streak ended when Ontjes, the Sooners' leading free-throw shooter, missed two free throws with ten seconds remaining in regulation. Missouri, trailing by only two points, tied the score on two last-second free throws and won the game in overtime, 83-81.

Prior to the game at the Hearnes Center, Sampson was introduced to Norm Stewart's courtside manner. Stewart was dean of the Big Eight coaches and had some friendly advice before the game for the young upstart from Oklahoma, Sampson, then thirty-eight years old and on a five-game winning streak going into Columbia.

"I always get out to the floor late, right before the game," Sampson said. "Norm was already out there. So I walked over to shake his hand on the way to the bench. He didn't say hello. He didn't say congratulations. He didn't say good luck. He said, 'You are winning too many damn games your first year. Slow down.' Then he just kind of walked back away from me."

After losing to the Tigers, Oklahoma finished third in the Big Eight behind regular-season champion Kansas and Oklahoma State. But because of defections from the Tubbs regime, the Sooners were down to eight scholarship players. And the team was getting worn down.

Sampson felt bad about the Missouri loss, but he also had to consider the depth problems. There were no subs for Minor. He could rotate the guards and the other forward spot and center. But Minor, starting with the victory at Colorado, had played every minute of four straight games, including the 45 minutes at Oklahoma State. And he followed with another 45-minute overtime haul at Missouri.

Sampson had Minor playing all over the court, depending on the match-ups.

"I saw how they were playing Ryan, then I would decide what we did on offense," Sampson said. As an example when Missouri put 6-4 Julian Winfield on Minor, OU tried to post up Minor inside. When Kansas put 6-11 Raef LaFrentz on him, Sampson moved Minor outside.

In the next two games in the Big Eight Post-Season Tournament, Minor followed with 39- and 38-minute efforts, scoring forty-five points and grabbing twenty-five total rebounds in the two games which the Sooners split, beating Colorado and losing to Oklahoma State in the Big Eight Conference semifinals.

But OU made it back to the NCAAs as a Top 16 seed in the 64-team field. Oklahoma, a No. 4 seed, lost, 77-67, to 13th-seeded Manhattan and Heshimu Evans, who later would transfer to Kentucky, in the first round of the NCAA Tournament in Memphis.

The Sooners had a five-point half time lead, but the Jaspers went ahead early in the second half. They then used a 22-8 run against a cold-shooting and turnover-prone OU team to take a thirteen-point lead with about seven minutes left in the game. Manhattan made thirteen of eighteen free throws down the stretch to win.

"I had eleven points and eleven assists in that game," Ontjes said. "It was difficult. I wanted to go pretty far. At least win a couple of games in the tournament. I didn't think it was Coach Sampson's fault. We had just peaked a little bit early, about two weeks early. That's when we played some of our best basketball all year. We kind of ran out of gas. I wish I had had a couple of more years under Coach Sampson."

Minor then faced a decision whether to return for his senior season or go to the NBA or play baseball.

"I didn't even realize he was contemplating the NBA," Sampson said. "It started getting in the newspapers. I called R.C. Buford, who was a scout for the San Antonio Spurs. Danny Manning's dad, Ed, had been to a lot of our games. And all of those guys told me they thought Ryan would be a first-round pick, but he wouldn't go in the Top Ten. That was the information I passed along to Ryan. If Ryan had been a lottery pick, then he wouldn't have had a choice. He would have had to have gone."

Minor had become an Oklahoma icon. The fans loved Ryan. He couldn't go anywhere without getting hounded for autographs. He did public service announcements. He was in the Yellow Pages. At each home game, one OU fan paraded around the court with a sign that read "Minor Meter," with Minor's current point total for the game. Some of his baseball teammates wore hard hats with flashlights taped to the brims and called themselves "Ryan's Minors."

"Ryan loved it here," Sampson said. "He loved playing in this system. He had lots of people telling him he should go pro. But Ryan, I think, wanted to stay. Hindsight being 20-20, maybe Ryan should have gone, because the next year, without John Ontjes and with a lot of new players, Ryan's role changed. Not a lot, because he was still our best player. Ryan didn't have as good a year. And I think his stock dropped a little bit."

Minor stayed for his senior season at Oklahoma and later said he had no second thoughts. He also had offers in baseball to jump to the pros.

"Who knows?" Minor said a year later. "If I had gone out maybe I would have had a good year or something."

Right after Sampson arrived in Norman, Minor, as a designated hitter, first baseman, and pitcher, had helped lead Oklahoma to the 1994 NCAA baseball title. He made three straight all-tournament teams that spring. Then, in June 1995, Minor batted .533 in an NCAA Regional Tournament, drawing the interest of scouts. A week later the New York Mets drafted Minor in the seventh round. He had been drafted out of high school in the eleventh round by the Baltimore Orioles.

Minor said no to baseball as well and returned to playing a second year for Sampson. But the time commitments of playing multiple sports—something Sampson had gone through as a baseball-basketball player at Pembroke State—may have hurt Minor.

"I think playing two sports was almost a detriment," Sampson said. "Because he was so good in both, he never made a commitment to one. In the summers, he played mostly baseball. When school started, he would come back to basketball. He was phenomenal. He was the best offensive player I have ever coached. I have never coached a kid who could score like him. He had the best hand-eye coordination of any kid I have ever seen. When the ball touched any part of his fingers, it was secure. He never bobbled the ball. He never missed a key free throw.

"And if he had made the commitment to basketball, there is no question in my mind he would be in the NBA right now. Or, if he had made the commitment to baseball, I think he would have been a 20-home-run, 80-RBI-a-year guy. Maybe 100 RBI."

In the spring of 2001 Minor was playing either for the Montreal Expos major league team or the club's Triple A affiliate in Ottawa after being traded by the Orioles.

"I also think Ryan had bad luck," Sampson said of the 1996 NBA Draft. "He was drafted by the Philadelphia 76ers. Their first pick was Allen Iverson. Ryan Minor, all of a sudden, was on the back burner. He also had a rookie coach. I was hoping he would get an older coach, like a Larry Brown or a Lenny Wilkens—a coach like that who would bring him along. Being on that team, which was poor at the time, they wanted somebody who could come in and help them right away."

"I liked him when he was a junior," the Spurs' Buford said. "But he didn't play very well in any of the post-season camps as a senior. It has been long enough ago I forget about why he failed. But he left [the NBA] so quickly, he didn't pursue it very hard."

Sampson saw Minor as a player who could have eased on to a pro team and then become a real factor his third or fourth season in the NBA. Instead, Minor was cut in the fall of 1996 and returned to baseball where he reached the major leagues in the late 1990s with the Orioles.

Ironically, Mark Hendrickson, Sampson's two-sport basketball-baseball star at Washington State, was drafted one spot ahead of Minor in the 1996 NBA draft's second round. Hendrickson was selected 31st and Minor 32nd overall. Both were picks of the 76ers.

"What happened was we played in the summer league," Hendrickson said, "I made the team, and he went to the CBA. He left the following spring before spring training and went to the Orioles."

Hendrickson played in the NBA for four years, for the 76ers, Sacramento, and New Jersey. But he is now back into baseball as a pitcher in the Toronto Blue Jays' Triple A farm club in Syracuse. He saw Minor in the spring of 2001 when their teams played. They are still good friends.

Minor's pro career may have been rocky. But there was no question he was the centerpiece of OU's first season under Sampson.

That same spring, Sampson also would sign maybe the most intriguing player of his coaching career, a rawboned kid from Chihuahua, Mexico, 6-7 Eduardo Najera. Little did Sampson know but Najera would work himself into a position to become the first player from Mexico drafted into the NBA after his career at Oklahoma.

Najera was an exchange student playing at San Antonio's Cornerstone Christian High School. The Sooners' staff first saw Najera at the Fort Worth Lions Club Tournament during December 1994. Najera, who had arrived in the United States a couple months earlier, spoke only bits of English.

"Having been here at UTEP for twenty-one months, I even have a greater appreciation for what Eduardo had to overcome," former OU assistant Jason Rabedeaux said. "Eduardo wasn't always the rough and tough player he evolved into. A lot of that was trying to figure out America."

The first time Sampson went to visit Najera he needed an interpreter. And Sampson's sense of humor didn't really come through. Sampson likes to have fun with the recruits. And he couldn't have fun with Najera because he was concentrating so hard on what Sampson was saying through an interpreter.

On April 19, 1995, the day the Alfred P. Murrah Federal Building in Oklahoma City was bombed and 168 people were killed, Sampson was on his way to San Antonio on a recruiting trip to see Najera.

"I remember talking to Eduardo," Sampson said. "He got worried about Oklahoma because he thought that was a place people bombed. I had to explain that was a one-time deal."

Oklahoma eventually won a recruiting battle with New Mexico, Oral Roberts, and Oklahoma State. But Najera was a partial qualifier. He had the grade point average, but not the test score. He went to OU as a part-time student (six or less hours) so he would not use up any eligibility. He kept taking the test in English, and on the fourth try he scored the necessary seventeen in December 1995.

"I will never forget the day he passed it," Sampson said. "He got his test score and he came up those stairs. He knew two words, really well, 'I pass.' He must have been saying it out in the parking lot, 'I pass, I pass.' As soon as he passed, I put him on scholarship."

Najera still had to be helped because of the language barrier. He lived in the dorm across the hall from OU basketball players Renzi Stone and Tim Heskett. He didn't know enough English to order pizza. He had a take-out menu, and he would look and point to what he wanted.

"All he would watch was Channel 49, the local Hispanic channel, when he first got here. And then he would start watching *The Andy Griffith Show*. This kid from Chihuahua, Mexico, was watching *The Andy Griffith Show* to learn how to speak English. I thought 'My God what do we have here?'"

CHAPTER 9
_____

Second-Year
Obstacles

Kelvin Sampson's second season at Oklahoma was strewn with hurdles. His health slid. The team struggled with chemistry. The nonconference schedule was brutal. And Sampson never really settled on a point guard.

It was a sophomore jinx of giant proportions.

Despite all of the problems the Sooner program endured during the last season for the old Big Eight Conference, Oklahoma still would wind up in the NCAA Tournament for a second straight year. Washington State transfer Nate Erdmann, by way of Hutchinson Community College, teamed with Ryan Minor, Ernie Abercrombie, and Dion Barnes to help the Sooners post seventeen victories.

The 1995-96 season was not an opportune time for Sampson's asthma to act up. He was also having trouble with his back, which had required surgery during his first season as head coach at Montana Tech nearly fifteen years earlier. The two health problems combined to drag Sampson down while coaching a team that was struggling to find an identity.

Oklahoma, fresh off its stunning first season under Sampson, was entered in the sixteen-team Preseason National Invitation Tournament (NIT) and opened with a 99-68 victory over Jackson State in the first round. But then the Sooners lost at Georgia Tech, 83-72, to start a three-game tailspin. The Sooners went under .500 for the first time under Sampson when they dropped their next game, 81-69, to a very talented Texas Tech team in Norman.

The OU team was in a state of disarray during the Texas Tech game.

Erdmann had an ankle injury that slowed him. Center Evan Wiley had been suspended for the game. And Minor, the team's star, played only seventeen minutes because he was ejected late in the first half by official David Libbey. Minor finished with just eight points, the first time in thirty-nine games he had not reached double figures in scoring.

The big story, though, was Kelvin Sampson's health. The Sampson family had pretty well concealed his asthma problems. But he coached that game with an intravenous tube in his left wrist because of his asthma, which had required hospitalization the week prior to the Texas Tech game. The family had to go public with his condition.

"I remember him being so sick then, he was in the hospital," OU assistant coach Ray Lopes said. "The doctor made him stay in the hospital for a thirty-hour period. But that week he was so concerned about his team, he walked into practice with IVs taped to his arm."

Oklahoma trainer Alex Brown has become an expert on Sampson's health.

"There are automatic times, like October and March, when the asthma kicks up," Brown said. "Stress is a major trigger for asthma. And because of his personal drive and intensity, his work ethic, the intensity of late in the season and the early preseason seem to bother him. The early preseason is the signing period. And there is always the stress of whether a player is going to sign with you or not."

Kelvin's asthma problems were old hat to Karen. In fact, she has a whole household of asthmatics. One of son Kellen's worst attacks came one night when he just was six months old. The Sampsons had just moved to Washington State where Kelvin had become an assistant coach in 1985.

"It took us three hours to stabilize Kellen," Karen said. "Asthmatics become fatigued and die. Their bodies just give up. We never thought Kellen would run and play basketball. But puberty has been a big help. We'd be on the way to Seattle and he would have just a cough and we would wind up in the hospital. If I couldn't stabilize him, I was in trouble. I am not a 911 person. But I would call the doctor and tell her what was going on and ask her to make the decision when to put him in the hospital."

Kelvin's asthma did not show up until he became head coach at Washington State in 1987. And he had a ritual he started that second season at OU when it became particularly bad again.

"He usually checks himself in and out of the Norman hospital," Karen said. "Once he was in the admitting room, and a fan asked him for an autograph." Kelvin, lying with his face down on a table, could barely sign his name. "My mom is such a fan of yours," the fan told a groggy Sampson.

"Nine times out of ten, he drives himself to the hospital," Karen said. "I have to be in the passenger's seat. A couple of times on the way to the hospital, he wanted to go see Kellen play basketball."

OU has an inhaler on the sideline. And there's a nebulizer in the locker room at Lloyd Noble Center. Sampson said Brown will take a battery-operated nebulizer on the plane in games this coming season. Brown keeps the inhaler in his pocket or in his kit on the bench. "At times he will get upset or very excited for a moment," Brown said. "He will get to yelling at someone."

Brown said that getting on top of it is the key. And since that second season, he has made it a priority.

"For the longest time, Kelvin would wait too long," Karen said. "And from twelve to three in the morning is when most asthmatics die. You may wait and not be able to get to the hospital. He did not take it seriously enough and react quickly enough. He was noncompliant. That is the most dangerous kind of asthmatic."

"When I would be hospitalized, I would check myself in," Sampson said. "Asthmatics have problems at night. I would talk the doctor into letting me go in at night. I would get IVs. And once I would get the drugs in me, I could check out."

Sampson continued to coach. After a 77-63 loss at Purdue dropped OU's record to 1-3, it was apparent Minor was in a shooting slump. In the first four games of the season, Minor had made only twenty-one of sixty-two shots. He had shot nearly 50 percent the previous season. Sampson had a heart-to-heart talk with Minor and told him he had gotten the big head. Minor admitted he hadn't been preparing himself for the game. He had been embarrassed with his ejection against Texas Tech.

"It just kind of slaps me in the face because my whole life I have never been like this," Minor told Bob Hersom of *The Daily Oklahoman.*

Minor broke out of the slump with thirty-three points in OU's 107-75 blowout of Texas-San Antonio, which started a six-game winning streak. Erdmann also sparkled with twenty-one points and started to live up to Sampson's expectations against UTSA. Sampson had moved Erdmann from shooting guard to forward, which pushed Abercrombie, at 6-4, to center. Barnes and junior college transfer Tyrone Foster were the starting backcourt.

In effect, Sampson was back to his old three-guard lineup after starting either sophomore Evan Wiley or senior Jason Yanish at center in the first four games.

Minor looked like the player he was the season before in this new lineup.

"I have never known a white kid to play as well as he did," said OU's Bobby Joe Evans, who was a freshman center on that team. "Everything he threw up went in. Ryan was a good basketball player. It was too bad he didn't play in the NBA like he should have. If someone would have picked him up, he would have been a good player."

It was Evans, a burly 6-foot-9, 270-pounder from McKinney, Texas, who Sampson had high hopes for in the future. And like Minor, Evans had NBA potential. But Evans, because of an assortment of injuries, did not participate in OU's fall conditioning. And he ballooned to 285 pounds during the fall much to Sampson's chagrin. Knee injuries would keep him from ever realizing his potential at OU. But at least in a two-game span against Oral Roberts and Drexel, he would star.

"He was a man child," OU assistant Jason Rabedeaux said. "He was such a great kid. There were so many expectations placed on him. He was the first big fish recruit for Coach Sampson at Oklahoma. If he had had a healthy pair of legs, he could have been as good a player as ever put on an Oklahoma uniform."

In OU's 87-53 victory over Oral Roberts, Evans played only 24 minutes off the bench, but he scored twenty points and grabbed eight rebounds. Then, playing head to head against Drexel's Malik Rose, one of the nation's top rebounders and scorers, Evans scored eighteen points and grabbed seven rebounds in the Sooners' 85-78 victory over the Dragons.

"I got a three-pointer right before half time to put us up by one," Evans said. "Rose wound up being an NBA draft pick and played for San Antonio. But that game we were holding each other. That game really stands out. I think I showed people I was an NBA draft pick.

The only thing that stopped me was bad wheels. I think they thought this kid could really play, if he had someone else's knees."

Oklahoma's six-game winning streak was broken in the title game of the All-College Tournament when the Sooners dropped a 76-72 decision in overtime to Florida. But before embarking on the last Big Eight schedule, the Sooners knocked off SMU by ten in Norman.

Then Sampson's back completely went out. He had suffered enough pain. He believed that steroids he was taking earlier for his asthma may have masked the pain he was having with his back.

"It was the next day after the SMU game," Sampson said. "The only person who knew about it was Alex. I was tired of taking drugs. I knew something was wrong with it because I had had back surgery before in Montana. It had started in August. And I thought if I rested it and didn't do much, it would go away because that will happen a lot with a herniated disc. It is kind of like a shock absorber in your car. This one wasn't getting any better, though. It was getting worse.

"Traveling kills your back, and I was traveling a lot of places. I didn't have time to take care of Kelvin. I can deal with pain. They were shooting me with shots to get me through. And for four or five days I wouldn't feel anything. I would take these painkillers and I would be drowsy the entire next day. I was tired of that. I couldn't move."

In early January Sampson went to get an MRI. And he was diagnosed with a ruptured disc. Surgery was scheduled for the next day.

"He was a real con man with his health," Brown remembered. "He wouldn't tell you what was going on until he had to, at least that is the way he used to be."

Three days later Sampson was back coaching after the surgery. He hadn't even seen his team and flew to the game on a private plane. He couldn't stand the thought of lying in bed and watching the game. Said Rabedeaux: "We didn't even know if he would show up. He was laying on his back at half time and before the game."

"I had to go to Wal-Mart in Manhattan to get him a stool to sit on during the game," Brown said. Coaching from that stool, from which he often had to be helped up by assistants, Sampson led by example. OU won its conference opener, 64-59, despite Minor shooting only five-for-eighteen. Tyrone Foster, the team's point guard had fifteen points and ten rebounds in a show of his athletic ability.

"Just knowing he [Sampson] was on the sidelines helped us win," Erdmann said. "It's real obvious in our organization how much he means to us."

Duke coach Mike Krzyzewski had a similar back ailment during the 1994-95 season and was told he needed a six- to eight- week recovery period. He returned in a week but then couldn't stand the pain and sat out the rest of the season.

"Sampson was back in a week," Abercrombie said. "That comes through in his coaching. He is such a mentally tough person. His pain threshold must be way up there. He had the asthma and IV in his hand. Plus, he had back surgery. Put all those together and the stress it takes to go through a season at a top program, and there you go."

Sampson didn't believe he could leave the team or it would end up much like Duke did the previous season when Pete Gaudet had to take over the reins. That Duke team finished 13-18.

"I didn't feel like I could afford to be away from that team," Sampson said. "Deep down in my heart I knew I couldn't be away from this team because it was too fragile. I don't think Ryan was ever happy that year, because he wanted that year to be like the year before. And it wasn't. We had different players. Nate Erdmann had sacrificed part of his career to follow me to Oklahoma. He had a pretty good junior year. But he struggled at times. It was important for me to get out of the hospital. I couldn't imagine my assistant coaches coaching that team."

Oklahoma returned from the Kansas State outing and faced a talented Nebraska team with such players as Jaron Boone and Erick Strickland. It took three overtimes for OU to win, 117-100.

But then the Sooners lost four straight games, before winning, 67-65, at Texas in the last nonconference game between the two teams. The point guard problems persisted. Roles were fuzzy.

"We didn't start recruiting a point guard until January or February [of 1995]," Sampson said when it was pretty apparent Prince Fowler was not going to work out. So Sampson went back to the old reliable Trinity Valley (Texas), which had produced Neil Derrick. Trinity Valley's Tyrone Foster, a 5-foot-11, 165-pounder from White Plains, New York, was more of a loner than Sampson liked. And that was not a good characteristic for a point guard in Sampson's system.

"Tyrone was all right," Abercrombie said. "But he was better off the court than on it. He was easy to get along with. But during

Ernie Abercrombie was a star for Kelvin Sampson in 1995-96.
Photo courtesy of OU Athletic Media Relations.

practice and games, everybody was on him and how hard he was [not] playing. And that hurt him."

In fact, at one of the team meetings at the sprawling Sampson home, especially built with eight-foot doorways on the ground floor for the tall players, Karen peered through her kitchen windows across the patio into the spacious team room. While many of the OU players were huddled around the television and pool table, Foster was in the corner by the windows, all by himself. She knew that wasn't good.

"He was a talented kid," Sampson said. "As far as pure talent, he was a much better player than John Ontjes. But not a point guard. He was not a great worker. But a talented kid. He could score twenty points a game. Tyrone could play. But he was just not a point guard in our system.

"Nate Erdmann sort of took some of Dion Barne's thunder. We had a lot of issues on this team. We had better players than we had at Washington State. But we did not have better chemistry. I learned a lot about recruiting that year. And that team still made the NCAA Tournament. If we were not going to make it one year, that was the year."

Furthermore, Oklahoma's 1995-96 nonconference schedule was brutal. The Sooners lost at Georgia Tech, which won the ACC regular-season title and made it to the NCAA Sweet 16. They lost at Purdue, which won the Big Ten Conference regular season title with a 15-3 record. Oklahoma also dropped home nonconference games to Texas Tech, which finished 30-2 and made the Sweet 16, and to Mississippi State, which advanced to the Final Four.

"Those were all hard games, and we were in a position to win all of those games," Sampson said. "But we were not close enough or tight enough to overcome adversity."

Oklahoma played six overtime games that season. The Sooners were 4-2 in those games, including a sweep of Nebraska in two overtime games. Oklahoma lost in the first round of the Big Eight Tournament to Missouri. And the Sooners nervously awaited the pairings show.

But Oklahoma was in again as a No. 10 seed and would play the Temple Owls, a No. 7 seed, in Orlando. The Owls, famous for their smothering match-up zone, were going to be a problem for the smaller Sooners. And Oklahoma managed only forty-three points in

Ryan Minor returned for his senior year in 1995-96 and averaged 21.3 points.
Photo by Lisa Hall/OU Athletic Media Relations.

an eighteen-point loss, the Sooners' lowest point total in thirteen years.

"If we had played Temple ten times, I don't think we could have beaten them," Sampson said. "We couldn't score the ball in the middle of their zone. Ernie was not effective in that game because they had a lot of big kids."

But Abercrombie had a big heart. And years later he still thanks Sampson for not only recruiting him to Oklahoma, but for giving him good advice.

"He just told me I should be disappointed if I didn't get a degree from Oklahoma," said Abercrombie, who is a regional sales manager in Houston for John Henry's Food Products. "He said it was a chance of a lifetime. I played in Spain for two years then came back to Houston. I could have gone back; instead I went back to OU, and I graduated in 1999 with a degree in sociology."

Following the 1995-96 season, North Carolina State coach Les Robinson resigned, and the Wolfpack made a run at Sampson at the Final Four.

"It was closer than we wanted him to be [to taking it]," Underwood said. "There were some things done by us contractually to counter that. But that is one job that really intrigued him. It was home for him. And North Carolina State is a state supported school. That appeals more to him. This probably could have been his job. I think a lot of it was his commitment. He had recruited some kids and told them he was going to be at Oklahoma."

A reporter from *The Dallas Morning News* approached Sampson at the New York Hilton, the coaches' hotel at the 1996 Final Four, and kidded him that North Carolina State was hot on his trail. The reporter had good sources, Sampson thought to himself with a little bit of trepidation. Even at that moment Sampson was on his way to a clandestine meeting with North Carolina State officials about the Wolfpack coaching vacancy.

"It was like some kind of treasure hunt," Sampson said. "I had to give an assumed name to the taxi driver. And he was going to take me somewhere in case I was followed. They were paranoid about it."

Sampson met undercover with North Carolina State but hadn't officially committed to going on to the next step, an official interview. Sampson flew back to Norman to ponder his future.

"I was really, really interested in that North Carolina State job," Sampson said. "That's when the plans for the new practice facilities

Nate Erdmann (22) was one of Kelvin Sampson's top captains.
Photo by Lisa Hall/OU Athletic Media Relations.

were hatched. I think Donnie Duncan, our athletic director at OU then, thought I was going to take the job because he invited me over to his house. We sat down at the table in his dinning room."

Sampson recalled that Duncan said, "I don't want to go through this every year, Kelvin. What do we have to do to make you not look at other jobs and stay at Oklahoma?"

"That's when we started talking about we have to have a place to practice every day where our kids can work out," Sampson said. "And it can be a destination spot for basketball. We have to make it more of a basketball school. And I kept thinking about Nate Erdmann. He left Washington State to follow me to Oklahoma. He spent a year of his life at a junior college before coming to Oklahoma. And I would have to go back to tell him I was going to leave him a second time? I had already done it once. I couldn't do it a second time."

Sampson canceled a meeting with North Carolina State in New Orleans because he knew if he got on a plane to New Orleans he was going to take the North Carolina State job.

"But I couldn't get on the plane to New Orleans because of timing," Sampson said. "I had only been at Oklahoma for two years. Kellen and Lauren were a factor. But the main factor was I could not leave Nate Erdmann."

"I don't know he ever came out and told me that," Erdmann said. "I think with the team coming back and just the whole process with the journey we had been through, it would have been tough for him to leave again. And I would let him know about it."

Sampson knew he had a good job at Oklahoma. And Karen wasn't pushing it either, although she would be back home in North Carolina.

"Sometimes, it is hard to go home," Sampson said. "What is best for other people is not always best for you."

CHAPTER 10

A Year in Transition

The troubling thing for Kelvin Sampson as he entered the third year at Oklahoma was still the point guard situation. He didn't have one on his roster. And running the 1-4 offense was not the job for some part-timer. That person had to be committed to getting the Sooners into their sets. The point guard couldn't be worried about his own shots in Sampson's system.

"The point guard is the most important part of his system," said OU assistant coach Bennie Seltzer. "He was a point guard. He coaches as if he were playing. He coaches through the point guard."

Opposing coaches and assistants have marveled at Sampson's ability to run the 1-4 offense, which puts a premium on ball placement by the point guard. The forwards have to be good passers who are mobile and can spot the guards on the perimeter or slashing to the basket. But the point guard got the ball to the best player at crunch time.

"Here's what I have always thought about Kelvin," said Kim Anderson, former Missouri assistant coach and current director of Big 12 Conference basketball operations. "He does the best job of getting his best player in the best position to succeed. You go back to Ryan Minor, Nate Erdmann, Corey Brewer, Eduardo Najera, Nolan Johnson. He could always take his best player and get him shots."

Since Ontjes left, Sampson had been searching for the man to run the 1-4. And once again, the 1996-97 season would be an experimental year. Tyrone Foster had left after playing just one season. The flamboyant Prince Fowler had transferred to TCU.

"The point guard had to be a high-energy guy," Sampson said. "He had to be able to handle adversity. He had to be able to drive the car, put the key in the ignition, and make sure all the passengers had their seat belts on and make sure they were all comfortable. Tyrone wasn't the guy. We had signed another point guard who didn't make his grades. So we didn't have a point guard."

But the Sooners did have a good freshman recruiting class coming in with forward Eduardo Najera, guard Tim Heskett, and center Renzi Stone. Heskett was not a point guard. He was a three-point shooter and a good passer. The other newcomer was Corey Brewer, from West Memphis, a raw-boned guard who played at Carl Albert Junior College in Oklahoma.

"All the kids who played for me the first two years were now gone," Sampson said. "It was really like starting over. The point guard for the first four or five games of the year was Nate Erdmann. The guy I had in mind to play point was Corey Brewer. He was tough. Corey had scars and welts on his body where he had been shot. I was in West Memphis the day he got drafted by the Miami Heat. It was a tough neighborhood. He overcame a lot.

"But the structure of our offense . . . there were days he would run up the tunnel crying because he didn't understand how things worked," Sampson said. "He ran up the tunnel because I made him dot every 'I' and cross every 'T.' I made him touch every line. He was not used to that. He just wanted to go. He was like a bull in the china shop. But I had to find a way to make him a point guard, because Nate was too valuable in other areas.

"There was one game where I only ran two plays the entire game. When John Ontjes was there, he was a true point guard and we could run a lot of stuff. When Corey was there, we had to really limit it. He didn't think like a point guard."

Brewer agreed with that assessment.

"It was a different experience for me," Brewer said. "I was used to being a two-guard and would score-score. I never had to get someone else involved. But I had Nate on my side, who was a great shooter. And I had to change my game. It was difficult at the beginning. Point guard was the most important position on the floor. You are running the team and you have to make everybody happy."

Oklahoma won its first six games, though, masking the deficiency. Included in that was an 82-58 victory over Purdue in Norman on ESPN. Center Bobby Joe Evans had seventeen points and looked like he was about to emerge. Then disaster struck.

"Bobby Joe got hurt in the Purdue game," Sampson said. "I knew I would never have him at full strength again. He already had had surgery once the previous summer. He had had surgery his senior year in high school. Then we had corrected it that summer. We found out he didn't have any cartilage in his knee. And when you don't have cartilage in your knee, it is like bone on bone. Cartilage is like a shock absorber. It reduces your blows."

Evans' injury meant mercurial center Evan "Hootie" Wiley would move more to the forefront as the season progressed.

"We also had a transfer that year from Indiana, Lou Moore," Sampson said of a 6-foot-6 forward. "He became eligible for the Purdue game. He was never the player we thought he would be because he was legally blind in his right eye. I remember talking to Ron Felling [former Indiana assistant coach] and telling him that. We had recruited him out of junior college. Wake Forest and Alabama also recruited him. But it came down to us and Indiana. He only stayed one year and he struggled with discipline."

The high-water mark for Moore was a nineteen-point, thirteen-rebound effort in a 76-66 loss at Texas in January of that season.

Kelvin had high hopes for Bobby Joe Evans (left).
Photo courtesy of OU Athletic Media Relations.

Sampson, armed with promises of improvements to Lloyd Noble Center after his brush with the North Carolina State job, then befriended one of the OU regents, Dr. Donald Halverstadt, who had played basketball at Princeton in the 1950s. Starting with the Memphis game in December 1996, Halverstadt has only missed one Oklahoma game home or away during the last five seasons.

"I think he invited me because he wanted to show me their facilities at The Pyramid," Dr. Halverstadt said. "We were trying to develop a plan for expanded facilities and upgrading facilities at Lloyd Noble. And he wanted me to see what he thought were some of the better facilities around the country."

But Dr. Halverstadt was stunned when Sampson hardly said two words to him the entire two-day trip. He didn't take it personally. Dr. Halverstadt was called to make the next charter trip. And he has missed only one since, when he was sick that season.

"Once, he gets his game face on, you might as well forget trying to reach him," Dr. Halverstadt said. "He is in a world of his own."

Sampson was too busy dealing with the complexities of his team to worry too much about Lloyd Noble. He was trying to develop a point guard. And he knew he had a budding star in the 6-foot-7, 232-pound freshman Eduardo Najera, who had his first double-double, ten points and thirteen rebounds, in OU's 61-47 loss to the Tigers at The Pyramid.

Najera, from Chihuahua, Mexico, had to sit out the previous season as a part-time student until he got his test score to become eligible.

"Eduardo played like a man against Memphis," Sampson said. "But he wasn't consistent. This is where I go back to adversity in our practices. Our kids would call it something else, I am sure. Eduardo went through a lot of adversity in our practices. I always thought Eduardo was soft. When he first got here, he wouldn't compete. He'd play hard. With our guys I always was trying to get them to understand there was a difference in playing hard and really competing. Most teams would play hard, but for us to survive we had to out-compete them. That's what I thought Eduardo had to do.

"Eduardo was a step slow in everything he did when he got here. A lot of it was his language barrier. But a lot of it was his personality. There was something hidden inside him that you could bring out. Eduardo was a nice kid. Corey was a nice kid, too. But Corey would rip your heart out and throw it at you. Eduardo wouldn't do that yet.

Playing with Corey, I was able to let Eduardo know how nasty, tough, and mean you could be. Playing with Nate Erdmann showed him what a captain was."

This was Erdmann's last go-around. And he served as buffer between Sampson and the team.

"Nate knew me so well," Sampson said. "He knew when I was getting ready to explode and get on the team. If I kicked the team out of practice, we were going to come back at six the next morning. Nate would have a great knack for saying, 'Coach, Coach, may I say something?' He would call the team around and start talking to them. The complexion of practice would change because of what Nate would say to pick it up. 'Let's go a little bit harder, let's talk a little bit more, compete harder, because if you don't Coach is getting ready to kick us out of practice. We will be back at six. You don't understand, we don't want to do that, because not only will we practice at six, we will come back and practice just as hard at three.' Nate knew how to do that. And he taught Tim and Eduardo. Erdmann was a senior and he took Renzi, Tim, and Eduardo under his wing. He was like the mother hen."

"Any coach, you can see it on his face," Erdmann said. When Sampson was going to toss the team, "He would give the captain a look. He wouldn't say anything. You just get a feeling, he is irritated and you stop the practice. He gives you that freedom. And eight hours from now, a lot of kids don't want to do it [practice]. They value their rest. That definitely comes into play."

The 6-foot-5 Erdmann, from Portales, New Mexico, was the son of a high school coach and would sometimes be reluctant to shoot. He was a multitalented player, who would just as soon pass as score. But Sampson could always push him competitively.

Erdmann said the maddest Sampson got at him was at half time of his junior year at Nebraska, when he had only two points at half time. Erdmann scored twenty-one in the second half as Oklahoma rallied for an 80-76 victory.

"I remember one time we played Colorado with Chauncey Billups," Sampson said. "It didn't take much to get Nate going. But I told Nate, 'There are nine NBA scouts here tonight and they all came to see Chauncey.' Nate had thirty-one that night. I always knew where to push the buttons with Nate. He had sacrificed a lot to come to OU, so it was personal with him.

"I have had some tough, tough competitors. Ryan, Corey Brewer, and Eduardo were my competitors. Nate grew into being a competitor. Nate and I had some of our most heated battles in practice to get Nate to compete hard and get out of his comfort zone. Nate had a lot of God-given ability."

Sampson credited Erdmann as the dominant force in a 66-60 victory at Texas Tech that season during "Nate Erdmann Day" before an estimated 300 to 400 fans from his hometown, Portales, about 100 miles from Lubbock. It was one of only two Oklahoma road victories that season. In the final standings the Texas Tech road victory was crucial because it gave the Sooners a 9-7 Big 12 record, good for sixth place.

The lack of true point guard translated into Oklahoma's problems on the road that year. The Sooners dropped a 73-72 overtime decision at Oklahoma State, in which the Sooners blew a fourteen-point second half lead. Renzi Stone remembered Najera crying in the locker room because he missed a key free throw late in the game and also Brewer wrecking the bathroom stall because he was so upset.

And there also was an 82-55 loss at Iowa State. That still ranked as the second worst conference loss on the road for an OU team under Sampson through his first seven seasons at the school.

"It was early in the second half and they had a breakaway and got their crowd fired up," remembers senior walk-on guard John Nash. "You couldn't hear yourself think. There was a time out and Coach Sampson just went off on us. It was the same thing we would get during a difficult practice. We would take a charge in practice. We were proud of doing it. But we weren't doing it in the game. We are down twenty-some-odd points, and he didn't get on us for not shooting the ball well. He got on us for not being good teammates.

"He was the same guy all the time in practice or in a game," Nash continued. "As a player that was reassuring. He may have been feeling more stress and excitement during a game, but he doesn't show it."

There was one practice that season, which stood out in everybody's mind, when Coach Sampson turned Corey Brewer loose on freshman Tim Heskett.

"If Tim didn't maximize his abilities, the quote overachiever unquote, he wasn't going to be effective unless he outcompeted his opponent," Sampson said of the freshman. "Everything being even, he was going to get beat. He was a step slow. He couldn't create his own shot. I told Tim this is not a platoon system. I can't bring you out here for offense and get you off for defense. You have to be a junk-yard dog. You have to be a warehouse rat. That is the only way you are going to survive.

"Corey was tough on Tim. I was tough on Tim. Everybody was tough on Tim. One of the things coaches coach against is recruiting mistakes. And there was a thing going around: 'Why was Tim at this level?' I didn't want Tim to fail. But I also know when I put my all-competitor team together when the party is over and my coaching career is all said and done, Tim Heskett will always be on my all-competitor team.

"Corey Brewer helped me get Tim there. Corey Brewer was a great athlete. He was strong, and he could go get his shot anytime he wanted it. And that's who Tim matched up with every day in prac-tice. We were teaching screening. My deal is, don't get screened. My deal to the screener is, make sure you set the screen. This was the immovable force against the immovable object. Somebody was going to lose. And whoever lost, I was going to get on. Tim was guarding Corey. And Corey would go through the screen by wrapping his arm around Tim and shoving him out of the way. Every time he did that, Tim would look at me and want me to call a foul.

"'Tim, I am not going to call a foul. Don't get screened. And don't let Corey whip you. You have a predicament here, son. You have a coach here biting you in the butt. You have 6-10, 250-pound Renzi Stone laying pipe to you; we are going to find out about Tim Heskett.' The kid grew up. It gave him a platform to build his tough-ness, his competitiveness.

"I love those situations. It is adversity. It is on the road. It is on the road at Texas. It is on the road at Kansas. What are you going to do in adversity? You want me to bail you out here? You figure it out. One of my responsibilities in our practices was to create adversity for our players. And I wanted them to be able to handle it. I am never going to let anything get out of control. And I have always been in control of all of our practices. But at the same time, a lot of our practices, to the casual observer, would be who is in charge here?"

Heskett said it was in that practice he basically had to stand up for himself. Heskett was named Big 12 Rookie of the Week the final two weeks of the regular season. He averaged 8.4 points and 2.3 rebounds while starting the last seven games of the season.

"Corey would punch me," Heskett said. "I wouldn't do anything back at first. There were times I couldn't get the ball across half court. I thought he was fouling me. I learned that was the way coach wanted us to practice. Around Christmas or January, he elbowed me and I elbowed him back. One day it got real intense. And I started standing up for myself. I started playing with more confidence. I became a tough kid, unlike before when I was softer."

Renzi Stone, as part of that freshman recruited class, was one who loved the whole atmosphere of the program, which personified itself in those practices.

"Oklahoma was not even on my map before Coach Sampson got here," said Stone, who was recruited by Arizona, Duke, Purdue, Maryland, and Oklahoma State. "Coach Sampson sold me on the way he plays. Basically, what it came down to was Coach Sampson and I were on the same page as far as what type of program he wanted to build and what type of program I wanted to be a part of. It stood for all the right things: hard work, dedication, hustle, the kind of blue-collar work ethic."

Sampson's practices were intimidating. Dr. Halverstadt observed that first season. But Dr. Halverstadt knows whence that style came, from Sampson's upbringing in North Carolina, the tough days at Montana Tech and Washington State.

"It is style of tough love," Dr. Halverstadt said. " . . . If these guys get on the floor and don't play to the maximum of their ability, there are suicides to run."

Erdmann knows all about that tough love.

"I didn't like him at Washington State," Erdmann said. "He was on me from day one, to make me better. At the time, I couldn't walk into the gym he didn't want me to do a drill all by myself or run extra. That's how he makes players better. That was definitely the hardest part. That's part of the reason why I love him."

"He talks about blue-collar workers and people who had it easy," Dr. Halverstadt said. "And he has great respect for the blue-collar worker who comes from a modest background or no background and manages to be successful in whatever he chooses to be successful in, whether it is basketball or whether it is in some other phase of life. Kelvin has this saying: 'Every journey has its end. But in the end, it is the journey that counts.' That is kind of how he leads his life. He is in the midst of a journey and he is doing the journey right."

The journey for Sampson had been difficult that season. Even in victory.

During an 83-69 victory over Texas that season before a packed Lloyd Noble, OU fans were yelling "UT sucks." Sampson didn't like that. He wanted OU fans to cheer for the Sooners not against UT. An official running backwards fell down, and several Oklahoma fans were laughing at him. Sampson got on the microphone and scolded the fans for not showing any class in those situations.

Sampson got letters that commended him for his showing of sportsmanship, but also some that said he didn't understand the OU-Texas rivalry.

The journey for Erdmann and Brewer was injurious.

Brewer suffered a gash above his nose that required four stitches in a regular-season game in Columbia. He said he was "bowed" by Missouri forward Derek Grimm.

"Corey got hit in the head and he was laying down face first in his blood," Sampson said. "They only thing Corey wanted to know was if he had to come out of the game. He was a man. Some of the kids would come in as boys and leave as men. Corey came in as a man and left as a man. He was one of those kids who would scrap. He was very similar to Neil Derrick."

In the Big 12 Tournament, Erdmann also suffered a short black-out and shoulder injury in his collision with Jason Sutherland, Missouri's resident bad boy. Erdmann dove for a loose ball and his forehead hit the press table. He actually wound up under the table.

"We had been going back and forth. Our fathers played college ball against each other, so there might be a little extra stuff going around there," Erdmann said.

Despite the Big 12 Tournament semifinal loss to Missouri, Oklahoma qualified for its third straight NCAA Tournament under Sampson and met Stanford in the first round. The sixth-seeded Cardinals, one year before making the Final Four, defeated 11th-seeded Oklahoma, 80-67, in Tucson. Erdmann led Oklahoma with twenty-two points and finished his two-year OU career with exactly 1,000 points.

"After that season I told that team don't ever be disappointed in this year," Sampson said. "We didn't have a point guard. I knew we were playing on borrowed time every game because we didn't have a point guard. Be disappointed that you lost, but don't be disappointed in your efforts and what you accomplished. Corey Brewer was a heck

The Sampson family: Karen (left), Kellen (center with ball),
and Lauren (right) after an OU-Texas football game in 1996.
Photo courtesy OU Athletic Media Relations.

of a player. Nate Erdmann was a heck of a player. Bobby Joe Evans didn't play the last month of the season because of a bad knee. Eric Martin had to have back surgery. Tim Heskett played his butt off. His best year at Oklahoma was his freshman year."

The season did have its light moments. The injury-riddled Evans didn't play much, but he at least got the menu changed for the chartered plane ride back to Norman for road games. The team, win or lose, usually got dried out turkey or ham sandwiches in a bag. But Evans struck a deal with Sampson during the road trip to Texas Tech.

"Those sandwiches were cold and they weren't any good at all," Evans said. "I asked if we won, if we could get Kentucky Fried Chicken." When the Sooners won from that point on, they got the bird.

And the Sooners did land the best recruit in the state of Oklahoma—forward Ryan Humphrey from Tulsa Washington. Humphrey was on virtually every high school All-America team.

"Ryan was a much ballyhooed high school star, probably the top recruit in the state of Oklahoma. I think there's always pressure on in-state schools to sign the best player. I remember Ryan was really hyped. I remember the first time I saw Ryan, I thought he was the best 6-foot-7 shot blocker I had ever seen. Arms forever. Infectious smile. He was not an easy kid to recruit because everybody was recruiting him. I don't know we ever knew where we were with him. Ray Lopes did such a great job recruiting him and spent a lot of man hours. He came from an All-American family."

Ryan's older brother, Rod, played football at Pittsburgh. Sampson always had a hunch Humphrey might end up in the Big East. Eventually, Humphrey would, but only after playing two seasons at Oklahoma first. OU pulled out all the stops in recruiting Humphrey. His official visit occurred on the weekend Oklahoma retired Wayman Tisdale's jersey. The Sooners beat Oklahoma State, 80-64, before the largest crowd in Lloyd Noble Center's history at that point.

"That was a big day for Oklahoma basketball," Sampson said. "It was important that Oklahoma sign Ryan. I thought he could be a terrific basketball player."

Defining Roles

There's nothing like September and October as far as Kelvin Sampson is concerned. There are no basketball games to interfere with what he loves most—building his team. And entering the 1997-98 season, he was putting his construction hat firmly on his head. The work was going to be long and intense.

Do-it-all Nate Erdmann was gone. Eduardo Najera was a budding sophomore star. Standout recruit Ryan Humphrey was a freshman. Sampson's point guard once again was a newcomer, junior college transfer Michael Johnson. And the offensive star of the show was guard Corey Brewer, one of three scholarship seniors on the team.

"It was tough," Brewer said of Sampson's conditioning and practices. "But it was learning. He made each guy turn it up. He always said, 'You have another level.' Sometimes we did. But if we went half speed he said, 'Get on the line.' That pushes you."

Before the 1997-98 season, Sampson wanted the conditioning to be the toughest the players had ever gone through.

"I always want to create adversity and find out who our tough guys are," Sampson said. "We start talking about winning on the road in September. I talk about when we go to Texas in front of 15,000 or to Kansas before 16,000. I don't think you can improve toughness. But I think you can teach courage. I think that is a learned attribute. You learn courage by battling through adversity. We are trying to build teamwork and team chemistry in September. The harder we push them in September, the easier October will become."

And October is when Sampson is in his real classroom when practice starts. Suicides (on the line), tip drills, screen drills, charge drills. You're in the army now, Coach Sampson's army.

"A lot of kids don't understand what he is doing," former OU player Nate Erdmann said. "You have what you do well, what you have done since high school. He will break you down and remake you as a player the best way he can. A lot of kids don't see that. After you are a senior, you realize that and what he does. It is pretty amazing."

"I enjoy coaching games," Sampson said. "But practice, I love practice. I am more intense in practice than I am in games. At game time I don't have to motivate much. Where you really need to coach and teach and be a motivator is every day in practice. Try going to practice on October 25 and your next game is three weeks away and you already have been practicing for ten days. That is when coaching really comes into play. Or, try coaching practice the day after losing a home game and you have a road game coming up. Those are the days you make your money coaching."

Sampson's practices have become legendary for their toughness, efficiency, and thoroughness.

"From the minute they step on the floor, they are organized," said Kim Anderson, who has been to several since becoming Big 12 Conference Director of Basketball Operations in 1999. "They do a lot of stuff by time or repetition. There is a very impressive precision in his practice sessions. There is not a lot of messing around."

OU assistant coach Bennie Seltzer, a former player of Sampson's at Washington State, has watched or participated in Sampson's practices for more than a decade.

"He has a lot more patience now," Seltzer said. "When I first was with him when a guy missed a block out, Coach used to go ballistic."

But the practices, which usually last three hours during the preseason and early in the season, can be grueling.

"It's a full day's work," said Ernie Abercrombie, an OU player from 1994-96. "There is no slacking off. Everybody is mentally there. If not, you hear about it."

Sampson's chore, entering the 1997-98 season, was developing a bond between these players.

"I had to somehow convince this group of kids, all individually talented, to play together," Sampson said. "Corey Brewer was a senior. Ryan was a freshman. Eduardo was a sophomore, who was now beginning to blossom and come into his own. And Michael Johnson was a first-year junior college kid. I had all of these kids. But they all wanted to be the reason why we won. And I knew we weren't going to win that way. It was tough to get them to play together collectively."

Humphrey, the much ballyhooed freshman forward, early on was introduced to Sampson's loose ball drill, remembers Rabedeaux. And the result was rather amusing.

"I think he was going against Eduardo," Rabedeaux said. "And he just kind of bent down to pick the ball up. That was not a drill they did at Booker T. Washington High School in Tulsa.

"There is a pecking order. As talented a kid as you are as a freshman, you are going to get knocked down. You are going to be a graduate assistant a little bit and earn your stripes on up. He made sure those freshmen earned it in the eyes of those upperclassmen."

The loose ball drill has always been one of Sampson's signature drills in early practices. "Coach Sampson would stand in the middle of the lane and he would roll out the ball," Seltzer said. "And the two players would dive for the ball."

"There was some blood shed in those," said guard Tim Heskett. "I will have four permanent scars on my knees."

But the charge drill may have been the most grueling.

"He spots a kid under the basket and another player will keep driving into him until the player under the basket takes a charge," Seltzer said. "Some kids are tough kids and will take the charge the first time. Sometimes kids shy away from contact and have to do it over again. Shying away from contact on a play could be the difference between losing and winning a game."

Rabedeaux added: "The upperclassmen would drill the freshmen and the junior college players. There was a pecking order there."

In many ways, Humphrey was one of the more difficult players for Sampson to coach because of his big buildup coming into the program as a consensus high school All-America.

"If he is being completely level, he would rather have a guy who doesn't have all the bells and whistles and has played in a system," Chicago Bulls coach Tim Floyd said. "He doesn't like players who play cool. If a player has a coolness coming into the program, he probably isn't going to fit. He asks guys to give that up."

"The recruiting environment is almost a culture," Sampson said. "I am not sure it makes kids understand the importance of being a teammate. So many kids are used to being *the* team, they don't know how to be a teammate. And in our system, it is important you be a good teammate. I was worried about that with the returning players. Eduardo always reached out for Ryan. He always extended his hand to make sure he fit. If I got on Ryan, Eduardo was always there to tell him, 'Don't listen to how Coach says it, listen to what he says.' He did a great job of getting Ryan through that."

Sampson fit the team together his way. He scrapped the three-guard offense and went with a bigger lineup.

"Ryan eventually started and I had to mix and match our team," Sampson said. "I had to play Eduardo out of position a lot. Eduardo's best position was always with three guards. In our system, we would usually play three guards and two posts. When Ryan was here we had to play [differently]. Ryan made tremendous progress that year. By the end of the year, he was becoming factors in those games. I think there are so many expectations of a kid like that, I don't know if he ever lives up to them. But he was one of the better freshmen in the league."

As always, Sampson had to figure out who was the go-to guy. And that was easy—Brewer.

Sampson liked Brewer because he continually had to find which button to push with him. The former junior college player from West

Renzi Stone (with towel), Kelvin Sampson, Eduardo Najera,
and Tim Heskett during a tense moment

Memphis was moody and had an edge to him. No one wanted to fight Brewer in practice. And no one would challenge him.

"He had a temper," Sampson said. "He loved basketball. It was the most important thing in the world to him. The thing I love about Corey is his girlfriend in high school is still his girlfriend. He was loyal, tough, competitive. And he took losing personally that year."

Brewer was not a good three-point shooter. But he was great at driving. Sampson gave Brewer the freedom to drive to the lane. The goal was to keep the game close until the end. Brewer could either score or get to the foul line and win the game. During the 1997-98 season, Brewer led Oklahoma in scoring in twenty-eight of thirty-three games. He was an aggressive, hungry player, who led by example.

"I remember the first time I ever saw Corey," Oklahoma forward Renzi Stone said. "I was in my dorm room. He came in with a cut-off T-shirt, a rubber-band necklace around his neck, and a pair of shorts. I don't think he brought much else with him from junior college. He was pretty rough around the edges."

"Corey Brewer was a prototype of a Kelvin Sampson player," Rabedeaux said. "You could cut him a mold with a guy like Ernie Abercrombie and Eduardo. All of them come from very little. And all of them have an exceedingly huge will to succeed and become better. Corey was a kid who wasn't good enough for Memphis or Arkansas to recruit him. He was recruited by Murray State, South Alabama, and Missouri Valley Conference schools. He was going to have a chip on his shoulder."

Brewer openly admits it years later.

"I wanted to prove to them I could play at the Division I level, whether it was Arkansas, Memphis, Texas, or Oklahoma," Brewer said.

Even with Brewer starring, it didn't take long for Sampson to butt heads with his team—exactly five games.

The Sooners opened with easy home wins over Jackson State, Texas-Arlington, and Southwest Texas. But then came back-to-back losses at the Big Island Invitational in Hilo, Hawaii, to Butler and Wisconsin. After the 75-64 defeat to the Badgers, Sampson kept the Sooners in the post-game locker room for three hours. So much for the beaches. Sampson even missed his radio show.

"The next game in the tournament after we had played had concluded," Rabedeaux said. "We were in the locker room from the time our game ended. They put thirty minutes on the clock, then the next game concluded. I just remember horns going off and teams coming back into the other locker rooms."

Sampson just wrote it off as an early-season curve in the road.

"Early in the season, you are going to have obstacles," Sampson said. "You are going to have curves where you don't see a deer run across the road. The obstacles that year were egos, a brand new point guard, kids not accepting their roles, and the coach not knowing what the roles were. It is kind of like chasing a cat. Once you get it cornered, you can catch it. I couldn't get the team cornered. They were up and down walls."

After an 80-78 home loss to Memphis, which dropped Oklahoma to 5-4, something had to give.

"That's when Corey and I had a man-to-man, come-to-Jesus talk," Sampson said. "In that Memphis game, Corey was our best player, but he was playing for Corey. It bothered me Corey was trying to do too much and not playing within the framework of how we had to play. Our sum always has to be greater than our parts. If I had three draft picks and a couple of lottery picks, I would allow for our parts to be a lot more free."

The Sooners took off and won their next eight games, and Michael Johnson, the junior college transfer, started to pick up the offense at point guard. He was inconsistent at times, but Sampson saw glimpses of how good he could be.

"I am harder on my point guards than anybody, except maybe freshmen," Sampson said. "Michael had good leadership traits. But I was brought up if you are not good at the point of attack on offense or defense you have no chance. Michael gave us a chance. He was one of the better defensive point guards I have ever coached. I remember when we beat Arizona in the NCAA Tournament the next season, he was guarding Jason Terry. And I thought he won that matchup because he could defend the dribble.

"But Michael had to learn to be a system point guard. He wasn't used to coming down, and if you didn't have the break, pulling it out and running a set. That year against North Texas he had eighteen assists. Then the next game he may have had eighteen turnovers. He was up and down early that year."

Oklahoma started 4-0 in the Big 12 with victories at Colorado and Texas A&M and home victories over Kansas State and then Texas on ESPN's Big Monday. In that game, Oklahoma's Stone and Texas's

Gabe Muoneke got into a verbal and physical spat for the entire country to see. But it showed Sampson's team would back down to no one, including the Big 12's known bad boy, Muoneke.

"I remember at half time," Stone said. "Coach Rab [Rabedeaux] got up in front of the team and said, 'If Gabe Muoneke runs by our bench one more time yelling whatever he had to yell, if he pushes you one more time and you don't push him back, then you are the ones who are going to be sorry the next time we practice.' I remember we came out in the second half and he pushed me after a bucket. And I kind of pushed him back. He swung at me. And I swung back. The play was going down to the other end. And the announcers said we should both be kicked out. But we had a rivalry. And we kept beating them."

The half time speech worked. Oklahoma turned a five-point half time deficit into a 91-75 victory. That was the first of a three-game sweep of Texas that season. But coaching wasn't getting any easier for Sampson.

Oklahoma was thin on the perimeter because Tim Heskett and Eric Martin, both good three-point shooters, were hurt. Heskett suffered a back injury (bulging disk) and missed all but the first two games that season.

Said Heskett: "I had two back surgeries. I was in and out of therapy. I was getting acupuncture. It was very frustrating. I was at practice and games and traveled with the team, but it was the first time I had been away from basketball."

Martin missed the last eleven games of the season with a similar injury. And center Bobby Joe Evans was finished as a player because of bad knees.

"I had sustained injures in high school and played before they healed," Evans said. "I had surgeries, but now I don't have any cartilage on the left side of my knee. I couldn't do much. And they made me a medical redshirt. But Coach was always around, and he let you know what you had to do to get through life."

The Sooners had to rely on role players such as the 6-10, 255-pound sophomore Stone, 6-5 senior Robert Allison, and 6-11 senior center Evan "Hootie" Wiley to mix and match down the stretch.

"Robert Allison was a tough kid," Sampson said. "Robert would compete with anybody, and he was a good three-point shooter. He was a typical role player for us. We could take a guy who had obvious weaknesses but play to his strengths. He helped that team."

To complicate matters, Najera suffered a stress fracture in his left foot and missed home games against Texas A&M and Texas Tech. He played the rest of the season nursing the injury. The Sooners survived Texas A&M, 80-71, by playing basically seven players. But they lost, 70-68 to Texas Tech, when six players played all but four minutes in the game. As usual, though, when needing a win, the Sooners got it, 81-74, at Texas.

Stone played the game of his life: thirteen points, ten rebounds, four assists, and two steals. He jumped outside his utility role, just when the Sooners needed him.

"I was sort of a glue guy," Stone said. "I held things together. I think Coach Sampson liked tough guys like that on the floor. He likes that one guy who doesn't worry about scoring. I saw that as my role."

"The thing that team learned to do during that stretch was how to win the game," Sampson said. "You knew how Kansas was going to win. You knew how Duke was going to win. But how was Oklahoma going to win? It is vital to look at your team's weaknesses. That's how I have always tried to coach. It is not our strengths as much as our weaknesses. Because if we can find out what our weaknesses are, we can stay away from them. As an example, Eduardo was not a good shooter. We were not going to win with Eduardo shooting threes. Ryan hadn't blossomed offensively yet. He was a shot blocker-rebounder. He had not developed into a great shooter yet."

Sampson could count on Stone to show up that season. But Wiley, a highly recruited player out of Lawton, Oklahoma, was up and down. He had been recruited by Billy Tubbs and sat out his freshman year as a Prop 48. Now, he was a mercurial player.

"Renzi was dependable," Sampson said. "I talked to our kids every day in practice about ability. I said the greatest ability you can have for us in our practices is dependability. Hootie wasn't dependable, and he probably had the most potential of all those kids. We have had four kids [at OU] drafted into the NBA. Hootie had the best chance to make it of anybody, had he loved the game, because of his size and skill."

Wiley, though, came to play against the better teams.

"He was an All-American when we played Kansas," Sampson said. "He could guard Raef LaFrentz better than anybody in our conference. I remember we played them in the Big 12 Tournament title game that season. We were ahead at half time. Hootie had like eight of our first ten points. If we played a nondescript team, which didn't have players with great reputations, you might as well put him in a bag and throw him in the ocean. We weren't going to have Evan Wiley. He just didn't have a passion for the game. Those kind of kids are the biggest challenge for me because you want them to match your passion."

This Oklahoma team was going to go as far as Brewer could take it. Case in point was Senior Day at OU when Brewer rallied the Sooners from a twelve-point second half deficit and scored a career-high tying thirty-six points in the Sooners' 80-76 victory over Missouri. He constantly beat the Tigers off the dribble and wound up shooting twenty free throws, making seventeen of them.

"I remember continuing to challenge Corey not to lose his Senior Day game," Sampson said. "We had this play called 'Down.' Anytime I would point down, Corey would get the ball on the opposite wing. He would pass it and go through the defense and get to the opposite wing. And we would go get Corey free with the dribble. We ran that one play the last ten minutes of that game."

Oklahoma finished tied for second in the Big 12 regular season. And Sampson was right. Wiley showed up for the good teams. He had eleven points vs. Missouri and fifteen the next game at Kansas, an 83-70 defeat. And in the Big 12 Tournament, he was named to the All-Tournament team when he found the opponents to his liking: Missouri, Texas, both Sooner victories, and Kansas. In the 72-58 title game loss to the Jayhawks, Wiley was one of two double-figure scorers for the Sooners along with Brewer.

There was little doubt Oklahoma would be invited to its fourth straight NCAA Tournament under Sampson. The opponent, though, would be key to advancing past the first round for the first time in Sampson's career. The Sooners were seeded 10th and played 7th-seeded Indiana in the East Region in Washington, D.C.

"As soon as I saw Indiana, I thought this is a hard match-up because they play five perimeter guys," Sampson said. "Indiana was a hard match-up for us because they didn't have a big man. Hootie was our five-man, and he had a hard time guarding a guy like Andrae Patterson who was going to float on the perimeter and shoot threes."

Indiana led by eleven at half time and took a nineteen-point lead in the second half before Brewer led a pulsating rally to tie the score in the final seconds and send the game into overtime. Patterson, as Sampson had predicted, was trouble with twenty-six points in the game.

"I remember Corey Brewer playing with exhaustion and playing too long before he asked for a breather," said Karen Sampson, who was watching from the stands. "I remember being down nineteen against Indiana and Corey coming down and getting fouled. He made a free throw to tie it. If there was any justice he would have been making a free throw to win it."

Brewer scored twenty-two points and played like a person possessed in leading the comeback.

"I was thinking I had to do something to keep the season alive," Brewer said. "That year we had a lot of people injured, and it put a lot more pressure on me every night. I had really enjoyed it at Oklahoma and didn't want it to end. I didn't want my relationship with Coach Sampson to end. I was just there for two years and it was over. But I definitely enjoyed the journey we took together."

Indiana outscored Oklahoma, 14-7, in the overtime and won, 94-87.

"I think in the NCAA Tournament, the day you play, your best player has to have his best game," Sampson said. "I was so mad at my seniors that last game. Corey didn't play well the first half. Hootie didn't play well the first half. I thought Eduardo, Ryan, and Michael were solid. They played OK. In the second half, we started playing Sooner basketball. I remember after the Indiana game thinking, 'Boy we could have used our shooters [who were injured] tonight.'"

That was the fourth straight first-round NCAA loss at Oklahoma for Sampson (Manhattan, Temple, Stanford, and the Hoosiers) and fifth overall, including a first-round loss to Boston College in 1994 when Sampson was coach at Washington State.

"What I didn't like, it was bothering him," Rabedeaux said. "He said, 'Rab, we are going to be measured at Oklahoma in terms of how we do in March. I am getting to the stage of my career I am going to be measured as a coach how our teams do in March.' A lot of this wouldn't even have come into play if, in our first year in the NCAA Tournament at Washington State, our starting center Fred Ferguson hadn't had a broken hand. If he is healthy, there is no telling what would have happened because that Boston College game went right down to the wire. And then Boston College beat North Carolina in the next round."

"I think an untold story of some of those NCAA games, those teams were picked to finish fifth or sixth in the league," Sampson said. "And they were probably NIT teams. And we had great years getting into the tournament."

Still, Sampson was excited about the future.

Part of that future would be without "00" forward-center Bobby Joe Evans, whose knees had given out. That didn't mean that Evans wasn't still a part of Sampson's extended basketball family.

"He wanted us to succeed in life, not just basketball," Evans said in the spring of 2001. "He really wants us to get that degree. I have one class to finish. And he's still pushing me. He calls me and says, 'Bobby Joe, finish that class.'"

And Brewer remains a close friend with Sampson, although he has been playing basketball overseas.

"The best advice he gave me: I was going to miss it when it's gone," Brewer said of his OU career. "And I miss everything...the people. I miss walking down the tunnel. He told us to put everything we could into it, otherwise you will miss out and you can't get it back. That's why I would go hard every day."

CHAPTER 12

Peaking Late

Kelvin Sampson went into the 1998-99 season with more confidence than he had had in four previous seasons at Oklahoma. He had a tough senior point guard in Michael Johnson and a star in Eduardo Najera, who combined work ethic with talent. That combination alone gave Sampson a heady feeling.

Throw in a bunch of role players, stars such as Renzi Stone, Alex Spaulding, Tim Heskett, Eric Martin, and Ryan Humphrey, and the Sooners would be formidable indeed—anywhere. That didn't mean there wouldn't be some bumps in the road. But this could be more of an interstate ride than the single-lane trips Sampson normally had taken during his head coaching career.

During the Big 12 season, Oklahoma won six of eight games on the road.

"I always had confidence if the game was close because we had an outstanding point guard in Michael Johnson and we had such a smart player in Eduardo," Sampson said. "Why was our team so good on the road? Our point guard and our best player were tough people. Your team will reflect those two. And if you are good in both those spots, you are going to be good on the road.

"Why do you think Duke has been good on the road? Look at Shane Battier. Eduardo was our Shane Battier. He was a poor man's version of Shane Battier. He had no weaknesses. He didn't have a lot of great strengths, but no weaknesses. And his greatest strength was his competitiveness. Eduardo was at his best when he was challenged.

"Michael Johnson was tough, so tough. He would get on those guys. He had a temper. He would scream at them. Eduardo knew how to calm Michael down and raise the self-esteem of someone else on the team."

But it didn't take long for the defining moment of the season to occur. Talk about the Murray State game three years later with former players and they wince.

Oklahoma won its first three games, including a 102-51 victory over Western Carolina in the first IGA SuperThrift Sooner Holiday Classic at Lloyd Noble Center. In the title game, however, Oklahoma fell, 68-64, to Murray State. The Sooners were out-rebounded, 46-23, by the Racers. And they had to accept the second-place trophy.

Sampson was livid. After the game, he merely told the team to meet him at six a.m. Monday morning.

"That following week defines Coach Sampson as a man," Stone said. "Coach Sampson is real adamant about playing a certain way and representing certain things: hustle, enthusiasm, emotion. The three Es he writes on the board before every game: Enthusiasm, Emotion, Energy. We went out that game, and it was the only time we didn't play with any of those. And they gave us the silver ball at our own tournament."

The early Monday morning film review of the Murray State game was not pleasant for the Sooners. It revealed an older referee beating one Sooner down the floor after a made basket.

Sampson took the players down to the court and ran them for an hour straight. Players were falling by the wayside. They ran that way the rest of the week. Each practice started off with the dreaded tip drill with a weighted ball with only ten players participating. The goal was to keep the ball alive on the backboard by ten players alternating tipping it on both ends. The walk-ons were exempt.

"All I know is that I lost twelve pounds in five days," Stone said. "The first day he put us through that, I said, 'He is going to break. He is not going to keep this up.' The second day he put us through it, I was kind of mad. By the third day, I was begging for mercy. It defined what he stood for. He was not going to stand for mediocrity. He was not going to stand for less than your best effort. He changed that team."

The Sooners practiced the entire week with the second-place trophy at mid-court.

"We were going through hell week," said trainer Alex Brown, who had to be in the training room by five a.m. for six a.m. practices in order to get the players ready.

Sampson kicked the Sooners out of their locker room shortly after the initial film session. He took players' shoes and clothes from the locker room and threw them in the hallway. "You guys don't deserve to be in this locker room," Sampson said. He made every player clean out his locker. Then he locked the door. And the players had to wash their own practice clothes.

If the Sooners wanted to play like an NAIA team, they would be treated like one. They spent the entire week in the visitors locker room, the Murray State locker room.

The following Saturday Oklahoma beat Arkansas, 87-57, and out-rebounded the Razorbacks, 45-31.

"We were embarrassed by our play against Murray State," said OU's Eric Martin, who scored a career-high twenty-three points against Arkansas. "We had something to prove."

It was nothing new for Sampson to push his team to such heights.

"The big thing he did," said Ernie Abercrombie, a star on Sampson's first two OU teams, "was get all the potential out of your talents. He pushed you to get all the God-given ability you have."

Sampson's biggest project was still Humphrey, the enigmatic star from Tulsa. He was starting on the front line with Najera and Stone.

Humphrey told *The Tulsa World* about his freshman season: "I didn't know what to expect. I was just out there. I felt like I was on my own. I didn't know what I was doing right and what I was doing wrong."

"The summer between his freshman and sophomore years would be when he would make the most progress and he did," Sampson said. "Ryan was limited on certain things he could do offensively. But I felt like it was important to get him to understand I could get him to be the best rebounder, shot blocker, and defender there was in the country and let his offense grow."

On the recruiting front, Kansas had finally arrived. At least that's what assistant coach Jason Rabedeaux believed.

Oklahoma was in a torrid recruiting battle with Kansas for guard Kirk Hinrich from Sioux City, Iowa. Rabedeaux had faxed Hinrich printouts from the Internet with Kansas fans talking about the limited playing time Hinrich would see at Kansas his freshman season the next year. OU promised Hinrich the ability to play a lot early. Kansas coach Roy Williams saw the faxes during a recruiting visit and called Sampson to complain.

"I know we are a threat if Roy is going to pick up the phone and call us," Rabedeaux said. "I told Coach we are not doing anything illegal." Kansas eventually signed Hinrich, but Oklahoma was in the ballpark.

Oklahoma was 6-1 going into the Puerto Rico Holiday Tournament. But Sampson had to put out a brush fire in mid-December when then Washington State athletic director Rick Dickson inferred that Samson and George Raveling did not run clean programs when they coached in Pullman. Dickson said, in a story in the *Spokane Spokesman-Review,* he had been told by Kansas coach Roy Williams and Oklahoma State coach Eddie Sutton: "All of us in the industry know that only two people have had significant success [at WSU] since Marv Harshman; well, we know how they did it." Both Williams and Sutton denied making the statements.

"The guy [Dickson] got caught in a lie," Sampson said. "I think a lot of that was Nate Erdmann leaving [Washington State] and coming here [to Oklahoma]. George Raveling called me and wanted to sue him [Dickson]."

With that annoyance behind him, Sampson didn't want a repeat of the previous season's tournament debacle in Hawaii. So he continued to push the Sooners even though the opening opponent was the host, American-Puerto Rico.

"We prepared for American-Puerto Rico like they were the Olympic team," Stone said. "And we get there and we are up 39-10 in the first half. And one of their players cold-cocks Tim Heskett. And the refs call the game."

Officially, Oklahoma won, 2-0, (a forfeit). But after playing only one-half of a game against a weak opponent, the Sooners were ill prepared and dropped the next two games: a three-point decision to Mississippi and a four-pointer to North Carolina State.

Oklahoma then won six straight, capped by a 54-43 victory at Oklahoma State. Humphrey appeared to be buying into Team Oklahoma. He didn't score a point, but Sampson believed he had a tremendous impact in the victory over the Cowboys by grabbing rebounds (seven), making steals (two), blocking shots (two), and hurrying several other shots.

"The thing I remember about the Oklahoma State game, we never trailed in forty minutes," Sampson said. "In fact, we never trailed for eighty that entire year in two regular-season games. Oklahoma State was really good. They had Desmond Mason, Doug

Gottlieb, and Brian Montonati. I had heard the local media talk about how fast Oklahoma State was. Our strategy was we couldn't run with them. We had to control the pace of the game with our offense and play smart. I convinced our kids if we utilized the shot clock and kept the score close down to the last two or three minutes, we would win the game."

Heskett remembers that in Sampson's scouting reports for such games he left nothing to chance. The Cowboys shot only 28.3 percent as the Sooners adjusted their defense.

"We were one of the few teams that swept Oklahoma State during the regular season," Heskett remembers. "Coach Sampson was good at knowing how to guard people. A lot of people we will beat, we have less talent than, because we know which way they favor and which way they don't."

Sampson blamed himself for scheduling a television game at Cincinnati. The Sooners had travel problems getting to Ohio because of a snowstorm in the area. They trudged into their hotel at two in the morning. Tip-off was early in the afternoon, less than twelve hours later. Cincinnati's big front line of Kenyon Martin and Pete Mickeal crushed the Sooners, 72-59.

"I thought that game took us into a funk," Sampson said of the first game of a four-loss streak. "Then we played probably the worst game I have ever had a team play—against Nebraska. We were down twenty and it probably felt like were down fifty."

After the 96-81 home defeat to Nebraska, losses followed to Kansas State and Texas. Najera was in a shooting slump that mirrored Oklahoma's losing streak. He was 4-for-15 against Cincinnati, 1-for-7 vs. Kansas State, 4-14 vs. Texas.

"I remember I sat him in a chair," Sampson said. "And he cried like a baby. And he wasn't coming out of it. I thought he was the key to the entire team. He was trying, but he wasn't getting anything done. The second Oklahoma State game, Eduardo had seventeen rebounds, twelve in the first half. That was Eduardo. We made a huge deal out of that. Eduardo was worried about making shots, shooting threes, making jump shots. And that wasn't his game. Eduardo had to get back being a get-in-your face, out-tough you, out-compete you type player.

"Eduardo could dominate a game and not make a shot. He could take a charge, go get a loose ball, pitch it ahead to somebody, offensive rebound, block a shot. That was his game. When he would run into trouble was when he worried about things he couldn't control like his jump shot."

Against Oklahoma State, Najera shot only 7-for-19.

"I was still struggling with my shooting," Najera said afterward. "I had in my mind I had to rebound my butt off. I think that was an important thing to do and that's why we won."

Oklahoma hit its stride and won six straight games, including road games at Texas Tech, Baylor, Texas, and Missouri. In the latter game, Najera scored twenty points and grabbed fifteen rebounds at the Hearnes Center.

"I remember when Eduardo slapped Missouri's Keyon Dooling in the back of the head when he was trying to block his shot," Sampson said. "Then everybody booed Eduardo every time he touched the ball. We have a rule: don't give up lay-ups or dunks. I didn't say maim him. And he didn't. But he tried to come from behind and slap the ball. He hit the back third of his head. And Dooling fell like someone had shot him from the upper deck. I am sure some of that was theatrics. Immediately, Eduardo reached down to help him up.

"When you are on the road and you are getting booed, use it to your advantage. That's when I found out who our toughest guys were. We got down in that game, but Michael Johnson, Eric Martin, and Eduardo came through. Sometimes kids don't understand the toughness and the competitive level you have to have to win on the road. Talent alone doesn't win on the road."

Najera was a player who used all the talent he had and then some. The 6-foot-8, 240-pound Najera had the same work ethic as his father, a waterworks employee back in Mexico.

"I saw how responsible my dad was," Najera said. "I felt like I am kind of like he is . . . . My high school coach taught me how to be consistent and how to be disciplined. But I learned the most from Coach Sampson. He taught me if I didn't work hard, practice hard, and play hard I am just an average player."

Down the stretch, Najera was hardly average. He was playing like an All-American.

Oklahoma was 10-3 in league play and had a shot at winning the Big 12 regular-season race, but they came up short with another poor shooting night, 26.5, and lost to Kansas in Norman, 60-50. A stinging 74-72 loss at Texas A&M the next game dropped OU out of the conference race. And the defeat drew Sampson's ire.

"He took all the chicken off the plane," OU trainer Alex Brown said of the post-game meal. "That was the only time we had lost to Texas A&M. I felt like he was right. We didn't deserve to eat. We weren't hungry on the court. Why should we be hungry now?"

After sweeping Oklahoma State during the regular season, the Sooners lost to the Cowboys, 60-57, possibly hurting Oklahoma's chances of making the NCAA Tournament. It also may have inflamed Sampson's old enemy—asthma. The Sampsons held an NCAA Tournament Selection party the following Sunday at their sprawling Norman home.

"He could barely make it down the steps at the seeding party," Karen Sampson said. "And he spoke to the press outside. Before everyone got there Eduardo had gone up to see him. He [Eduardo] was nervous because he didn't know if we were in the NCAA Tournament. We checked Kelvin into the hospital as soon as the press left. I think it is the end of the season and there is stress and fatigue."

When Sampson saw that Oklahoma was the No. 13 seed (maybe the last at-large selection in the field) and would be facing No. 4 seed Arizona in Milwaukee, he didn't feel any better. In his seven seasons at Washington State, Sampson had failed to beat Arizona (0-15). Arizona was the only team in the Pac-10 he hadn't beaten.

"I was feeling awful," Sampson said. "Then, when I saw Arizona go up, I thought I would vomit. I thought, 'God, are we ever going to win a first-round game?' That's your first reaction. I knew that was a tough draw. The thing I kept telling our kids was, 'We were 6-2 on the road in the Big 12. And we had Arizona on a neutral court.' And I thought that was to our advantage. Our league that year had really prepared us. We had won at Oklahoma State. We had won at Texas. We had won at Missouri. We had won at Iowa State. Those were four of the top teams in the league. We could play with anybody."

Sampson's hotel room in Milwaukee was complete with oxygen and other hospital amenities to keep his asthma in check. He had checked out of the Norman hospital where he had set up his office with VCR, phone, and television. And he had continued to conduct interviews with the media and view film of Arizona.

"I remember talking to James Worthy and Tim Brando [of CBS]," Sampson said. "They asked me if we have to play our best game of the year to win this game. I said no because they're not. Our greatest strength is we can make you not play your best game. That's what defense, toughness, and rebounding can do. Tom Izzo of Michigan

State has become a legend coaching like that. I told our kids we could win this game. This is not a game we are going to win because we are better. This is a game we can win because we're going to be tougher. We would out-scrap them."

The announcers asked Sampson if both teams played their "A" game who would win?

"Nobody is going to play their A game against us," Sampson said "I said we don't have an A game. I said if we play the best we can play, it's going to be a B. Our B is going to be good enough to beat you because we are pretty good at making you be a B team."

Rabedeaux remembers the mindset: "Here we are with a chip on our shoulder. They say we don't belong there. We are going up there to make some noise. And Arizona is looking toward who they are going to play in the next round. That was kind of the theme. As Coach Sampson evolved as a tournament coach, the team was relaxed and it was an almost nothing-to-lose type of thing. It tells you about his progression as a coach."

Strategically, Lopes said the Sooners tried to funnel the Arizona offense to the baseline where the Sooners would trap the Wildcats. Sampson believed Oklahoma could control the pace of the game. And he was counting on Oklahoma's Michael Johnson to shut down Arizona's high-scoring guard Jason Terry, who was the trigger in Arizona's offense. Terry would make just four of seventeen shots in the game.

"I got to the floor first and remember Lute Olson coming down," Sampson said. "The NCAA asks coaches to shake hands with each other before the game. I remember Lute said when we shook hands, 'You have come a long way.' I said, 'Good luck.' I wanted to win this game so badly. Not because I hadn't won a game in the NCAAs. It was because we had good kids."

Stone said Sampson gave the haves vs. have nots speech. The Sooners were pumped. Maybe a little too pumped. The first half was ugly. Both teams shot poorly. Oklahoma trailed 27-24 at half time. The Sooners didn't take their first lead until eight minutes remained when Najera began to assert himself. Oklahoma's "Superman" finished with seventeen points, thirteen rebounds, three steals, and two blocks.

With 48 seconds remaining, Arizona's Michael Wright turned the ball over. That allowed Oklahoma to register the winning basket when the Sooners scored on a controversial follow tip-in by

Humphrey with 21 seconds remaining. Humphrey was close to goal tending on a lay-up by Najera. Arizona had four shots at victory in the final seconds but missed them all. Oklahoma won, 61-60.

Arizona athletic director Jim Livengood, who had been with Sampson at Washington State, watched the game from a CBS truck in Denver where he was serving as a NCAA Tournament Basketball Committee representative.

"It was bittersweet in a lot of ways," Livengood said. "I was sad for our team and Lute. On the other side—and I know a lot of Wildcat fans wouldn't understand it—but if you are going to get beat, I felt good it was Kelvin. And it was strictly Kelvin, not the Sooners. That's the toughest of all games. It's not fun to play your friends, regardless of how your team does."

Karen was sitting in the stands.

"I was so glad Kelvin had won a first-round game," Karen said. "I wish it hadn't been Arizona. As happy as I was for us, I was sad for them. I was looking at Bobbi Olson. When the ball didn't go in, her hands went down. I thought to myself, 'Oh, Bobbi, I know exactly

The OU bench erupts after beating Arizona in the 1999 NCAA Tournament.
Photo by Lisa Hall/OU Athletic Media Relations.

how you feel.' At that moment you are hugging everybody, then you are sad."

Sampson knew he would never have to answer the first-round loss question again.

"There were a lot of emotions," Sampson said. "I had started at Washington State and tried to rebuild that program. I remember in the early days at Washington State thinking we had no chance. It probably helped me prepare our team to play Arizona because we hadn't beaten them. And that was in my craw. As a coach, when you are a competitor, you think you can beat anybody. But we hadn't beaten Lute until then.

"He was always a coach I admired. In the summertime when I would see coaches out recruiting I didn't see anybody working harder than Lute. That always stood out to me. And his wife, Bobbi, was always gracious. When Karen and I were in our early thirties at Washington State, she was the only coach's wife who ever traveled with her husband to Pullman. She always made it a point to seek out Karen. And she would always come up to me and say something nice. Always. She was Karen's mentor.

"Lute, when you get to know him, is a little bit shy. A lot of times people confuse that with being arrogant or aloof. There were a lot of times when Lute and I were among five coaches in a gym late at night watching somebody playing. And he would say, 'What are you doing for dinner?' Lute and I would go grab a burger or pizza and beer and talk.

But the first victory over Olson was a sweet one because it ended all the stories about Sampson's first-round NCAA Tournament losing string.

"Lute was a great role model for me," Sampson said. "He taught me the value of running a system and sticking to your guns."

The Oklahoma team swarmed Sampson after the upset. And the Sooners also helped name assistant coach Ray Lopes' newly born third child, Trey, when they made ten three-pointers in the victory. Lopes had decided on that name if the Sooners' made at least ten three-pointers against the Wildcats.

The second-round opponent was Charlotte. And outgoing Marquette coach Mike Deane called Sampson and asked if he wanted a scouting report on the fifth-seeded 49ers. Deane had been a former assistant coach for Jud Heathcote at Michigan State. And his Golden Eagles had split two games with the 49ers that season.

"The Charlotte game was the most relaxed game we had played all year. After the first five minutes, I thought we are going to kill them," Sampson said.

For the second straight game the Sooners got an unexpected scoring surge from Alex Spaulding, a 6-3, 190-pound sophomore, who had averaged just 3.4 points a game during the season. He scored ten against Arizona and added twelve against Charlotte. Oklahoma jumped out to a 21-5 lead and coasted behind Martin's six three-pointers and Najera's twenty points and fifteen rebounds.

For only the third time, a 13th seed had advanced to the Sweet 16.

After the North Carolina-Charlotte game, Najera and Johnson jumped on Sampson. And Heskett and Stone did a dance under the rim. They chanted, "Sweet 16, Sweet 16."

"We are Cinderella," Sampson said. "Before the tournament started, it was you haven't won a first-round game. Nobody was talking about that anymore. But we were not a 13th seed. We just happened to be seeded 13th. There were teams in our league we were better than seeded higher than us. But that shows you how that seeding thing goes.

"We had been close to being a Sweet 16 team. We had not been that far away. We just hadn't done it yet. For some programs that is a huge leap. For us, it was just a small step. We had been a No. 4 seed. We had been to the NCAAs every year I had been at Oklahoma. I told our kids we have our IDs. We didn't slip in the back door. Let's not run in here and act like we stole something. Let's walk in here and act like we belong here."

Sampson would have to beat the region's top seed, Michigan State, at the Trans World Dome to advance to the Midwest Region final.

"As Coach approached it, we were a poor man's Michigan State," Rabedeaux said.

"All I remember about the game is they were a mirror image of us, but maybe a little bit better than us at every position," Stone said. "It was a cat fight the entire game."

Sampson said Michigan State was the best offensive rebounding team he had ever seen. He told the Sooners to find ways to get easy shots and go hard to the boards. Those would be the keys to victory. For added spice, Heathcote was in the stands rooting for the Spartans.

"Jud wanted it to be a close game and wanted our team to look good and play well, but he wanted Michigan State to win," Sampson said.

And it was a close game. In the first half there were five ties and twelve lead changes. Michigan State crept ahead in the second half. Then, with 9:34 remaining in the game, Najera collided with Michigan State's Mateen Cleaves in one of the most violent collisions in college basketball history. Najera's chin hit Cleaves' forehead.

"They banged so hard, I was feeling it hurt up in the stands," Heathcote said. "It was the collision to beat all collisions."

"My first thought is, 'My God, he is dead!'" Sampson said. "At that point, I didn't care about winning or losing because I loved that kid so much. The game didn't matter anymore."

Oklahoma center Victor Avila and Michael Johnson were crying. There were 42,440 people at the game. But it was so quiet Sampson could hear CBS announcers Billy Packer and Jim Nance talking at mid-court.

"It took a long time for him to clear the fog," said Dr. Donald Halverstadt, who, along with trainer Alex Brown and Dr. Brock Schnebel, rushed on to the floor. "And he had this huge laceration on his chin. Apparently, he didn't have a neck injury. We took him out under the stands."

"Kelvin instills a toughness in a kid," Brown said. "As a freshman, Eduardo would not have come back. As a junior, his persona had changed into more of an hombre, so to speak. We teach our players pain is only an opinion and to have a low opinion of pain."

Sampson didn't know if Najera would return. He had sustained a grade-one concussion, a bruised breastbone, a chin laceration that required six stitches, and a chipped tooth while trying to set a pick for teammate Michael Johnson.

"I had to get our kids back to reality," Sampson said. "Eduardo was our heart and soul. And they were taking him off the court. As he was going off court, I shed a tear. I knew I had to get that team back together. We win this game and we are in the Final Eight. I got my emotions under control. But I kept looking to the locker room for Eduardo. There was no one there to tell me how he was. Our medical staff was in the back with Eduardo.

"All of a sudden I hear this roar. And it was the loudest roar at a sporting event I have ever heard. It was like a car you hear coming around the curve and all of a sudden it is upon you and you see it.

That is how that roar was. It started cascading down. I looked up on the overheard scoreboard. It showed Eduardo running out of the tunnel onto the floor, through the path by the fans. He barely stopped by me. I still think the kid was knocked out.

"Eduardo says, 'Who do you want me to go in for?'"

Sampson doesn't remember telling him to substitute for anybody. He just went to the scorer's table.

"I don't even know who he went in for," Sampson said. "That's the first time I have never sent anybody into the game. And the first thing he did when he went into the game, he set a screen on Mateen Cleaves. And that's on TV."

Najera recounted later: "One thing I remember is I couldn't drink anything cold for awhile because I had the chipped tooth. I try not to think about it."

Oklahoma lost, 54-46, but gained all the respect from Michigan State coach Tom Izzo. The Spartans won their twenty-first straight game by limiting Oklahoma to 33.3 percent shooting.

"His energy and enthusiasm are second to none," Izzo said of Sampson. "And, after competing against him in the Sweet 16, I thoroughly understand why he is a coach in demand. His blue-collar approach and the work ethic of his players are as good as any team we have played. There is no doubt in my mind Kelvin Sampson will bring the Sooners a national championship someday."

Before the 1999-2000 season, Sampson would suffer two unexpected losses: Humphrey and Rabedeaux.

In the final game against Michigan State, Humphrey scored ten points and added ten rebounds. On the season, he averaged 11.1 points and 7.6 rebounds a game. He had a high of twenty-one points against North Carolina State.

"The biggest issue with Ryan was he didn't want to play the role we had given him," Sampson said. "And there was pressure on him. He was a high school All-American. And I really understood him. I had talked to his father a couple of times about his role. His family wanted his role to be more offense. And that never upset me. It really didn't. But I had to do what was best for our team.

"I always thought it was my job to develop the kids to the best of their best abilities, maximize strengths, and win games. My father taught me a great lesson in my second year at Montana Tech. I had to deal with a parent. I called him for advice. And I never will forget him saying this: 'Most parents would rather their son make

All-Conference than your team win the conference championship.' And I have always used that as a foundation for kids now and dealing with parents.

"The thing that disappointed me about Ryan leaving, had he stayed at Oklahoma he would have become a great player for us in his own way eventually. He wanted to be more prominent in the offense. Ryan and I had a great visit recently. He has developed into an outstanding player at Notre Dame."

Humphrey asked for, and was granted, his release. He visited Pittsburgh. He also visited Notre Dame and UCLA. He wound up transferring to Notre Dame.

"And I think he may have visited Kentucky," Sampson said. "But Ryan and I had a good relationship. There was no bitterness between us. But when he left, we had to go get a front line player who could at least help us some. I had to recruit a fourth post. We had Renzi, Eduardo, Victor. We knew Ryan was unhappy so we weren't completely caught with our pants down. We had been talking with some second-tier kids. And that's when we got Jameel Heywood."

The next loss came several months later.

It was early September when Sampson lost Rabedeaux. In late August Don Haskins suddenly retired as the Texas-El Paso coach after thirty-eight years on the job.

"Rab was not a guy who looked for jobs," Sampson said. "He was so loyal and tuned into me and the program. Rab went from being my whipping boy as a graduate assistant to my sounding board. That is a wide scope—someone who can go from being your son to being your brother. He went from the kid I gave a start to maybe my best friend."

Rabedeaux wanted to be talked out of taking the UTEP job.

"I told him this is why you coach, to run the show," Sampson said "You can blow the whistle in practice and put your stuff in and make a difference. That is what coaching is all about."

While recruiting in Minnesota, Sampson got the word from Rabedeaux he was going to UTEP. Rabedeaux broke down and cried on the phone. And so did Sampson.

"I looked at it this way," Sampson said. "A pigeon was shot in the wing. And this lady took the pigeon in and nursed it back to health. And when the bird was healthy she let it go. And she knew it was gone forever. That might sound a little mushy but that's the way I felt when Rab left. He had been such a big part of our program over the years. He had seen the worst year I had ever had at Washington State. But he also was there for the Sweet 16 trip and everything in between."

Rabedeaux left behind his old driver with a note for Sampson, a lefty golfer. The driver was a relic left over from their golfing days, which began on a nine-hole course back in Pullman. Rabedeaux assured Sampson he wouldn't forget his roots.

"When I had to leave, it was a difficult split," Rabedeaux said. "In so many ways I had evolved into Kelvin Sampson Jr. in terms of how I approached basketball and things. There is a part of Coach [that feels]: 'Rab will always be my assistant.'"

CHAPTER 13

Najera's Show

Sampson looked at the 1999-2000 season as a rebuilding one. The starting five, except for Eduardo Najera, had been wiped out. There were promising newcomers on the Sooner horizon, however.

During Oklahoma's Sweet 16 year, guard J.R. Raymond sat out as a partial qualifier and practiced with the Sooners. Now he would become eligible. Two guards—Hollis Price, a freshman, and Nolan Johnson, a junior college transfer—were unproven. Oklahoma had lost its three starting perimeter players: Michael Johnson, Alex Spaulding, and Eric Martin.

Two other three-point specialists, Kelley Newton and Tim Heskett, were back but coming off injuries. Newton had a torn ACL and had red-shirted during the 1998-99 season. Heskett had suffered a broken hand.

"It was going to be a little bit of a rebuilding year," Sampson said. "And there were a lot of teams in our league who had everybody back. Our team lost four starters. We may have to take a step back and rebuild.

"I was around Hollis in June. He came up that summer. And J.R. Raymond was a talent who I knew could play. Kelley, Tim Heskett, and Renzi Stone—I knew what I had there. And I had my best player back—Eduardo. That was the only year we would have only one captain—Eduardo. I told him you have to be more than a leader on this team. You have to take ownership. This has to be your team."

Practices went badly early that season. Sampson kicked the team out of practice, which meant players reported at six a.m. and at three p.m., the next day.

"The managers and trainers have a pool when he will kick the team out of practice for the first time," said Oklahoma trainer Alex Brown. "He is testing their mental toughness. I warn the new kids,

'You better get it right the first time. I don't like to get out of bed any more than you do.'"

Najera called Sampson crying after early practices didn't go well.

"It is my senior year and I am going to break the streak here and not go to the NCAA Tournament," Eduardo said. "Our team won't go the NCAA tournament.

"Coach, we are not very good, are we?"

Sampson: "Eduardo, we don't know how to compete."

Najera: "Do you think we are going to get better?"

Sampson: "I don't know, Eduardo. What do you think? That is up to you."

Eduardo was worried, but Sampson believed that showed he cared.

"Nolan is like a zombie," Sampson said. "You can look into Nolan's eyes and see all the way to Wyoming. And he has no clue as to what's going on. Hollis weighs 150 pounds. We recruited Hollis as a guard, and we are not even sure he can dribble at this point. J.R. I have never seen play in a game. But in my mind, that's OK. I don't mind them going through this adversity. If I can't find something to kick them out of practice over a couple of times in October, I will invent something."

Oklahoma opened the 1999-2000 season in the Top of the World Classic in Fairbanks, Alaska. The Sooners swept the three games by an average of seventeen points and beat Cal, 75-58, in the title game.

That Najera, a senior, was named the MVP of the tournament was not a surprise. But Raymond scored twenty-nine points in the opener against Montana State and was named to the all-tournament team. Although Stone and Heskett might have gone unnoticed in the box score, Sampson knew their importance.

"We played Cal in the title game, and that's when I realized the importance of seniors and experience," Sampson said. "They had some talented, talented kids. But we had Old Man River, Tim Heskett [a fourth-year junior], who was starting now. He couldn't outrun me. I'm not sure he could even touch the rim. Renzi [a senior like Eduardo] was not a great athlete but was tough and a winner.

"But Renzi could set screens," Sampson said. "Renzi was a point center. Renzi knew the offense better than any point guard I ever had. Renzi knew how to screen and make people better. Look at the stat line and people would wonder why is Renzi starting. Because he knows how to win.

"I found out a lot about our athletic director Joe Castiglione when he hired Renzi. People say, 'Boy, Joe knows how to pick a winner.' You look at Bob Stoops. He also hired Renzi. I know that doesn't compare. But Renzi has done an unbelievable job with Sooner Sports Properties. Renzi was a winner and he cared so much. This year, when I didn't have Renzi and Eduardo, I almost felt naked. It was like I was walking into the gym with no clothes on. Those guys were my security blanket."

Renzi looked at himself as an Eduardo Najera-type player.

"Eduardo did everything I did good, but he did it better," Stone said. "He did all the little things I took pride in doing. And that is what made him such a good player. Not only would he score and rebound, he would set a screen. He would tell a point guard where to run a play. He would pick a guy up off the floor. He would take a charge. That's stuff that stars don't always do. He might not be a star in the NBA, but he will have a long career because he does those things."

Stone also had a fondness for Sampson and his ability to motivate players.

"He has a saying for every day of the week," Stone said with a laugh. "His favorite sayings are when he is trying to tell a player he doesn't know what he is talking about. He would say, 'Son, you don't know whether you are pitching or catching,' 'Son, you are like a fart in a skillet. You are jumping around everywhere,' 'Son, you don't know whether you are on foot or on horseback.'"

Former assistant coach Jason Rabedeaux had a few more Sampsonisms: "He would always say, 'I don't have time to coach the coaches.' In other words, he doesn't need to be out of his office, coaching you into what you need to do. Some of the other ones... 'I was born at night, but not last night.'... 'That player doesn't know whether he is washin' or dryin'.' 'He thinks defense is something running around the back 40—de-fence.'"

The whimsical Sampson was winning.

With the leadership of Stone-Najera-Heskett, the Sooners started 9-0, which was their best start since a 10-0 beginning under Billy Tubbs during the 1991-92 season.

Arkansas was a big game because the Sooners had beaten the Razorbacks by thirty the previous season in Norman. Arkansas players wanted revenge.

Eduardo Najera's passion matched Sampson's.
Photo by Lisa Hall/OU Athletic Media Relations.

"The media was playing it up in Arkansas," Sampson said. "We knew what we are walking into. J.R. was technically a redshirt freshman. Hollis was a true freshman. And Nolan was a first-year junior college player. But I had the three [Heskett, Stone, Najera] who had Sooner basketball stamped on their foreheads. They knew exactly how to play on the road. And they knew how to win."

And the Sooners did, 66-52, before the 19,316 howling Hog fans in Fayetteville.

"Eduardo could have the worst shooting percentage I have ever seen and be the best player on the floor," Sampson said. "He was five-for-fourteen in that game against Arkansas, but was the best player on the floor. That's the thing I told the NBA guys. They would say, 'What about his shot?' I would say, 'What about it? He doesn't have one. He is not a good shooter. He shot 60 some percent from the foul line. If you are asking about Eduardo's shooting, that's not what his value is. He knows how to win the game. He knows how to influence the game.'"

And at least one NBA coach, Chicago's Tim Floyd, has appreciated Sampson's frankness.

"I think he is one of the good guys in the business," Floyd said. "He will level with you. If you make a call and want an evaluation of a player, something along that line, sometimes you are looking out of the corner of your eye at the guy you are talking to, but not Kelvin."

The Sooners' winning streak came to an end with a 72-57 loss to Cincinnati in Norman right before Christmas. But the Sooners won their next five and stood 14-1 on Jan. 11. The last time OU had been 14-1 was in 1987-88.

"We weren't on anybody's radar," Sampson said. "This team was picked to finish fifth or sixth in the Big 12. But here we were ranked. I was on the 'Don Fortune Show' out of Kansas City. And the guy says, 'Aren't you guys playing a little bit over your head? You are not nearly as good as your ranking.' That is not the thing to say to me. He called and apologized to me after that. We won the All-College Tournament and we were 14-1 going to Texas. I am thinking we are not quite as good as our record, but we are a little bit better than I thought we would be."

Assistant coach Ray Lopes added: "We work hard from the managers to the assistant coaches to the secretaries. But to say that we are overachievers, that's not fair to the players we recruit. We have guys who can play. We have won fifty-three games the last two years and ninety-seven the last four. It takes players to win that many games."

Oklahoma needed more stars than Najera, however. Sampson had returned to his three-guard offense, with Price, Johnson, and Raymond. Heskett was coming off the bench.

"But Nolan, I didn't know if he would ever come around," Sampson said. "Nolan looked like he was walking through a mine field. There was a three- or four-game stretch where I sat him down and wouldn't let him play. He was soft. He wasn't rebounding. He wasn't competing. And I was on him pretty good. I had to get off him. He couldn't handle struggling and me getting on him."

Oklahoma lost at Texas, 79-66, when Gabe Muoneke scored thirty. That didn't bother Sampson. But the next game did, an 80-68 loss at Colorado. Colorado guard Jaquay Walls scored twenty-eight points. And through seven seasons at OU it was the only time Sampson lost to the Buffaloes.

"Nobody was guarding him," Sampson said of Walls. "Nolan Johnson couldn't have guarded the back door with two cannons that night. I was disappointed in everybody's effort. I am an effort guy. I know some nights you are not going to play well. But I cannot comprehend why a kid can't give great effort."

Sampson had the chicken tossed off of the plane before the team even started back to Norman. And the day after the Colorado game was the most intense film room OU had had since Murray State the previous season.

"The more I watched the Colorado tape the madder I got," Sampson said. "Our problem had nothing to do with Xs and Os, it had to do with effort. Nolan Johnson and J.R. Raymond played like sieves. They were stealing from the state. They were getting $11,000 scholarships. And it was just like highway robbery. I said, 'You guys need to reimburse the University of Oklahoma for what you did.'"

During practice that day, Johnson walked out he was so frustrated.

"I said you are either part of the problem or you are part of the solution," Sampson said. "I said right now you are part of the problem. We are not playing nearly as hard as we need to play. Here you are, I am getting on you, and you want to quit. So why would I want you to stay? So, Nolan walks out."

Najera went after Johnson but couldn't find him. Sampson sent Seltzer after him. Seltzer eventually found Johnson in his apartment lying on the bed and talking to his mother about how he was going to return to his home in New York.

"It was hard for me," Johnson said. "Basically I had come from street ball. I didn't know how to play in a structured offense. Coach Sampson taught me a lot of things, running an offense and learning how to score in an offense. All I knew was how to drive and score. I was a Junior College All-American. But we had Eduardo that season, and he was doing a lot of scoring. I had to take the back seat to him.

"That was the low point. I was serious about going home. I had missed two days of practice. I was on the way out. I was lying on my bed talking to my mom. I was hiding in my room. But I forgot I told Coach Seltzer how to get into my apartment if the door was locked. And here he comes through the window. Coach Seltzer had played for Coach Sampson, and he told me it was not the end of the world. I went back to practice. And the second half of the season made me a better person."

Oklahoma would lose only two regular-season games the rest of the season. And Johnson would become a force eventually.

After the Colorado debacle the Sooners rebounded against Iowa State.

But it took two overtimes in Norman for the Sooners to win, 80-75. Najera turned in a dazzling performance: twenty-five points and fourteen rebounds. He was making himself into an NBA Draft choice by his play every night. Sampson finally had a player who matched his passion. Najera had a great desire to play in the NBA. Eventually Najera would fulfill that dream during the 2000-01 season with the Dallas Mavericks.

Sampson said, "You look in Eduardo's eyes you could see his passion. He would never hide it. Eduardo was always a factor in something, always. He cared so much.

"He would come in my office and have heart to heart talks. He would be so passionate about being the first player from Mexico to be drafted into the NBA, he would start crying. Eduardo had gotten hurt. I think it was shin splints. And I was playing him way too many minutes. The fact we had lost Ryan Humphrey was beginning to have a little bit of an effect on us in my mind. I had done a poor job substituting for Eduardo. But I couldn't take him out. I was just riding Eduardo. It was his team. And I put that saddle on him. I was just going to ride him as long and as hard as I could."

During that season *The Sporting News* sent a reporter to Norman to spend a week with Sampson as part of a story on rivalries such as North Carolina-Duke, Indiana-Purdue, and Oklahoma-Oklahoma State. The reporter went to Sampson's house to observe the team meeting/film session on Friday night before a home game against Oklahoma State in the middle of the Big 12 season.

The basketball room in the Sampson home has a "Kelvin's Diner" neon sign on one wall. The room has series of long windows, which allows for a view of the back patio, a basketball goal, and a swimming pool. There's a large-screen TV and basketball memorabilia on the other walls. It's a very homey atmosphere for the players. Karen put the "Kelvin's Diner" sign on the wall because Kelvin likes greasy spoons. Quipped Karen: "The kind that were on *Alice,* you know, the ones where the waitresses wear the white aprons. One time he mentioned he would like to own a diner. This is probably as close as he gets."

Such was the setting for Friday night film sessions for home games.

"He really leaves no stone unturned in terms of preparation," Rabedeaux said. "He does it at home because it takes the kids out of the gymnasium and locker room environment. The kids would have light snacks they could munch on, maybe pizza. One of the assistant coaches gets up in front, hands out the report, goes over it, and pops the tape in the VCR. It was more of an informal setting, although the kids, trust me, were on the edge of their seats. It was all business. If you didn't get there on time, the door was locked. If you missed the film session, you didn't start or you were not playing. Coach is a huge stickler for time."

The next day at Lloyd Noble Center, the Sooners set an attendance record with a crowd of 13,280, but Oklahoma State beat the Sooners, 74-71, to end OU's five-game winning streak. Glendon Alexander came off the bench and made three three-pointers to spark the Cowboys.

OU had to leave the next day, a Sunday, for a Big Monday game at Nebraska and fly through a snowstorm to get there. It was another Waterloo game for Sampson and the Sooners.

"On Monday I told Alex we are going to tape them at shoot around," Sampson said. "Most teams don't go hard the day before the game and certainly not the day of the game. But we had a spirited, tough practice that day. And I wanted our kids to get in the mindset this was an important game. We had lost a home game. But if we could win this game, we still had a chance to win the league. The first half we played about as good as we can play. And we ended up winning, 62-54."

The following Saturday the Sooners lost at Kansas, 53-50, and could never catch Iowa State, which won the Big 12 regular-season race by a game over Texas. Oklahoma still could finish in a tie for third place with Oklahoma State. The Sooners, however, had to win the last game ever played at the old Gallagher-Iba Arena. Oklahoma State fans were in a festive mood. It was Senior Night at OSU.

With about ten minutes left in the game, Oklahoma trailed, 52-39. Sampson called time out.

"We were having a hard time running our stuff," Sampson said. "They were making tough shots. Desmond Mason didn't hurt us. He didn't make a field goal that night. Our goal was to hang in there. I think that's one thing we had established in our program. We were pretty good on the road."

Oklahoma rallied behind Johnson, who was getting the ball and creating scoring opportunities in Sampson's 1-4 offense. The Sooners outscored Oklahoma State 15-4 in the final seven minutes to hand

Senior Night 2000 before OU's victory over Missouri in Norman.
Photo by Chuck Porter/OU Athletic Media Relations.

Senior Night is always emotional for Kelvin Sampson
as he embraces Eduardo Najera.
Photo by Chuck Porter/OU Athletic Media Relations

the Cowboys their first home loss in fifteen games that season. One of the more interesting quotes of the season came from Oklahoma State's Brian Montonati, who told *The Daily Oklahoman*: "We just put our hands on our throat and squeezed as hard as we could. We choked this off ourselves, with a little help from them."

"I thought that was a great win," Sampson said. "And I don't think people were realizing what a great year we were having considering we had lost four starters."

"It was one of my top five wins at Oklahoma," Stone said. "It was just incredible."

Missouri was the next opponent in the quarterfinals of the Big 12 Tournament. Having to play Missouri in the state of Missouri frequently in the post-season tournament is one of the reasons Sampson is glad the 2003 and 2004 tournaments will be in Dallas.

"Missouri is always a hard game in the Big 12 Tournament," Sampson said. "It's on a neutral floor, but the advantage always goes to the team that has the most fans. I always thought as long as the tournament remained in Kansas City it would never be the Big 12 because Kansas City would always be linked to the old Big Eight. We had to do something to incorporate the South."

The Missouri game went into overtime. Najera fouled out with 2:32 remaining in regulation. That's when Sampson knew he had a strong supporting cast. Price, only a freshman, gave the team the pep talk it could win without Najera. And then Newton scored five points, on a three-pointer and two free throws, in the final 22.2 seconds to win the game, 84-80.

"The thing Quin Snyder [Missouri coach] does is get his team to play hard," Sampson said. "And I think we bring that out in teams, too. The other coach talks so much about how tough we are and how hard we play. Missouri and Oklahoma are very similar. But if you look at the strengths of the coaches in this league, it is usually from the defensive end. When you have two teams who play similar to each other, you are going to have a hard fought, hard-nosed game."

Najera bounced back with a career-high thirty-one points in the semifinal against Texas. And OU came from behind to win, 81-65. That put the Sooners in their second Big 12 title game in three years. "Tonight was a want-to game," Najera said. "And we wanted it more."

The title game was a rematch with regular-season champion Iowa State, which had lost only to the Sooners and to Missouri during the Big 12 season.

"There were 19,900 fans and 16,000 or 17,000 were Iowa State fans," Sampson. "We had 1,000. Talk about the Roman Empire days. I thought we were out there performing for Caesar. It was a close game early. Then all of a sudden their kids fed off their emotion. We didn't play well that day. But we had won twenty-six games and that wasn't bad for a team that had lost four starters. And we still had a chance for a pretty good seed."

The Sooners returned to the hotel in Kansas City. And Sampson was surprised the Sooners received a No. 3 seed in the NCAA Tournament in what he believed was a rebuilding year.

Oklahoma would face 14th-seeded Winthrop in the first round of the tournament. That was no contest as the Sooners sprinted out to a 39-23 half-time lead in a game that started at 10:30 a.m. in Tucson. The Sooners shot 51 percent and 47.6 percent from the three-point range.

That set up a second-round meeting against sixth-seeded Purdue, which, in many ways, was a lot like the Sooners. At least two of the players were mirror images: Najera and Purdue's Brian Cardinal. "They dive on the floor, they take charges, they post up, and they hit threes," said Purdue coach Gene Keady. "They play hard on defense. They don't leave anything out on the floor."

Najera won the individual battle statistically but fouled out of his final collegiate game. And it was Cardinal who deflected a loose ball and kept alive a sequence that led to Purdue's go-ahead free throws with 43.7 seconds remaining. The Boilermakers put the game away, 66-62, with three more free throws in the final 21.3 seconds.

"I was real emotional in the locker room after the game," Sampson said. "Losing the game was clouding the fact I wouldn't get to coach Eduardo anymore. I had only been at Oklahoma six years, but Eduardo had been there for five. This kid had come in as a boy and become a man. And now I realized for the first time in five years he wouldn't be around anymore.

"I loved Eduardo and Renzi. And they were loyal to this school and program. When a recruit would come on campus, those two would say, 'He won't fit us' or 'He is one of us.' I loved that because they took ownership in the program. They wanted the right kind of kids to play with them. They didn't want jerks on their teams. And I respected them for that."

On the plane trip back to Norman, Sampson already was looking to the future.

"On the way back he told me that to succeed you have to fail," said guard Hollis Price. "I had seven turnovers in that game and we lost it. He told me I would do better the next year. And the next year, better things did happen for me."

Before the 2000-01 season Sampson had a brush with another job.

Lon Kruger decided to leave Illinois to take the Atlanta Hawks head coaching job. Sampson's name was linked to the Illinois job. And Illinois athletic director Ron Guenther actually flew to Oklahoma City and checked into an airport hotel.

"I had a lot of interest in the Illinois job," Sampson said. "I am not sure if I could explain how that came down in the end. We had agreed to agree to get together and talk about the job. He was moving quickly. He was not devoid of candidates. Jud thought it was one of the top jobs in the Big Ten.

"We talked on the phone and we discussed the job. But we never could get together. If we could have sat down and gotten face-to-face ...but we never did. I never met Ron. I talked to him on the phone two or three times."

It was a media circus. Television reporters even came over to Sampson's house and tried to peer with their camera crews through the Sampsons' windows. And reporters had staked out the Oklahoma City hotel where Guenther was registered, just waiting for Sampson to walk into the lobby.

"I believe things happen for a reason. I have an unbelievable job working for a great person, Joe Castiglione, and an impact president in David Boren. My entire family is very happy at OU. My daughter, Lauren, is a sophomore at Oklahoma. And that's a great selling point for a recruit."

CHAPTER 14

That Roller Coaster of a Season

Kelvin Sampson's seventh season at Oklahoma was a roller coaster ride.

There was the low of dropping to 1-3 in the Big 12 after a one-point loss at Texas Tech.

There was the high four days later—a miraculous last-second overtime victory over Kansas State that turned around the Sooners' Big 12 season.

There was the high of OU's twenty-one-point blowout of Texas in Austin. But four days later Sampson suffered another low, his worst road loss in seven seasons at OU. The Sooners dropped a 72-44 decision at Oklahoma State.

There was the high of winning the Big 12 Post-Season Tournament for the first time.

There was the low of losing in the first round of the NCAA Tournament to Indiana State.

Get the picture?

For the first time in his career, a Sampson-coached Sooner team lost an exhibition game. Considering Sampson was recovering from the loss of the previous spring's senior class—Renzi Stone, Eduardo Najera, Victor Avila—he wasn't all that concerned.

"Early in the year nobody is going to be as good as they are going to be later," Sampson said. "We lost an exhibition game. I know the night we played them we had no one who could have started for them. We didn't have anything in. We didn't know any of our half court offense. But the older I got the more secure I got with our journey. I am not interested in how good we are in November anymore. Don't worry about it.

"I remember we used to start practice on October 15, and we would have a master plan for each daily practice. You wouldn't play a game until Friday after Thanksgiving. We had forty-six practices. Now you play a game after twenty. We used to have everything ready. Now when we play in the first week of November, we have nothing ready. I would just walk into the locker room and write 'improve.'"

The irony of the situation was for the second straight season Oklahoma would win three early-season tournaments, including the Big Island Invitational in Hilo, Hawaii. The Sooners won both of their tournaments, the Sooner Classic and the All-College Tournament in Oklahoma City. But it took a 79-78 overtime victory over SMU to win the All-College. And Oklahoma also needed overtime to defeat Arkansas, 88-79, in Norman in a single game.

"And after we won the All-College Tournament in late December, I said to my assistant coach Ray Lopes, 'We are a phony. We are not near as good as our record. We are the most deceptive 11-1 team ever,'" Sampson said. "We had been lucky to beat Arkansas, because we had to come back from nine points down. The SMU game in the championship of the All-College we weren't very good. Tim Heskett and Kelley Newton bailed us with threes."

"But they kept getting better and better as the season went along," SMU coach Mike Dement said. "They had a great year. They played really hard defensively in that game. They played harder defensively than some of the other top teams we played early [such as Tennessee]."

OU's best guard, J.R. Raymond, had been nabbed on a shoplifting offense at a Wal-Mart in July 2000. And he was suspended for the first three games, including two exhibitions. He had lost his confidence and wasn't playing well. The Sooners were using Hollis Price as the point guard and Kelley Newton as the shooting guard to begin the season. Sampson tried to rotate Raymond in off the bench.

"Our big guys had no clue how they would fit in," Sampson said. "We have three positions: point, post, and perimeter positions. But in those twelve games, I never saw the three parts play equally. We were winning on tradition. We were winning because we were a little bit tougher and when it got down to it, we could make the play when we had to. And that caught up with us."

The Sooners ran into problems in the first Big 12 Conference game, at Iowa State.

"I knew when we went into half time of that game against Iowa State, we were in trouble," Sampson said. "Iowa State was a great defensive team, and we had forty-nine points. If you have forty-nine points against Iowa State, you better be up more than eight. That was not a good sign. I told them we were not going to win this game on the offensive end. The first five baskets of the second half were three-pointers by them."

After a 100-80 loss to Iowa State, Oklahoma returned home to face Texas A&M and Kansas. The A&M game was a routine OU victory.

"I wish the Kansas game had been later in the year," Sampson said. "We really didn't have J.R. yet. Our two best scorers I thought would be going into this season were Aaron McGhee and J.R. Raymond. And combined, they didn't score a point against Kansas. We lost, 69-61. The alarms were starting to go off.

"I didn't know how to coach Daryan Selvy [a 6-foot-6 junior forward]. He wasn't a perimeter player. He wasn't a post. And he certainly wasn't a point. McGhee was a good player. But he didn't have a feel. He could only do one thing to help us win and that was make a basket. If he wasn't making a basket, he wasn't doing anything else to help us win. We were a team playing hard but not getting anything done. It was the treadmill effect. We were burning calories, running on the treadmill. We were stuck in neutral. The engine was racing, but we were spinning out."

Sampson knew the team chemistry was not good. Oklahoma was 1-2 going to Texas Tech. And Oklahoma trailed almost the entire game before taking the lead in the last minute. But Texas Tech point guard Jamal Brown banked in an eight-foot shot as time expired to beat the Sooners, 60-59.

In the second half of the Texas Tech game, Sampson had a conversation with a struggling Selvy, a junior college transfer. And then Ronnie Griffin, another junior college player in his first year in the OU program, and Selvy started arguing at the end of the bench. Sampson went ballistic He chewed both kids out.

"That was totally out of character," Sampson said. "The teams at Montana Tech, Washington State, and Oklahoma, regardless of what you said to them, the players would nod their heads and say, 'Yes, sir, I am going to try better.' I had four or five kids who would run through a brick wall, but most of them would look around and see if the other ones would. That wasn't Sooner basketball. I didn't let either one of them play the rest of the game. I was upset to the point I got distracted. That's one of the few times that has happened."

Sampson believed the team was playing way below its level. After the Texas Tech loss, Sampson was volatile in the locker room and dumped over an ice chest. He was disappointed in this team because it was not living up to what the program had established the previous six seasons with Ryan Minor, Corey Brewer, Eduardo Najera, Renzi Stone, and Ernie Abercrombie.

After the game OU trainer Alex Brown told Sampson he had a bit of bad news.

"I asked what could possibly be worse than what I just watched?" Sampson remembers.

A snowstorm had moved into Texas. And the Sooners would have to bus four hours in the snow to Abilene to catch a plane back to Oklahoma.

"The weather was one bit of bad news, the other was Kansas State had beaten Missouri by twenty that night," Sampson said. "Our next game was at Kansas State. We are 1-3. And we are playing at Kansas State. And they are going to think they are really good. They will have their biggest crowd of the year. We are coming apart at the seams. This is when you shake things up.

"It's like there are three routes in front of us, and we keep taking the wrong road which ends in a dead end. We have to know how to choose the right road. There has to be a thought behind what we do. There has to be purpose."

Sampson opted to take the team on a very long road that night—a ten-hour bus ride from Lubbock to Norman—instead of riding four hours to Abilene to catch a plane. This was back to the Montana Tech days. Snow. Roughing it. Hard times.

"There was dead silence in the bus," Oklahoma's senior guard Tim Heskett said. "Well, the players were talking among themselves. We were checking ourselves. But we play best when things are against us. Coach Sampson does his best coaching then. People were jumping off the bandwagon and shoveling dirt on us."

Sampson got on the bus and took his customary seat on the left behind the driver. He watched the bus's windshield swipe the snow off, back and forth, back and forth, in rhythmic strokes. And he plotted the moves he had to make.

"We are 1-3 and four of the next seven games are on the road," Sampson said. "I believe this is where Montana Tech and Washington State helped me. You solve the problem or find a solution. When you solve the problem, you may be putting a band-aid on it. I wanted to build toward February and March. I had one of the best guards in the conference on my bench wallowing in self-pity, J.R. Raymond. We are 1-3 in the Big 12 and not getting any better. And I know our best guard was J.R., plain and simple.

"I knew I had to make some crucial decisions," Samson said. "The first thing I had to do was rectify our chemistry situation. I was going to suspend Ronnie Griffin from the team because he had the wrong attitude. When you are twenty-two, in your fourth year of college and at your fifth school, you should have it figured out. That was the last game he ever suited up for Oklahoma. But he left in good standing and is now at Southern Indiana. That was my fault. I shouldn't have recruited him. I had doubts when I recruited him. I couldn't let him fester and pull someone in with him."

Price added: "I think it was a good call making us ride that bus. He showed how much he cared for us. Kelley Newton and I sat on the back of the bus and stayed up until 3 a.m. talking. That made us think about what we had to do the next game."

Sampson told the team about the personnel moves when they returned to Norman. Raymond would be the starter at point guard. Price would move to the shooting guard. And Newton would come off the bench. The other new development was for the first time in Sampson's seven seasons at Oklahoma, the Sooners didn't leave until the day of the game in which they had to fly.

Sampson was just trying to shake things up. He even forgot his dress shoes and had to borrow a pair from the strength coach, Scott Kolok, on game day.

"J.R. was playing well, but Hollis didn't know whether he was on foot or horseback in that game," Sampson said. "Aaron was trying hard, but he was suffering the treadmill effect. Nolan was in a daze. Selvy had no idea. We have all these problems popping up. At half time we are down nine. I would have gotten upset, but I realized this team had to be nurtured. Tim Heskett wanted to go into the game. He had earned the right to say that, but I didn't agree. 'If you want to win, put me in,' he said. I love your effort, son, but I don't agree."

At one point Oklahoma trailed by thirteen points. Sampson got in Newton's face because he wasn't defending hard enough. Slowly, though, Oklahoma clawed back into the game. The Sooners trailed by two points with under ten seconds remaining in regulation when freshman forward Johnnie Gilbert was fouled. Gilbert was a 29.1 percent free throw shooter.

"There is probably a better chance for the grandson I have never seen to win the lottery," Sampson said of Gilbert making the free throws. "I looked at the tape later. And Johnnie is actually praying when the referee gives him the ball. He has his eyes closed and is saying a prayer. When he released the ball, you couldn't have put a safety pin in his behind with a jackhammer. He misses the first one."

Sampson called time-out and told Gilbert to miss the second free throw purposely either right or left. The plan, in a play called "Boomer," was for Daryan Selvy to flash across the lane and take a defender with him and Nolan Johnson to slide into the spot Selvy once occupied and score off the miss. The strategy worked perfectly. Gilbert missed it. And Johnson laid in the missed free throw with two seconds to tie the score at 55 and send the game into overtime.

It took a couple more odd twists for Oklahoma to win the game.

During the overtime, Kansas State missed eight free throws. But Oklahoma still needed two stellar defensive plays to pull the game out. Price made a steal and the winning basket with 10.5 seconds remaining in overtime. Raymond then stole the ball on the ensuing Kansas State possession to preserve a 64-63 OU victory.

Oklahoma players dog piled on the floor as the team raised its league record to 2-3.

"They won, but they had no chance to win at Kansas State," said Charlie Spoonhour, who was on the Sooner Sports Network television broadcast. "Kelvin's guys fought uphill all night. At the end, the way they won it was amazing. Everything had to break right. I remember late in the overtime, Dean Blevins said we had a problem. I said no, Kansas State had to miss a couple free throws, Oklahoma had to steal it and lay it in, and we would be a winner. Dad gummed if something like that didn't happen. It was just one of those things you will yourself to win."

"It was a springboard for the rest of the season," OU assistant coach Bennie Seltzer said.

The Kansas State victory was the first of seven straight for the Sooners, who were breezing along with the personnel changes Sampson had made. Raymond came out of his funk. During the seven-game winning streak, he averaged 18.8 points per game.

"It came back to getting a chemistry problem fixed and a point guard who could change speeds for us," Sampson said. "Hollis is a point guard, but he couldn't change speeds as well or as quick as J.R. With Hollis we didn't play as fast. The game came easier to J.R with the ball in his hands. Hollis is really good at scoring. He is not as good a ball-handler-dribbler and couldn't maneuver in traffic and make plays as well as J.R. But no one scored or defended as well as Hollis."

And McGhee, who played his freshman season at Cincinnati before transferring to junior college, was finally conforming to Sampson's system, giving the Sooners another scoring threat.

"At first Aaron looked like Godzilla," Sampson said. "He had the tattoos and the muscles. But he played like a nun. I had to teach him to play physical."

The Sooners won four road games during that stretch—at Kansas State, at Baylor, at Texas A&M, and at Texas, which had a twenty-five-game home-court winning streak. That continued a trademark of Sampson's teams. Through the 2000-2001 season, Oklahoma had the second best road record in Big 12 games (24-16) behind Kansas (28-12). Texas (21-19) was the only league team with a .500 road record in Big 12 play.

"Road games are who he is," Renzi Stone said of Sampson. "He loves road games. He loves keeping a group together, a small intimate group of guys who go into an arena that is loud. And we are at our best as a team when we play road games against teams we are not supposed to beat."

The Texas victory on ESPN's Big Monday pushed Sampson's record to 11-3 against Texas, 4-2 at the Erwin Center in Austin.

"Why do we win on the road?" Lopes hypothesized. "We have great focus and preparation. From a coach's standpoint that's why we win on the road. We don't change the way we play. We play the same on the road as we do at home from an effort and intelligence standpoint."

But the next road game, at Oklahoma State, was unlike any in Sampson's career. It was the first meeting between the two instate rivals since the January 27, 2001 plane crash in Colorado that killed ten people in the Cowboys' traveling party, including two players.

One of the crash victims was Bill Teegins, an Oklahoma City sports television anchor who co-hosted Sampson's television show, "Inside Sooner Basketball with Kelvin Sampson." Sampson also knew

Will Hancock, the Oklahoma State basketball information director, who died in the crash.

Sampson had orange T-shirts made. The names of the ten people killed in the crash were printed on the backs. The Sooners donned them when they came out of the locker room for the last time. And the appreciative Oklahoma State fans gave the Sooners an ovation.

"We walk in there and they are clapping for us," Seltzer said. "We took off the shirts and threw them into the crowd. We feel all warm and fuzzy. And then they unloaded on us."

Heskett added: "We were being nice to them. Then, it was like they let a pit bull loose on us."

The seven-game winning streak came to an end as Oklahoma State won, 72-44, in a game that wasn't even that close. It was the worst loss in Sampson's seven seasons at Oklahoma. Oklahoma made only two of thirteen three-point shots.

"That was the hardest game I have ever coached," Sampson said. "If we had played good we still would have lost. I don't think there was any way we were going to win that game in that gym, in that environment, in that situation.

"But I could have cared less. The more I sat there and we got down 28, I wanted us to compete and come back. It was the first game I had ever coached in my life like that. Bill Teegins hosted my television show. I looked so forward to talking with him. I have worked with a lot of people on television shows, no one as good as Bill. And every time we went to Stillwater, I enjoyed talking to Bill. I got to thinking about Bill. I got to thinking about Bill Hancock [director of the NCAA Division I Men's Basketball Tournament] and his son Will. I got to thinking about those things."

Sampson, to this day, has never looked at the tape of that game. The Sooners put that game behind them and blasted Baylor, 82-60, back in Norman, preceding a two-game road swing to Missouri and Maryland. Before the season Sampson had looked at the four road games, including those at Texas and Oklahoma State, and imagined Oklahoma would be doing good to win one of the four road games.

"We got ahead in the second half at Missouri," Sampson said. "And one of the things I remember we had a stud officiating crew. They were veteran refs. You can't win big road games without veteran refs. Inexperienced, weak referees will get influenced by home crowds. When I go on the road, one of the first things I do is look at the crew. If it is a veteran crew, I feel a little bit better. If it is a young or weak crew, I think we better play good to win."

The crew for the Missouri game was Tom Rucker, Ted Hillary, and John Clougherty, who had all officiated games in the Final Four.

"That Missouri game was a culmination of what I believe," Sampson said. "If you are a good kid and you work hard and you hang in there and you believe in your coaches and you believe in yourself, good things will happen. Jameel Heywood had backed up Eduardo Najera his junior year. And Eduardo played nearly every minute. Jameel got down on himself. I talked to him about attitude and character and being a part of a team."

Heywood, a 6-6, 230-pound senior, who averaged less than four points a game, came up with the biggest offensive rebound of his career to win the game.

With the scored tied, 61-61, with 17.5 seconds remaining, Sampson called time out.

"Everybody in the gym knew what we were going to do; we were going to run flat for Nolan," Sampson said.

"The two things we wanted were a shot and an offensive rebound. And the best way to get an offense rebound is off offensive penetration. If Nolan can get into the lane and by his man and force help, that will allow someone else to rebound. Nolan is like a thick piece of bacon; you can't get to the other side of him. He is uncanny turning the corner; once he gets that shoulder by you, he is by you."

Nolan missed the shot, but he penetrated enough to free up Heywood, who snared the rebound and scored as the buzzer sounded. It was a bang-bang play the officials went to the monitor to review. But the basket was good. And the Sooners won, 63-61, snapping the Tigers' thirteen-game home winning streak.

In the cramped Missouri locker room, which Sampson says is smaller than his wife's walk-in closet, he reminded the team of the Lubbock trip and how far they had come. This was a Big Monday game on ESPN. The league leaders Iowa State and Kansas had both lost in Columbia. And now the last two times the Sooners had played on national television they had won, including the Texas game nine days earlier.

"I told the team, 'you should feel good about yourself, but Jameel, you should especially, what you have gone through to get yourself to this point,'" Sampson said.

The next day, Wednesday, Sampson went recruiting. But the players were going to be drug tested back in Norman.

"J.R. had had a history, but he had been clean," Sampson said. "In the back of my mind I hoped he was being honest with me. We had him seeing people, and he had tested negative. I didn't anticipate a problem."

On Thursday Sampson started off with ten minutes of tape and talked to the team about how it was going to defend Maryland's flex offense with a zone and different switches. Trainer Alex Brown told Sampson during practice it was urgent athletic director Joe Castiglione see him before he left for Maryland. Sampson figured it out right away. J.R. had tested positive. Later Raymond revealed it was marijuana.

"I thought to myself J.R. will never play for Oklahoma again," Sampson said.

Under NCAA and Big 12 rules, Raymond could have returned in a week and played against Oklahoma State if he had gone through rehab. "But my deal with J.R. was not the NCAA, Big 12, or school policies, it was his track record with me and our responsibility to rules," Sampson said. "He had tested positive before."

Sampson told Raymond he wasn't making the trip. Raymond started crying.

"You bring J.R. back, you still have the team intact," Sampson said. "This was a good team. We could strap it on with anybody. We were going to be on ABC National Television against Maryland. You just feel sick to your stomach. I felt like somebody had taken a baseball bat and rapped me in the solar plexus. I told Joe [Castiglione] I couldn't bring J.R. back. I said winning is important. But it was other things like his class attendance and the trouble in the summer before that bothered me. He was a kid who came from a tough, tough, background and had a hard time handling temptations.

"J.R. was one of the best guards I have ever coached. From three to six in the afternoon, he was phenomenal; from six p.m. to three a.m. you needed to have a beeper on his ankle. You had no idea what he was going to do. His biggest enemy was never the other team; it was always himself. Sometimes we search and we search and we get to the last peak of the highest mountain. And there's a mirror there and we look in it. And it is us. That was J.R."

On the bus ride from the airport in Washington, D.C., to the hotel, Sampson made the decision to remove Raymond from the team permanently. Sampson called Castiglione and told him. And shortly after arriving at the hotel, Sampson called a team meeting at two a.m. He told them Raymond would not be back.

"We knew something was wrong," Johnson said. "We were on the bus back in Norman and we saw J.R. pull off in his car."

Sampson had always been taught the foundation of any program was discipline.

"You have to have rules and do things right," Sampson. "Here I am as a coach and arguably our best player has screwed up numerous times. I have done everything in my heart to help this kid get better and do better. Am I going to keep him because I want to win games? Or, do I do what is right, because it is right?"

Price waited until after the meeting and shook Sampson's hand.

"Don't worry, Coach, we will be fine," Price said.

At three a.m. Sampson wasn't so sure. He started watching film.

"I was rationalizing," Sampson said. "This was not a tragedy. Tragedy is what we saw in Stillwater. We will get through this. But don't tell me, 'You don't have J.R.; you can't win.' That's all I needed to tell myself. I wanted to grab Hollis out of his bed and show him how we were going to win this game."

One of Sampson's most ardent supporters at Washington State, Dennis DeYoung, wasn't surprised by Sampson's decision on Raymond.

"That's the Kelvin Sampson I know," DeYoung said. "Kelvin sticks by his guns. That may have cost wins in the tournament. But that is what he thought was needed for the student and the program."

"It is easy to have principles some of the time," said John Nash, a former OU walk-on. "It is hard all the time. He has them all the time."

Sampson's immediate concern was Maryland's trapping press. Hollis wasn't good at breaking a press. Sampson told his team to shorten the game by lengthening the possessions. Sampson wanted Maryland to guard OU in half court unless McGhee was near the bucket, Newton had an open three, or Johnson had a lane to slash to the basket.

At Cole Field House, Dick Vitale and Brent Musburger, the ABC Sports announcing team, came by before the game and extended their sympathies to Sampson over the fact Raymond was not playing. They were both complimentary. But there was a hint of resignation in their voices that Oklahoma's season was over. Sampson was fueled by such talk.

"It gets back to toughness," Price said. "We didn't want one person to spoil our season because he got kicked off the team."

OU fell behind Maryland, 10-2. Price was playing nervous against the press, and Maryland was dominating the boards. But Heskett hit a three-pointer to make it 14-7. Sampson told his team they had to tighten up the defense and not allow second shots. At half time, OU had nearly caught up, trailing only 27-25. The game was going the way Sampson wanted it. But OU could not guard Juan Dixon's three-point shooting. He made three three-pointers in four possessions in the second half.

Maryland won, 68-60, with Dixon scoring twenty-three. But the Terrapins had to work for their 77th straight nonconference home victory.

"Hollis had to play forty minutes, and I told him that was the last time I wouldn't rest him," Sampson said. "He was the only one to play the point. I was encouraged the way we played. I thought, we can still win."

Johnson said: "Even though we didn't win that game, we knew we could win."

On the way back to Norman, the Oklahoma party had a startling reminder of the Oklahoma State tragedy less than a month earlier. The team's charter was struck in flight by lightning shortly after refueling in Louisville on the trip back to Oklahoma.

"We set down in Oklahoma City, and there were lightning marks on the aircraft," said Dr. Don Halverstadt, part of the OU travel party. "We came very close to a significant problem. That was the worst plane trip I have ever been on, commercial or charter." And for the frequent flyer Dr. Halverstadt, who had made every OU trip for the past five seasons, that was saying something.

"Bad things come in threes," Sampson said. "I had just lost my best player, lightning struck the plane. I wondered what was next."

The Sooners finished the regular season with home games against Colorado and a return match with Oklahoma State. Sampson needled OU players they couldn't win because of Raymond's absence. Sampson went back to harder practices that week. The team regrouped. And Johnson, the 6-4, 220-pound senior, would become the focal point of OU's 1-4 offense.

"You would turn on ESPN and they would say the Sooners' season was over," Johnson said. "I knew I had to step up my scoring and other things I did for the team. He [Coach Samson] challenged me and I enjoyed challenges."

"I would tell Nolan he would have to get a double-double," Sampson said. "You could tell when Nolan was going to play well. That was when he was offensive rebounding and he got to the line at least ten times."

Kim Anderson, former Missouri assistant coach and now Big 12 Director of Basketball Operations, added: "Kelvin convinces his team who gives them the best opportunity to succeed. And he would build the team around that guy. He is good at putting the other four guys on the floor in the best position for them to succeed. That is not only scoring. He does a great job to get them in position to rebound. He has guys who are not big guys who are 6-5 and 6-6 guys. He gets them to the boards where they can rebound."

Sampson was finding all sorts of ways to spring the bull-like Johnson on the Big 12. It would eventually result in Johnson being named the Most Outstanding Player of the Big 12 Tournament.

"We started spreading the floor," Sampson said. "A lot of times, when teams started flattening out for Nolan they would jump into a 2-3 zone, so they took away his penetration angles. So we put Nolan on baseline, and he became more effective. I needed another scoring option.

"Selvy was a good one-on-one player. He was not a good system guy. We started playing Selvy like Nolan, except on the front line. Against Kansas, whoever was guarding Selvy, we would clear out one-on-one in the paint. He would penetrate and draw the defense and pitch it out. Kelley got involved. Hollis got involved. Our team did a great job adjusting."

Oklahoma crushed Colorado by nineteen and beat Oklahoma State by twelve to finish tied for second with Kansas in the Big 12 Conference's regular-season race, only a game behind Iowa State. In the first five years of Big 12 competition, Oklahoma boasted a 55-25 (.688) league regular-season record—second only to Kansas' 64-16 (.800) mark.

But off the floor, Sampson's family was deeply hurt by an illustration that accompanied a story in *The Daily Oklahoman*. The story talked about the popularity of OU football coach Bob Stoops, Oklahoma State basketball coach Eddie Sutton, and OU women's basketball coach Sherri Coale. Sampson was depicted as the low man on the totem pole, a direct shot (although the paper said inadvertent) at his Native American ancestry.

The Daily Oklahoman story focused on the theory Sampson had to fight for recognition of his program in a state where Stoops, Sutton, and Coale coached.

"I couldn't believe that something like that [illustration] would occur in a state like Oklahoma," said Oklahoma athletic director Joe Castiglione. "That's especially with all the sensitivity that we have for diversity in our state. To go that far using that vehicle to make that point, particularly when you are talking about a Native American, was deplorable. If the roles had been reversed, we would have been ripped to shreds and probably run out of the state.

"It was hurtful," Castiglione said. "Karen and Kelvin are mature enough to handle the situation. What hurt them the most is how it affected their children and comments people made. First of all it was a horrible story to begin with, but to use that tool to make a point, even if it is a figure of speech, to illustrate and use that symbol...it can appear to some to be derogatory."

Later Sampson was e-mailed an apology for the use of the symbol by the writer and received a call from a sports editor.

"I didn't understand it," Sampson said. "I thought it was unnecessary. What is your point? In this profession, what you realize over time is some people will like you and some won't. There are some reporters who will either like you or like your style of play. And I think their writing will reflect whether they agree with any of that. I think that was a reflection of his feelings toward our program."

In the landscaping behind the pool at their home, the Sampsons have a small totem pole amid the shrubs as a token remembrance of the story.

"Maybe people don't like the grind-it-out defensive matchups," Oklahoma guard Tim Heskett said. "Sometimes we win and it's not pretty."

Despite the flashiness of Tubbs' teams, the eight largest crowds ever at Lloyd Noble have all come under Sampson. Although Sampson's teams are defensive-oriented, they have been popular with OU fans for their grittiness.

The Daily Oklahoman illustration and story only served to turn on the Sooners, who won their first Big 12 Tournament in Kansas City, Missouri.

They beat Missouri (67-65), No. 9 Kansas (62-57), and No. 20 Texas (54-45). Johnson averaged 18.0 points and 6.7 rebounds during the three victories. Oklahoma trailed by double digits in each game, but outscored the three teams by a combined 120-80 margin in the second half.

"Friday night against Missouri was a bloodbath," Sampson said. "Saturday against Kansas was an endurance test. The Texas game was an emotional game. That's when it becomes mind over matter. Jud Heathcote used to say it is mind over matter. If you don't have a mind, it don't matter. I remember telling our assistant coaches that before we played Texas. This was a mental game."

Oklahoma fell behind the Longhorns, 26-8. Texas, which had lost the two previous meetings to OU, was obviously inspired. The Longhorns led by twelve at half time. But the two teams are alike in many ways.

"We were making shots early," Barnes said. "They weren't. Then it flipped . . . I just know this. When we get ready to play Oklahoma, there is not going to be anything easy. They are not going to give us anything, like step out of the way and give us what we want. They are going to make you work for everything you get. He believes in hard-nosed, tough defensive basketball."

Samspon added: "I think it is easy to coach against somebody whose coaching philosophy is entirely different from yours. I think it is a lot more difficult to coach against like teams. And the problem with our league is we have a lot of guys who coach alike. But I always have had great respect for Rick."

Before shutting down Texas, Sampson believed his players were making excuses they had had a rough draw beating both Missouri and Kansas in Kansas City, Missouri, only 40 miles from Lawrence and 120 from Columbia.

Sampson backed off and let assistant coach Ray Lopes scold the team. Sampson already had punched a hole in the white board in the locker room at half time of the Missouri game because the Tigers were mauling the Sooners on the offensive boards. It was still there. "I can't punch another hole in this thing," Sampson said. "About that time, Ray starts into his oratory."

Sampson calls Lopes "Joe Friday" because of his matter of fact nature. Kids Sampson: "Just the facts, ma'am." The half-time outburst was totally out of character for Lopes.

"I was really upset," Lopes said. "We had been at Oklahoma for seven years and we had been so close. We had missed the regular-season championship by a game. We had been to the tournament championship three times, and Kansas and Iowa State had beaten us. We had been so close to cutting down some kind of net. When we beat Missouri and Kansas, I knew we could win the championship and beat Texas.

"We were playing soft, playing lethargic. We had no purpose. Texas was whipping our tails. That was not an Oklahoma team out on the floor...I said that's not our team. Jim Shaw gives me a stat sheet. I looked at it and crumpled it.... This is not about stats. I have lost it a few times when we have been at practice, but never during a game. It was all sincere."

Johnson certainly got the message. He had eighteen points, a career-high thirteen rebounds, two assists, and two steals. He had fifteen points and eleven rebounds in the second half as Oklahoma beat Texas for the twenty-first time in the last twenty-five meetings and for the fifth straight time.

"Nolan's a load," Sampson said. "Your team is a reflection of your best players. During time-outs in the second half, I kept telling Nolan to get to the foul line. Nolan wasn't a guy who was going to relate to six different things. When he got to the foul line, he played his best. In some ways, he was our best player, even with J.R. J.R. was our best scorer. Nolan was our best defender, and if we needed a key rebound, Nolan could go get a rebound."

Sampson was assured his eighth straight NCAA Tournament appearance as a head coach (seven with Oklahoma and one with Washington State). That consecutive tournament string trails only Arizona's Lute Olson (17), Temple's John Chaney (12), Kansas' Roy Williams (12), and Cincinnati's Bob Huggins (10). Kentucky's Tubby Smith and Maryland's Gary Williams also have been to eight straight tournaments.

Oklahoma was rewarded with a No. 4 seed in the South Region and was paired against 13th-seeded Indiana State. With Price suffering a key injury late in regulation, the Sooners were upset by the Sycamores, 70-68, in overtime. Oklahoma led 47-34 with sixteen and a half minutes remaining in the game.

"In 1999 when we lost to Oklahoma State in the first round of the Big 12 Tournament; we were a thirteen seed and had an agenda that season," Sampson said. "Had we lost to Missouri this year, it is a lot

Ray Lopes, the trusty assistant who was vocal at half time of the title game.
Photo by Lisa Hall/OU Athletic Media Relations.

easier to convince your team they are not as good as they think they are coming off a loss. We had an emotional investment that weekend at the Big 12 Tournament. But the bottom line in the Indiana State game we were up thirteen points and we didn't find a way to put it away."

Late in the game, Price drove the lane and was fouled by Kelyn Block. As the two stumbled to the floor, Price struck Block in the face with an inadvertent elbow. Block had three teeth either chipped or lost, but Price's triceps tendon was torn. Price returned only briefly and didn't play in the overtime. Block returned and scored five of his seventeen points in overtime.

"It has to be the most unusual injury I have ever had," Price said. "Right after the game, they took an X ray and it showed a little tooth in there [in his tendon]. It was real frustrating. I was one of the leaders of the team. I wanted to compete with the team. We lost the game. It hurt my feelings that I had to sit and watch the last five minutes of the game."

Without Price and despite a career-high tying twenty-six points by Newton, Oklahoma lost, 70-68, when Johnson's jumper rolled off the rim as time expired in overtime.

"When you lose your last game and it's the first round, there is a little bit of a hollow feeling," Sampson said. "Time hasn't cured this wound. I liked coaching this team because it had heart. There was an involvement of adversity we all endured together, and it bonded us."

CHAPTER 15

Looking to the Future

The University of Oklahoma made a serious statement about its basketball program with the $16.8 million renovation and expansion of twenty-six-year-old Lloyd Noble Center. Armed with an improved facility, Kelvin Sampson hopes to raise the Sooner program to among the very elite in college basketball.

The renovation will make Lloyd Noble Center a "state of the art" college basketball facility. There will be an additional 628 seats nearer the floor, separate practice facilities for both the men's and women's basketball teams, improvements in the locker rooms, rest rooms, and concession stands, and ceiling and lighting upgrades.

It took five years and three OU athletic directors to make the renovation and expansion projects a reality. But the seeds for renovation were first planted in the mind of Sampson when he interviewed for the OU job in April 1994.

"There was no weight room," Sampson said of his initial tour of the facility. "Paint was peeling in the locker room. It was a mess. I rationalized Billy Tubbs had just resigned. And no one was taking care of this. But I couldn't get over how small the locker room and training room were, and they didn't have a whirlpool. The scoreboard and facilities were ancient.

"I looked at Lloyd Noble. It was a beautiful arena, but there was no floor down there. There was a tartan surface down there. They were getting ready for graduation. They told me when the season is over they take the floor up and use the arena for multipurpose events. I asked where's the trophy cases? They said up in the coaches' offices. I thought that was strange there was no place to display your tradition. OU had a great tradition and I wanted to see that displayed."

Sampson's interest in the North Carolina State job after his second season at Oklahoma in 1996 caused then OU athletic director Donnie Duncan to summon Sampson to his house. Initially, that's when the laborious process of getting Lloyd Noble Center updated started.

"I told Donnie in this profession I think we have journey jobs and we have destination jobs," Sampson said. "A journey job is where you go and wait for a destination job. And Donnie asked me is OU a journey or destination job? I told him this can be a destination job if we will make a statement about basketball. We don't have anywhere to practice."

Other facilities on campus were difficult to get into to practice. And after the basketball season, Lloyd Noble Center was used for other events, causing the basketball floor to be taken up.

"We need a place to practice," Sampson told Duncan. "We need a trophy case. We need a locker room. That's how you make a statement and make it a destination place. I said we need a basketball SID. And that's when we hired Mike Houck. We had a student intern. I made a list of all those things. The budget was fine. The idea was hatched with Donnie. He had great vision. I respected him greatly."

Shortly after the meeting, Dr. Don Halverstadt, a member of the Board of Regents of the University of Oklahoma, began traveling with Sampson on game trips. Together, they began looking at the top college arenas and devising a plan for Lloyd Noble Center.

Then in July 1998 Joe Castiglione left Missouri and became the Oklahoma athletic director. Nothing had been done with Lloyd Noble Center, except for a new scoreboard.

"I was here two or three months and learned of the development of an addition to Lloyd Noble Center and other ancillary team related areas in both men's and women's basketball," Castiglione said. "Our locker room for basketball was not up to standards for Division I programs. The ceiling was low.

"I walked in there the first time and I said, 'Gee, Coach, no wonder it is tough to recruit seven-footers. They can't fit in here.' They would have to walk around the entire time with their heads bent over, it was such a low ceiling. The women's basketball locker room was on the second floor. That was totally unusable."

The renovation and additions plan kept growing and evolving. Castiglione's question: "What are we trying to accomplish?" The fixes kept reminding Castiglione of short-term solutions or band-aid approaches. Castiglione told both coaches he believed the plan, asking for only $400,000-$500,000 from the Lloyd Noble Foundation, was insufficient for what had grown to a multimillion-dollar project.

"My first meeting with the Noble Foundation was to ask them to disregard the proposal," Castiglione said. But he told the Foundation he would return with a larger request. Eventually the Foundation contributed $8.5 million for renovation and expansion of Lloyd Noble Center.

"We went out and saw what the best programs had done or were about to do," Castiglione said. "It has everything we could possibly want. It has more seats and baby basketball arenas [practice facilities]. In terms of team-related facilities, it is state of the art. And I think it clearly demonstrates the commitment of the University of Oklahoma to its basketball programs."

Will the new arena finally end the talk of Sampson leaving? Castiglione hopes so. Sampson has a buyout clause if he leaves during the next seven years before the completion of his contract. According to Sampson the buyout ranges from $500,000 to $900,000 for the school that wants his services.

Sampson says the two most serious brushes with possibly leaving Oklahoma were for jobs at North Carolina State in 1996 and Illinois in 2000. Inquiries from one pro team, the Vancouver Grizzlies, and schools such as Michigan, LSU, Texas, and Arizona State were never that serious.

"Certain positions would open and names would be mentioned as successors for jobs," Castiglione said. "And Kelvin's name would constantly come up. I knew Kelvin wasn't interested in just any job. I started thinking about that. People would think another job would come along and he would leave. That was incorrect. Whether or not Kelvin was interested in the job, it created a hesitation on the part of Oklahoma fans to totally fall in love with the guy. It was almost like a courtship. The two sides enjoy each other's company but for some reason can't allow themselves to go to that next step emotionally. Maybe there's a fear you take that step, they may not be around.

"I was talking to him about it after this past season. It hit me. The last two years jobs have come open, and it is the annual rite of spring. I don't know if someone hits a button on the computer like spell check. Who are the respective coaches out there? Kelvin Sampson, and the rest fall in behind."

During this past off-season, Sampson had feelers for vacant Tennessee and South Carolina jobs, which didn't even reach the media. He doused any talk of his name being linked to those jobs before the media could write about them.

"I think I have been criticized being involved in so many jobs," Sampson said. "The thing people don't realize is you don't go asking for this. You want to get to the point your job is better than all of these other jobs. I wouldn't have traded my job for any of those jobs that opened up this year. You get to the point you try and keep your name out of it.

"I think this new facility makes a statement that basketball is important at the University of Oklahoma," Sampson said. "Whether you want to admit it, football is king here. I don't argue with it or fight it. But my point is basketball can be really, really good. Equally as good? That depends on the administration, the coach, and the players."

This past season the Sooners compiled a 13-1 record at Lloyd Noble Center, although it wasn't always full. Oklahoma averaged 10,324 fans a game at the 11,100-seat facility. But no-shows at OU basketball games are hardly a phenomenon during the Sampson era.

"When Billy had Stacey King and we went to the Final Four [1988], we didn't always sell out those games in December because people had Christmas on their minds and they had a football bowl game on January 1," said former OU associate athletic director John Underwood. "I think a little bit of that syndrome occurred after OU won the football championship this past year. Peoples' appetites were full."

And even when full, the atmosphere at Lloyd Noble Center isn't quite as hostile as some other arenas in the Big 12.

"It was not an opposing atmosphere, like, for instance, Allen Field House or at Missouri," Halverstadt said. "The fans there are right down on the floor. It's like a six-point home-court advantage because of the noise and fan support. So Kelvin said if we could do it, we need to get the fans down to the floor."

"Lloyd Noble is a pretty arena," Sampson said. "But a pretty arena doesn't always make a hostile environment. We have great crowds. We won thirteen of fourteen games at home. But we don't have a hostile arena. Ultimately your goal is to have a home-court advantage. Our arena, because of the way it is set up, you have a rectangular floor and built-in space pockets on the side in which no one sits. I have never liked the wall. It is a subliminal thing. You all stay behind the wall, don't come across the wall. You have to take the walls down. When you do that, I think you change attitudes. Make the fans part of the game. We do have great fans."

Oklahoma officials have taken the first rows out behind the wall, and from that point, will slant everything down to the floor. There will be 314 additional seats on each side. And the wall will be eliminated.

"It is going to make it a more intimate environment and make it more hostile," Sampson said. "I think it will change the attitude of the fans in the arena."

And the 2001-2002 Sooners, Sampson believes, will be deeper than his teams in the past. Thus, the Sooners will be able to overcome injuries or unforeseen circumstances.

"We have had a lot of bad luck here in the past," Sampson said. "The best big kid I have had here was Bobby Joe Evans. My best guard was J.R. Raymond. The kid who was most athletic was Ryan Humphrey. Evans got hurt. J.R. we had to dismiss from the team. And Ryan transferred. We have had to win with guile and guts. Charlie Spoonhour always said you are good at trickin' them. We have figured out how to do more with less. But I think our talent level has gone up. The thing I am excited about is we have good parts.

"My biggest concern about this coming year's team is outside shooting, because we lost Tim Heskett, J.R. Raymond, and Kelley Newton—three great three-point shooters. We have replaced them with better size and more athleticism. Another thing is leadership. When you lose a tremendous senior class, who is going to step up? Even though Hollis Price is a kid I expect to be a leader, my two seniors are Aaron McGhee and Daryan Selvy, who will be in their second years in the program. We have to establish consistent leadership. And we have to have new kids play major roles."

But Sampson has several new players who could step up.

The last OU signee, 6-5 Ebi Ere, a second-team All-American from Barton County (Kansas) Community College and originally from Tulsa McLain, caps off maybe the best class Sampson has had at Oklahoma. Auburn, Illinois, and Michigan State were among the pursuers of the talented wing player. He averaged 32.3 points in the national junior college tournament last spring.

Others to be counted upon heavily are first-team junior college All-American 6-5 Jason Detrick from Southwest Missouri State at West Plains and 6-1 Quannas White from Midland (Texas) Community College. White figures to be the Sooners' starting point guard.

"An intriguing backcourt will be White and Hollis Price," Sampson said. "When Hollis was a senior in high school they won the state title together in New Orleans." And a freshman "with a load of potential," according to Sampson, is Matt Gipson, a 6-foot-9 three-point shooter from Burkburnett, Texas.

"He will have a chance to contribute and help, but we are not depending on him," Sampson said. "I think when you get to the point you are not depending on freshmen, your program is getting stronger. Johnnie Gilbert will make tremendous strides. Kids always improve the most between their freshmen and sophomore years because their summers are different. They prepare differently. They know what to expect."

And Sampson could have his best interior defender during his OU tenure, 6-10 Jabahri Brown, a transfer from Florida International.

"Jabahri gives us something we have never had here—a shot-blocking and interior presence," Sampson said. "Jabahri is going to change a lot of shots inside. He is every bit of 6-10. He's a tremendous athlete and he is a quick, quicker jumper. He has tremendous timing. He has to get bigger and stronger. It is a lot easier to develop strength and weight than it is size and quickness. He has size and quickness. He has to sit out the first six games. It will take him into February until he is comfortable.

"But this is the best depth and quality we have ever had on the front line. Talent to me comes down to presence and impact. Eduardo had the most presence of any front-line player I have had. I have never seen Jabahri play a game. How does he factor in winning and losing? If he blocks five shots and he doesn't affect the game because they regain possession and they still score, I don't want that. How is he going to handle Chris Owens with an elbow in his throat? How is he going to handle September? I can tell a lot about what they will be like in January, February, and March by how they handle September."

Yes, that is September, when Kelvin Sampson's conditioning begins and his players run in the heat and under his demanding presence. Then it is on to October, when he tosses them out of practice, when he challenges them with the tip drill, the suicides, the charge drill, the screen drill, and he tries to test their toughness.

However Sampson has learned to ease up and peak for the end of the season.

"I was up there two years ago, and I noticed something different from when we were there," said Ernie Abercrombie, an undersized post player on the 1994-95 and 1995-96 teams. "We practiced harder the latter part of the season. In those end-of-season tournaments we would be exhausted, almost burned out from the entire season. He still has some long practices, which are extremely hard. But he gives them more time to get away from the game and come back and freshen up at the end of season. I think that is why they made it to the Sweet 16 and why they did well in the Big 12 Tournament this past year."

"He has built the program to such a level, we should be on the next tier," said former OU player Renzi Stone. "It should be on the Sweet 16, Elite Eight level every year and a Final Four every now and then. When that happens, we will know the program has arrived."

Former Michigan State coach Jud Heathcote, Sampson's mentor, was sitting in a bar in O'Hare Airport in March 2001, when OU rallied to beat Texas in the Big 12 Tournament title game. Three Oklahoma fans were watching the game, but they did not know Heathcote. They were talking about how Sampson was not appreciated in Oklahoma.

"Sometimes I don't think the people at Oklahoma understand what a good job he has done," Heathcote said. "Some people say he can't do anything in the tournament, even though they have a great season. I think it is a shame when a coach's and team's season is judged by how far they go in the NCAA Tournament. He has done a tremendous job with limited material in a very tough conference."

As a part of OU's appreciation, Sampson's coaching salary was increased to a guaranteed $800,000 annually, when his base pay was raised from $150,000 to $200,000, effective on July 1, 2001. The $800,000 compensation figure doesn't include camps, speaking engagements, and incentives. The contract is effective through July 2008. So Sampson is in the Sooners' plans for some time to come.

"They are so consistent in every way," Chicago Bulls coach Tim Floyd said. "They have grown to where they expect Kelvin to be good, win 20-plus games, compete for a league title, and make the

NCAA Tournament. There is going to be a year when he takes them to the Final Four and they win it all. There is no doubt in my mind."

"I think it is only a matter of time before he takes a team to the Final Four and wins a national championship," Dr. Halverstadt said. "How soon will he do it? It is hard to tell. When you get to that point in the NCAA Tournament, a lot of what happens depends on the schedule [opponent], luck, and injuries. You can't put that on a piece of paper.... Injuries have played a significant role a number of years for our team. But one of these years there will be no injuries, the schedule will fall right, and we will be there in the Final Four."

And from those early days in Pembroke comes this closing word, from one who saw all this potential long ago in Kelvin Sampson.

"He is organized and hungry," said Joe Gallagher, Sampson's basketball coach at Pembroke State. "And he knows what he is looking for. I think he is firm, but he is fair. He can carry a heavy stick, but when he doesn't have to, he doesn't. He has great common sense. I wouldn't be surprised someday he doesn't win a national championship. If not at Oklahoma, then some place. He can deal with kids. He has a rapport with them."

CHAPTER 16

Settling into the Top 10

In September 2001 Sampson welcomed six new players—five of them transfers—into the Sooner basketball program.

There would be growing pains for the new players as they learned the Sooner system. They had to grasp what the word intensity on the back of their practice shorts meant. But in the end, the Oklahoma basketball team would rise to heights not reached in Norman in 14 seasons since the Sooners made their most recent Final Four under Billy Tubbs.

There was a bedrock of leadership beneath the newcomers Sampson had brought into the program.

"I think back to the Tuesday before Labor Day when six new kids walked into our program and didn't know what Sooner basketball was all about," Sampson said. "I thank the Good Lord for guys like Hollis Price, Daryan Selvy, Aaron McGhee, Michael Cano, and Richard Ainooson. Those kids are great leaders."

Sampson knew this would be his best offensive team and overall his most talented at Oklahoma. But the defense would have to come around for the Sooners to become national title contenders and fixtures in the Top 10 during the 2001-02 season.

"We knew we had more kids who could score the basketball," Sampson said of the newcomers. "We knew we were better offensively. But you never know how they will accept each other. A lot of teams when they fail, their greatest enemy is not the other team. It is themselves. I didn't worry about offense early.

"I didn't know how Ebi Ere, Quannas White, and Jason Detrick [junior college transfers] would buy into defense. We got them to guard. We got them to run downhill at both ends of the floor. With some players it is like running downhill on the offensive end, but uphill on the defensive end. And they don't want to run uphill."

Sampson called it an "eclectic" group because there were different categories. White, Ere, and Detrick were junior college transfers in their first seasons at OU. Center Jabahri Brown had already sat out a semester at OU after transferring from Florida International. Center Jozsef Szendrei, a junior college transfer, had sat out last season after an ACL surgery on his knee. He had a second operation on the other knee in the spring of 2001. Guard Blake Johnston was a redshirt freshman.

"I really didn't know what to expect when I came in here," Ere said. "It was kind of tough, the conditioning, the practices, at first—especially on the defensive end. Coach Sampson really taught us and helped us out along the way. It was tough at first. I sort of got the hang of it now."

The early leader of the OU program by example was Price, the 6-foot-1, 165-pound junior, who had learned several years ago about the sacrifices players had to make in September and October for Sampson.

"He had a clear understanding of what our program was," Sampson said. "I think one of the best things that happened to Hollis was getting to play with Eduardo Najera his freshman year when Eduardo was a senior. That was really important.... Teams or programs that have great player leadership tend to maximize their potential. I think a big key for us, we've had great player leadership."

Sampson put the 2001-02 nonconference schedule together with several things in mind: build confidence among the newcomers, play some nationally ranked programs, win, and take the program to the next level.

The Sooners were playing in the Pre-Season National Invitation Tournament on Nov. 12. And that could be a positive as well. OU could get some early exposure by playing in Madison Square Garden in the semifinals if it won its first two games.

Sampson had hoped to play two games in Norman, where the Sooners would prove to be invincible during the 2001-02 season (16-0). He only got to play one NIT game at home.

The Sooners defeated Central Connecticut, 66-44, in Norman, in the first round and then had to travel to East Lansing, Michigan, to play the Spartans. The Sooners were more talented. But Michigan

Oklahoma's junior guard Hollis Price was named the Most Outstanding Player of both the Big12 Conference Tournament and the NCAA West Region.
Photo by Jerry Laizure.

State, coming off three straight Final Fours, had Division I's longest home-court winning streak at the time—45 straight games.

Oklahoma was playing without Brown, who had to sit out until mid-December under transfer rules. And senior forward Aaron McGhee had yet to become a scoring and rebounding force. The Sooners lost to Michigan State, 67-55. This was not only an aberration to the season, it became one of the launching pads.

McGhee was 2-for-10 from the field, scored four points, failed to grab a rebound and committed three turnovers against Michigan State. Oklahoma shot just 32.3 percent, was out-rebounded by five, and allowed the Spartans to shoot 56.1 percent. The 32.3 percent tied for Oklahoma's worst shooting effort of the season.

"I tried to tell Aaron he was playing with six guys he had never played with before," Sampson said. "They didn't know how to make Aaron better. They didn't know how to get him the ball. I told him not to get frustrated. He had to be patient with this team. We are going to get him the ball.

"Aaron responds well to positive reinforcement. His confidence is tied to self-esteem. If he thinks things are going pretty good, then everything around him progresses. I wanted him to play like he's the baddest dude in the gym. Get a little bit of swagger." Later in the season, he would. But first a lot of the newcomers had to grow up.

Oklahoma lost to Michigan State on November 14. And because the Sooners were eliminated from the NIT, they would not be playing again until November 28 against Central Michigan in Norman.

"During those two weeks we emphasized half-court defense, not giving up easy baskets, and being maniacs on the boards," Sampson said.

And on the flight back from the Michigan State game, Sampson had a heart-to-heart talk with his assistant coaches.

Sampson had a conflict with them. They believed Price should be the point guard and Detrick and Ere should play on the wings. Sampson told them Price couldn't be a great scorer if he was playing the point and they needed to get Quannas White ready to play point guard. They spent the next two weeks doing that.

"I have been around programs which have had two point guards," Sampson said. "It is kind of like a two-quarterback situation. If you have two starting quarterbacks, you don't have one. Same thing with point guards. That meant either Jason or Ebi would have to come off the bench. Jason wasn't as physically mature as Ebi was."

A decision was made early by Kelvin Sampson that Quannas White would be the Sooners' starting point guard. Photo by Jerry Laizure.

When Brown became eligible in mid-December, he would be in the OU starting lineup along with McGhee, White, Price, and Ere. Sophomore Johnnie Gilbert was awarded a medical redshirt after six games because of hip and shoulder injuries.

"The biggest obstacle was getting Jason Detrick and Daryan Selvy to buy into coming off the bench," Sampson said. "Could they be starters? Absolutely. I pulled out a chart and showed them of all the Sixth Man Award winners in the NBA. I showed them the list all the way back to the days Kevin McHale was a sixth man for the Boston Celtics. You have to make it a big deal. Where they had played they were always stars. They were both junior college All-Americas. We got those kids to buy into what was best for the team. Our salvation is they were great kids. Did it hurt their pride? Yes. But I told them your minutes and what we want you to do will be no different than when you were starting. But I can only start five guys."

The practices for a couple of weeks before the Sooners beat Central Michigan, 81-64, were tough.

"I think our practices are probably among the most brutal in America," McGhee said. "There are no out-of-bounds lines. There's a big plastic bubble they put on the rim every day. There's no possible way a shot can go in. It's kind of like a war down there. There are bodies flying everywhere, scratches and bruises. But I think that carries over to our toughness on the court [in games]."

Getting a dose of Michigan State was good for the Sooners as well. They saw a future reflection of themselves in the mirror.

"Michigan State is about rebounding and defense," Price said. "They were a team which had been to the Final Four three years in a row. If we can do what they do, I would be happy to be compared with those guys."

The Michigan State loss would be OU's last loss for more than two months. Oklahoma would win 13 straight games.

Once through the practice boot camp, Sampson had the task of exposing his junior college players to basically a December home schedule, preceded by an ESPN2 game at Arkansas on November 30.

Sampson never has been averse to recruiting junior college players. It went back to his days at Montana Tech when he had to claw and scratch for players from anywhere. It went back to those days in North Carolina when he was stigmatized because he was a different race at the predominantly white military academy.

For those reasons, Sampson can identify with junior college players who are looked at differently.

"So many junior college players get overlooked," Sampson said. "There is a stigma with junior college. People will ask me how do you do it with junior college kids? What's the difference? Jozsef Szendrei had a 24 or 25 on his ACT. Quannas White had a 3.0 grade-point average in high school. He just didn't test well…. The common denominator is they are smart. Ebi Ere is sharp. Not only are they smart, they have good families. You get a junior college kid who is 20 years old compared to a high school kid who is 17. The junior college players handle adversity better. They have a little bit of an edge to them."

The Arkansas game would be Oklahoma's second and last road test of the calendar year. And the game would be a major measuring stick for improvement. The Sooners were carrying a three-game winning streak over the Razorbacks into Bud Walton Arena. So they wouldn't be sneaking up on Arkansas.

"At Arkansas, it was how we won the game," Sampson said. "We had been emphasizing offensive and defensive rebounding from day one. And this was when Arkansas was playing well. Arkansas had just beaten Tulsa. And there were more than 19,000 fans at the game. This was our litmus test. We dominated them. We could win games with rebounding and defense. A lot of teams have to shoot it well to win games, but we didn't have to do it that way. At the Arkansas game on the road we realized how offensive rebounds (+10 on the offensive boards against Arkansas) could be a weapon for us."

Oklahoma out-rebounded Arkansas, 42-24. The Sooners scored 17 points off turnovers to Arkansas' eight. Oklahoma shot only 44.1 percent and just 26.7 percent from 3-point range. Arkansas was worse in all of those categories. The defense and rebounding were encouraging for Oklahoma. And so was the shooting of one of the junior college players.

The Arkansas game was the coming out party for the 6-foot-5 Ere, the junior college star from Tulsa, who Oklahoma had signed out of McLain High School. Ere didn't qualify academically for a Division I scholarship and played two seasons at Barton County (Kan.) Community College before joining the Sooners for the 2001-02 season.

Against Arkansas, Ere made 10 of 14 shots and scored 29 points in the rather easy 69-54 victory over the Razorbacks. Instead of settling for 3-point shots, he took several mid-range jumpers and drove with a purpose.

"Tonight I went to the bucket more," said Ere, who also had been told by Sampson to go up with the ball stronger to prevent opponents from stripping the ball.

The Sooners followed the Arkansas victory with two close home victories over St. Bonaventure and Louisiana Tech, before the 6-11 Brown became eligible against High Point (N.C.). He came off the bench for that game and one against Bethune-Cookman, then finally started against Eastern Illinois, a game in which Sampson said his team finally "got it." Oklahoma won by 59 points against a team that had made the NCAA Tournament the previous season. OU pulled down 57 rebounds.

The Sooners, prepping for their showdown against Maryland, for the first time in the Sampson era scored more than 100 points in the three straight games against High Point, Bethune-Cookman, and Eastern Illinois.

Incredibly, the Sooners shot exactly 57.4 percent by making 39 of 68 shots in all three games as they won by an average of 40 points over the three-game span. If Oklahoma shot well, it could blow teams out.

"Maryland was the first-semester final," Sampson said. "Everything was leading up to that game. We were so scattered early, but we were coming together. By the time we got to Maryland, we knew who should be taking the shots. Jason and Selvy were entrenched in their roles. And Aaron was a big game waiting to happen. Hollis was just old man river. He just kept flowing. Ebi was dynamite waiting to blow up; Jabahri was a novelty. For these kids, this was their chance on the national stage. We realized Maryland was good, but they were not invincible. We weren't selling wolf tickets here."

Against Maryland, Sampson was able to move McGhee to power forward and play Brown at center. This was critical against the Terrapins' big front line. In addition to his shot blocking and rebounding, Brown was another good passer in the Sooners' offense.

"The Maryland game was a key game for Aaron McGhee because it was a big game," Sampson said. "The Michigan State game was a lot like he played last year. The bigger the game, the more Aaron would disappear. The Maryland game was a huge game for him because he had a double-double against one of the best teams in the nation. That was the game he started taking off. Early in the year he

Guard Ebi Ere had his ups and downs during the 2001-02 season, but in the end he was a scoring ace for the Sooners. Photo by Jerry Laizure.

was our third scoring option. Hollis was No. 1, and Ebi was No. 2. Aaron was third. As we got into the conference season, Ebi hit a slide and Hollis-Aaron were 1-2. And by the middle and end of the conference season, Aaron was our No. 1 option. But to take advantage of him, you just couldn't go 100 miles an hour. I had to pull the reins back on this team. Aaron was rebounding better. When Aaron became a tough scorer for us inside, that's when we slowed it down and started running more half-court offense. If we shot the ball in transition, Aaron would have gotten stuck between the top of the keys."

Just before the Maryland game, four days before Christmas, Karen Sampson appeared anxious but hopeful. She knew the importance of this game, which was going to be shown nationally by ESPN. A Sooner victory could vault the Sooners into the Top 15 possibly the Top 10. Maryland was ranked No. 2 in the country and Oklahoma, No. 22 in the AP poll. With a victory, Oklahoma would knock off its first Top 5 team during the Sampson era at home other than Kansas.

Standing in the tunnel at Lloyd Noble before the game, Karen said Kelvin hadn't been nervous all week. The reason? He knew the Sooners had the talent to play with Maryland.

"They are going to take it right inside and try and get us into foul trouble," Karen said, echoing the thoughts of her husband and the OU coaching staff.

McGhee did pick up four fouls. But Oklahoma was able to effectively battle the wider Terrapins, with Brown grabbing 14 rebounds to go along with eight points, two steals, and two blocked shots. McGhee still scored 16 points and grabbed 11 rebounds. And Ere had 19 points.

"We saw one tape on him," Maryland coach Gary Williams said of Brown. "You can't tell how quick he is. He has quickness and speed and good timing. They have guys who can slash to the basket and guys who make threes. And they have a post player in Aaron McGhee. He [Brown] gives them a guy who blocks shots. They are a good team, but he [Brown] makes them better."

Maryland shot just 38.6 percent and was blown out in the final 10 minutes of the game when Oklahoma ran away with an impressive 72-56 victory. Brown remarked after the game: "This is why I came to Oklahoma, to play in games like these."

Sampson saw the Maryland game as another steppingstone.

"It was a game where our junior college players came of age," Sampson said. "Sometimes junior college players try to whirl through three people and score. We beat a really good team that night. We didn't upset anybody that night. We beat them."

The Maryland game stamped Oklahoma as a bona fide national power. Even the often-skeptical *Daily Oklahoman* had to admit the Sooners' victory over Maryland was no fluke. The Sooners jumped from No. 22 in the Associated Press poll to No. 12 after beating the eventual NCAA champions.

After the game, Sampson admitted to reporters that this team had the "greatest ceiling" of any of his teams at Oklahoma to grow.

The following week the Sooners breezed past Texas Southern by 42 in the All-College Classic and moved into the AP Top 10 at No. 10

Center Jabahri Brown was an effective shot blocker and rebounder when he could stay out of foul trouble during his first season with the Sooners.
Photo by Jerry Laizure.

for the first time under Samspon. They would not drop below No. 6 the rest of the season.

After dispatching Texas A&M by 26 in the Big 12 Conference opener on Jan. 5 in Norman, the Sooners traveled to Connecticut two days later for another ESPN affair as part of the Big 12 Conference's Big Monday package.

The Connecticut game was in Hartford and provided a rare Sooner showcase to the Eastern media, which Sampson knew was important. It would do little good for the Big 12, which was an emerging powerhouse conference, to lose to a Big East team. Oklahoma, which had won 10 straight going into the UConn game, had just risen to a No. 5 ranking nationally, which was its highest ranking under Sampson.

The Sooners, though blowing a lead, got the blessing of such influential Eastern writers as Dick "Hoops" Weiss of *The New York Daily News* and Mark Blaudschun of *The Boston Globe,* who were in attendance at the game. Oklahoma held off the Huskies for a 69-67 victory at the Hartford Civic Center.

On the morning of the game, OU's starting point guard Quannas White was late for the 9:45 a.m. bus for the 10 a.m. shoot around. Because the hotel was adjacent to the arena, White still showed up for practice on time. But he didn't start that night. Jason Detrick started in his place and responded with 12 points.

It was a discipline thing for Sampson. Touching the lines at Montana Tech was important. So was this.

"I have always been a stickler for details," Sampson said. "Sometimes adversity makes men out of us. Sometimes prosperity creates monsters. The problem with kids we work with is how much emphasis they put on sleep. This team loved to sleep. We are not an NBA team. Don't meet me at the arena."

Sampson got on the bus and took the seat by his top assistant, Ray Lopes.

Lopes said, "Where's Q? Somebody go get Q."

"Go get Q my butt," Sampson said. "Let's go. As soon as I sit down, it is time to go. We leave and nobody says a word. I am getting steamed at Quannas. I know why he is late. That guy loves to sleep. Why would you put sleep above a team rule? To me that is the most selfish act in the world to put your comfort level above your teammates. I am in a bad mood now."

Once at the arena, Sampson considered asking the ESPN crew to leave the practice and keep his venting private, but decided to let it stay. Sampson didn't have the players taped. And they practiced hard for 45 minutes. He didn't care if there were sprained ankles. Sampson didn't speak to White, who he believed disrespected the program. He was going to make him sweat and at the same time make a point to the team about discipline. He called out the starters, the red team, and White wasn't among them.

"I knew he was sorry," Sampson said. "But I wanted to really, really, really drive the point home of not being on time. And that was the only discipline problem we had all year. But I think the reason that was the only problem we had all year is because we made a really big deal out of it."

Oklahoma didn't shoot well against UConn (36.6 percent), but like Sampson said earlier, so what? The Sooners out-rebounded the Huskies, 45-32. Oklahoma had 28 offensive boards, which caused UConn coach Jim Calhoun to say he liked the Sooners' focus and hunger, "particularly on the glass."

Oklahoma's three starting guards, Ere, Price, and Detrick, accounted for 53 of OU's points as the dominating presence of the Huskies' freshman, Emeka Okafor (eight blocked shots), kept the Sooners bottled up inside. Brown fouled out of the game with 5:35 remaining, but the Sooners, leading by 12, never trailed. Sampson left knowing that UConn forward Caron Butler (25 points) was one of the best in college basketball.

With the last nonconference game out of the way, Sampson and the Sooners could concentrate on the Big 12 now. The big games would start coming one after another now.

Next up was Texas Tech in Norman. In recent years this would have been a sleepy Saturday afternoon affair, and the buildup would have gotten lost in football recruiting stories in the Oklahoma newspapers. Not this year. Bob Knight was coming to town with his Texas Tech Red Raiders. A sellout crowd was in place.

Sampson appreciated Knight's place in basketball history. And he knew that his history against Knight had been 0-3. Sampson had lost to Knight twice while coach at Washington State. And the Knight-led Hoosiers had beaten the Sooners in overtime in the first round of the NCAA Tournament in 1998.

Forget all the past controversies Knight had had at Indiana. He was doing an excellent job coaching this Texas Tech team. And even

Guard Jason Detrick could have started for most teams,
but accepted his role off the bench. Photo by Jerry Laizure.

after the Sooners' 98-72 victory over the Red Raiders on January 12 in Norman, Sampson still believed this Texas Tech team was going places. Two weeks later Sampson would be proven right.

But in the first meeting against Texas Tech, OU's guards were just too quick. The Sooners jumped to a 16-4 lead after the first 5½ minutes of the game. Texas Tech committed 20 turnovers on the way to seeing its 10-game winning streak snapped. Price, Ere, and Detrick combined for 69 points for OU.

Knight basically gave his blessing to the Sooners: "They present problems for you on the defensive end and they get after you on the offensive end. They've done a really good job of putting the team together."

After its 78-51 blowout victory at Nebraska, Oklahoma would travel to Lawrence for its only regularly scheduled game against the No. 4-ranked Jayhawks. It would be a pivotal game in the Big 12 Conference regular-season race because Kansas would not play in Norman this season. And the Jayhawks were coming off an impressive 79-61 victory over Oklahoma State in Stillwater. Both teams were 3-0 in the league race. And the No. 5-ranked Sooners were riding a 13-game winning streak since the loss to Michigan State way back in mid-November.

There were eight lead changes and two ties during the first half. Kansas emerged with a 30-25 half-time lead and then made 10 of its first 12 shots of the second half to take a 22-point lead with 12:07 remaining. Brown, from the Virgin Islands, picked up two early fouls and had to go to the bench by the first TV time out. He wound up playing 19 minutes.

"Jabahri's immaturity on the road came into play," Sampson said. "Jabahri's comfort level was in Lloyd Noble. The thing that people forget about Jabahri, he's an island kid. He's not an inner city kid. And there's a big difference. He is not used to physical adversity. When things got tough for Jabahri he always had a comfort zone to go to—go hang out. All of sudden Kansas' post players were beating the crap out of him. Sometimes a kid who wants to get out of the game will get a foul called on him. Jabahri wanted to do well, but he didn't know how to get himself out of trouble. He's a smart player, but at that point he didn't know how to use his quickness to his advantage. He has tremendous weakness with his body size. Most of Jabahri's fouls came because he was out of position."

KU forward Drew Gooden, who had failed to reach double figures in scoring in two previous games against Oklahoma, would lead all scorers and rebounders with 19 points and 10 boards.

Even so Oklahoma started to come back behind point guard White, who would have his highest scoring total of the season to that juncture with 17 points. White played an all-around great game with five rebounds, four assists, and four steals. Oklahoma went on an 11-0 run and sliced the Jayhawks' lead to six with 3:18 remaining before Kansas hung on for a 74-67 victory. At that point of the season, it was the Jayhawks' lowest scoring game.

"The thing about Quannas, he has no ego about basketball," Sampson said. "He doesn't require shots to be happy. He's one we had to make shoot. He's real quiet. He has the perfect temperament to be a point guard." It was a breakthrough game for White, who gained assurances about his game in just about all areas in a hostile environment.

The seeds were sown for a possible rematch in the Big 12 Tournament in Kansas City, Mo., in March. The game made White a stronger player and gave Oklahoma confidence it could play Kansas away from Allen Field House in Lawrence. And Gooden did nothing to ingratiate himself to the Sooner players when he called them "dirty" in a *Sports Illustrated* article a few days later.

"We read in *Sports Illustrated* where Drew Gooden [of Kansas] thought we were a dirty team," Price said. "But we don't think we're dirty. We think we're a tough team. It all starts in September, waking up at 5:45 a.m. for lifting weights and conditioning. I think that's where we get a lot our toughness from."

There was a quick turnaround for the Big Monday game in Norman. Luckily for the Sooners, who had to spend a lot of emotion and physical effort in the KU game, Missouri was the opponent. OU has owned the Tigers in recent years.

Oklahoma scored on 14 straight possessions in the middle of the game to win its eighth straight against the Tigers, who actually were picked to finish ahead of Oklahoma in the Big 12 race before the season.

Little did anybody know at the time but this would be a preview of the NCAA West Region final two months later.

Oklahoma had four days off before playing Texas Tech in Lubbock. Sampson knew the game wouldn't be easy despite the Sooners' easy victory over the Red Raiders two weeks earlier.

Basically, Knight had taken the same team that was 9-19 the season before, put in the motion offense, defined roles better, and instilled the fear of God in the returning players. If they didn't listen to him, they wouldn't play.

Sampson said the fact Knight had big man Andy Ellis facing the basket and scoring off screens on the perimeter had made Texas Tech a much better team. The Sooners, like the previous season, came out of Lubbock with a bad taste in their mouths.

Only this time they didn't have to ride the bus all the way back to Norman. Still, Sampson was livid with the outcome. Texas Tech shot 56.7 percent against the Sooners—the best anybody would shoot all season against OU. Sampson called it the worst defensive performance he had seen since he had been at Oklahoma, when the Sooners lost, 92-79, in what would be their worst defeat of the season.

"Texas Tech was sharp and ran its motion offense to perfection," Sampson said. "I thought Quannas was really bad that day. And Jason Detrick was our worst defender, no question, this year. And if you have a bad defensive player on the floor against a team as smart as Texas Tech the way they screen, they are going to find you. At some point they are going to find you with a down screen, a cross screen, or back screen."

Kansas now was two games ahead of the Sooners in the loss column in the Big 12 Conference race and would be hard to catch for first place. But the Sooners were playing for a high seed in the NCAA Tournament, perhaps a No. 1 seed in one of the four regions.

Games against Oklahoma State in Norman and at Texas completed Oklahoma's toughest stretch of the season. And the Sooners were victorious in both. OU won the first Bedlam matchup, 58-53. And then the Sooners went into Austin and beat the Longhorns, 85-84, in overtime on February 2. Sampson felt like his team had to win the Texas game twice.

Oklahoma let a 17-point lead fritter away in the last 7 minutes of regulation and gave up a score-tying Texas three-pointer as time ran out.

"The most fun player to watch in the league was T.J. Ford," Sampson said of Texas's freshman point guard. "When we got up 17, it was like something got in that kid's head. He took the game over down the stretch."

With seven-tenths of a second left in regulation and trailing 74-71, Texas coach Rick Barnes drew up an out-of-bounds play, which found Brandon Mouton coming off a double screen and making the tying three-pointer.

"We could have gone zone, but why change what you have been doing in every game in that situation?" Sampson said. "All we do is switch every screen. Daryan Selvy and Aaron McGhee did a poor job of communicating. Hollis was guarding Mouton and got screened. All we do is switch on those.

"I still remember watching the highlights, and when the ball was almost in the cylinder the clock still hadn't moved. It was still at 00.7. And I called Kim Anderson at the Big 12 office and complained because there was a point there in the overtime period where they didn't run the clock for eight seconds when we had the ball. There was obvious clock mismanagement. When it happens two or three times, you have to wonder if it is intentional.

"We had had trouble with the clock guy at Texas before. Michael Johnson hit a runner in the lane, the year we went to the Sweet 16 [1999] to win the game. After Johnson's basket there was one second to go in the game. I remember they ran a great play for Chris Mihm and they missed the shot to win the game. And the clock should have been out. They got two more shots after that. That is how long the Longhorns' second is with that guy on the clock. Low and behold if history didn't repeat itself."

The Texas victory served as a springboard for McGhee, who was sizzling the entire month of February.

"When we got Aaron he was an offensive guy," Sampson said. "And offensive players tend to be bad defensive players. He treated rebounding and defense as a disease. Aaron would have been a heck of a football player because you could trot him out there on offense and take him out on defense. But you can't do that in basketball."

The left-handed McGhee had seven double-figure scoring and rebounding games in the last 10 games of the regular season heading into the Big 12 Tournament. And six of those performances were 20 points or more. He was shooting more than 40 percent from 3-point range during the final 12 games of the regular season and playing the kind of defense Sampson demanded.

Assistant coach Ray Lopes worked with McGhee in practice to develop turnaround jumpers from either his right or left shoulder.

"His improvement from last year to this year is probably the best I have seen around," Price said. "Last year, he really wasn't that good of a rebounder. This year he has worked on the offense so hard on his body, his feet, his quickness, and everything. Aaron made a big adjustment because he matured so much this year."

Early in the fall, Sampson had kicked him out of the gym, "when he did not want to work hard.

"I screamed at him," Sampson said. "I told him I am not going to let you get 17 points and two rebounds. I told him if you get 17 points and two rebounds, we are going to get out-rebounded by 12 and we are going to lose. In essence, you have to make a decision. Are you going to be the player we need you to be, or are you going to be the player just scraping by?"

On the day Sampson kicked McGhee out of the gym, OU chose its captains for the 2001-02 season. And McGhee wasn't there to be selected.

"After one game later in the season, I said, 'Aaron you were not elected captain. But you are our captain because of the transformation you made inside your head and your heart,'" Sampson said. "I don't know that I ever had a player make such a transformation."

OU's final loss of the regular season occurred on February 13—a 79-72 overtime defeat at Oklahoma State. Sampson did not believe some of his players were tough enough in that game. Lineup changes would be forthcoming.

"Oklahoma State out-toughed us," Sampson said. "I thought the tougher team won, not the best team. And that is something we take pride in . . . I thought Jabahri was soft. I could look in Ebi's eyes and see all the way to Saskatchewan . . . . He was way out there in the wilderness now. I put them on the bench. I thought this team needs to be shaken up.

"I don't think our kids understood who we were," Sampson added. "We had been underdogs and had been so far under the radar. Now all of a sudden we were ranked among the Top 10 in the nation. When teams prepared for us, they weren't preparing for a tough Oklahoma team, as in years past. They were preparing for a really tough, good Oklahoma team. We were getting everybody's best shot."

The next three games against Kansas State, Baylor, and Texas, Ere came out of the starting lineup in favor of Detrick and the 6-11 Brown was replaced by the 6-9, 240-pound Szendrei. Sampson had a motive to all of this shuffling as well. He also was building some depth, which would prove crucial in March. And he wanted to keep his team's attention and all the players hungry for playing time.

"Jozsef's breakout game was when he had 11 rebounds against Oklahoma State in Stillwater," Sampson said of the player from Hungary. "It was one of those games where Jabahri had it on Caribbean Cruise. Jozsef is a tough kid. He is not as athletic as some of the other players, but one of the things he takes pride in is his rebounding. He had total reconstructive knee surgery in the spring, and five months later he is practicing. And he's playing games sixth months later. We probably brought him back too soon. His knee was swelling. And there was some psychological damage. In January he was doing better.

"There is no way we would have gotten to the Final Four with three post players. Jozsef is our fourth post. And we had to have him. He was a life saver."

With Detrick in the starting lineup, this also took some pressure off Ere, who hit the wall in mid-season. On a Sunday afternoon in early February, Ere called Sampson and wanted a meeting with Sampson following a victory over Texas A&M.

"He talked about how everybody expected this or that out of him. At the beginning of the year he was below everybody's radar. But the expectation level rose. He felt pressure he wasn't producing. It got to his confidence. I told him it was okay if he got eight rebounds and eight points. His scoring took a dip when he wasn't doing the dirty work, rebounding and playing defense. Once he started doing that, his offense got better.

"Ebi had been part of a triangle and one of three guys we depended on every night," Sampson said of the threesome, which included Price and McGhee. "First-year kids often hit the wall, and he dipped down into a valley. Fortunately, someone else fit into the triangle. We knew at some point he would bounce back. During his dip we knew we were good because we were winning without Ebi contributing much. Once we got to Kansas City and the Big 12 Tournament, he came back and we saw a new energy level."

After the loss to Oklahoma State, the Sooners watched as Kansas won the Big 12 Conference regular season race by three games. But Oklahoma won its last five regular season games—all by 11 points or more—to finish a solid second in what would turn out to be college basketball's most powerful conference during the 2001-02 season.

The Sooners' overall record of 24-4 was the best during the Sampson era at OU entering the Big 12 Tourney.

"We weren't picked to win our league, so we snuck up on people," McGhee said. "It wasn't until the end of the year people recognized we were a pretty good team."

Sampson really didn't mind.

"We had a 13-3 conference record and that was special," Sampson said. "And that was special because of how good the league was. There were two reasons we were under the radar. Kansas went undefeated in our league, and everywhere we went they talked about Coach Knight and what a great year he was having."

But in the next month the perception of OU basketball would change.

CHAPTER 17

Reaching the Promised Land

Kelvin Sampson had mixed emotions about the 2002 Big 12 Post-Season Tournament.

The Sooners had won their first Big 12 Tournament in 2001 and had exerted a lot of energy during the three days, including a big second-half comeback to beat archrival Texas in the second half of the title game. Then Oklahoma and Texas both turned around and lost in the first round of the 2001 NCAA Tournament to lower-seeded teams.

Would it be so bad to lose in the semifinals, take Sunday off, watch the NCAA pairings show with an extra day's rest? The carrots, though, for the Sooners were two-fold.

If they made the title game, they probably would get to settle an old score against Kansas, even if it was before a partisan Jayhawk crowd at Kemper Arena, KU's home away from home 40 miles from Lawrence. At least it wouldn't be in Allen Field House where Sampson had yet to win a game.

And the Sooners, who entered the Big 12 Tournament with a No. 4 ranking in the AP poll, were very much in contention for one of the four No. 1 seeds in the NCAA Basketball Tournament. Duke, Maryland, and Kansas were considered cinch No. 1 seeds. But Cincinnati and OU were vying for the fourth No. 1 seed.

Weighing this scenario vs. rest for next week. How much difference would there be in getting a No. 1 or No. 2 seed anyway?

"That debate will go on forever," said Texas coach Rick Barnes about advancing in the league post-season tournaments vs. the rest issue. "I know when I was in the ACC and the Big East, you get done around 6 o'clock. And then they would have the selection show. I know the year we won the Big East Tournament [when he was at Providence] they had all the presentations and the ceremony, then they had this room upstairs for us. And I remember our name came up and that was the least excited of any team I have coached. They were extremely excited to win the championship. . . .

"I remember that night, I sensed that about our guys. We were going to work hard to try and rest them. We wound up playing Alabama in the first round and we lost in that game in 1994. We never had the excitement in that game like we did toward winning the championship."

Barnes wouldn't blame the fatigue or disinterest on losing to Temple last season in the first round. Neither would Sampson use that as an excuse for losing to Indiana State in 2001. Still, it was something to think about.

"Aaron McGhee and Daryan Selvy, our two senior starters, wanted to play Kansas," Sampson said. "Everybody talked all year about how great Kansas was. We had played them. And we had great respect for them. We knew they were really good. But we knew we were really good, too.

"I thought the worst thing that could happen is we would leave Kansas City as a 2 seed. But the thing that kept coming back to me was I wanted to go to Dallas [for the first and second rounds of the NCAA Tournament]. Did I want another shot at Kansas? That wasn't that big of a deal. I remembered winning the Big 12 Tournament the previous year, and I remembered no one remembered what we did in the Big 12 Tournament after we lost to Indiana State in the NCAA Tournament."

The Sooners entered the Big 12 Tournament as the No. 2 seed behind Kansas and would play Kansas State in the quarterfinals after the Wildcats defeated Baylor in overtime in the first round. Three weeks earlier in Norman, Oklahoma had defeated Kansas State, 73-62, in one of the uglier games of the season.

Knowing he couldn't match OU in talent, Kansas State coach Jim Woolridge played a zone defense, which slowed down the game and forced the Sooners to pick it apart. This time, Oklahoma won by 11 again, 63-52, and did it the blue-collar, lunch pail way.

Oklahoma shot only 32.3 percent (tying the season low at Michigan State) but out-rebounded the Wildcats, 54-30. Kansas State ended its season with a 13-16 record by taking 15 fewer shots than the Sooners, who had 28 offensive rebounds. Oklahoma countered with a 1-3-1 trapping defense, enough to smother the Wildcats' triangle offense. A 19-3 second-half OU run advanced the Sooners to a semifinal meeting against Texas.

"They kept attacking, five guys at a time, it seemed," Kansas State forward Matt Siebrandt said after the game.

As is often the case when the Kansas area media is in the building, Sampson had to answer questions about winning ugly. The Jayhawks looked like perfect thoroughbreds in their quarter-final victory over Colorado, 102-73. So the beauty contest was on between the Big 12's top two teams. Sampson's Sooners rarely win these in the media.

"I don't know how you make a kid shoot good," Sampson told the media after the Kansas State game. "But I don't negotiate or discuss rebounding. Effort, intensity, and out-competing people—those things don't take nights off. That's a mark of a good team—when you are missing shots, you find a way to manufacture points."

In fact, the Sooners wouldn't shoot better than 42.1 percent in the Big 12 Tournament and still win it for the second straight season. In the three-game set, Oklahoma shot just 35.8 percent and only 60 percent from the free-throw line, but they limited the three Big 12 Tournament opponents to an average shooting percentage of 34.8.

In the semifinals, Oklahoma played Texas for a third time during the 2001-02 season. But the Sooners would have nothing of the old axiom, "it's difficult to beat a good team three times in one season." Once again the Longhorns had trouble guarding Oklahoma's three-point shooters, who made 10 of 21 (47.6 percent). In the previous two games, OU had made 12 and 10 three-pointers against the Longhorns and had won both times.

Oklahoma jumped on Texas and never let the Longhorns off the mat. Oklahoma made six three-pointers in the first 11:50 to take a 26-16 lead. Oklahoma lengthened that lead to 38-23 at half time. Oklahoma forced 22 Texas turnovers and bottled up UT center James Thomas, who scored just one point. It was Sampson's eighth straight victory over the Longhorns and 15 in 18 games against Texas.

Texas couldn't guard all of OU's scoring options.

"By that time," Sampson said, "we could automatically flip to the channel the show was on. If you guard us like this, this is what we would do. We knew exactly how to react. For every action, there was reaction. We were a great counter-punch team."

Kansas, meanwhile, crushed Texas Tech, 90-50, in the other semifinal, setting up the battle between the Big 12's two best teams.

Top-ranked Kansas had won 18 straight games against Big 12 opponents. In fact, the last Big 12 team the Jayhawks had lost to was Oklahoma in the semifinals of the 2001 league tournament.

Oklahoma unleashed a defense that shocked the Jayhawks. Big men Drew Gooden and Nick Collison combined for 37 points, but the rest of the Jayhawks, who had won 16 straight games, could manage just 18 points.

"After we beat Texas, we went right to our room and we didn't even work on offense," Sampson said of preparations for KU. "I knew Kansas was going to take our sets away. So we just tried to spread the floor and get to the free-throw line. If we could get dribble penetration and force them to help on defense, we could make a living on the offensive glass. I told our team we were going to win this at the defensive end of the floor."

Oklahoma forced the normally sure-handed Jayhawk guards into 12 turnovers in the first half when the Sooners emerged with a 29-19 lead. Kansas guard Kirk Hinrich was 0-for-10 from the floor and scored only four points. Oklahoma's 64-55 victory over Kansas was the Jayhawks' lowest point total of the season.

"It definitely wasn't very pretty out there," Collison said, echoing KU's theme that OU plays ugly. "They give you an extra bump, but that's good, physical basketball."

Oklahoma shot only 33.8 percent, but Kansas was at 33.3 percent in what Sampson called the best defensive game he ever had had a team play.

"It was us in every sense of the word," Sampson said. "The story that wasn't told there was these were the two best defensive teams in the Big 12. They would say, 'Coach, you didn't make baskets.' That was a tribute to Kansas' defense. They're a great defensive team also. Oklahoma was a combination of many things this year. We were a team that could score 90 and win. But we were one of the few teams that could score 60 and win because we could beat you so many different ways.

"I told them in the locker room, our team had been slighted a little bit. It was a little bit unfortunate the No. 1 team in the nation was in the Big 12. We were stuck between that and Bob Knight at Texas Tech. We were kind of a sidebar story. Sometimes to get the respect you deserve, you have to make your own noise. This was our one chance."

The fact there was a veteran officiating crew of Scott Thornley, Tom O'Neill, and Steve Welmer, Sampson said, was a positive for OU because they would not be swayed by the partisan Jayhawk crowd and would let the game flow. "When we played at Kansas, Jabahri had two fouls by the first TV time out," Sampson said. "He was out of it."

Sampson said he never spoke to Kansas coach Roy Williams about Gooden's comments that OU was a dirty team after the first game.

"I am used to it," Sampson said. "Norm Stewart said the same thing when Eduardo Najera accidentally smacked Keyon Dooling on the forehead. I use that to our advantage. There's always a little bit of a fear factor. They always look sideways when they think you are dirty. We know we are not. But that's okay if they want to think that. I think every referee that has ever called an Oklahoma game would say Oklahoma is very aggressive. There's a big difference in being aggressive and being dirty."

Oklahoma guard Hollis Price was named the Big 12 Tournament's MVP and made two big three-point shots in the closing minutes over KU's Jeff Boschee. Price scored a game-high 23 points—12 in the final 8:26 when the Sooners put the game away. And Price was helping, of course, shut down Hinrich.

"Hollis brings a tenacity to our team that most teams don't have," Oklahoma's Aaron McGhee said. "Most of the time he's stuck on one of the best players on the other team on the perimeter. He usually does a good job of defending the ball. He's just tenacious on D."

Hollis and the Sooners had little time to celebrate because the NCAA Tournament pairings came out after the game. And Oklahoma, despite winning the Big 12 Tournament, was still the No. 2 seed in the West behind No. 1 seed Cincinnati, which had won the Conference USA regular-season and tournament titles.

"I felt a little bit like I was punched in the gut," Sampson said. "I felt like we had earned a No. 1 seed. I was a little bit confused. But I made a pact with myself a long time ago. I saw so many programs that didn't make the tournament...Virginia, Michigan, North Carolina, Syracuse didn't make it in 2002. I thought what a great year Butler had. They didn't make it. Who am I to be holier than thou? I thought we had earned a No. 1 seed. But when I saw we were a No. 2 seed and were playing our first two games in Dallas, that was good enough for me.

"I didn't want the story to be one of being a sourpuss. I didn't want us to forget where we had come from. I didn't want us to forget we had been a 13 seed [in 1999]. We had been a lower seeded team before that had worked its butt off just to make the tournament."

Sampson instructed his players to not say they were disappointed with being a No. 2 seed because that would become the story in the news media the next day.

"Our kids were like POWs in Germany," Sampson said. "They gave reporters name, rank, and serial number. 'My name is Hollis Price, we're a 2 seed, we're happy, we're playing Illinois-Chicago on Friday.' 'But are you a little upset you're not a 1 seed?' a reporter would ask. 'My name is Hollis Price…'."

On the bus back to the airport, OU players told Sampson they were bombarded by those questions. The party line was OU was happy.

And the next weekend was a great one for the Big 12 in Dallas. Texas and Oklahoma were both playing at the American Airlines Center (AAC) in the first college games ever played at the less-than-one-year-old arena. Of course, OU and Texas fans weren't cheering for each others' teams when Texas played Boston College and the Sooners met Illinois-Chicago in the first round. That would be too much to ask for the two bitter rivals.

"Oklahoma fans and the Texas fans would both be surprised what good friends Rick and I are," Sampson said. "I was pulling for Texas. I was pulling for Rick. There was a story that had come out that week in *The Dallas Morning News* that said Rick and I hadn't won a lot in the tournament. My record was 3-8 going into the tournament and Rick's was 3-9. And the longer I coach, the more I realize that is important. If you are good enough to get to the tournament, then they are going to keep score once you get there. I was thinking about my record. And I was thinking about Rick's record. That's why I wanted Rick to win because people don't know what a great coach he is."

Sampson said the ghosts of his past five first-round NCAA Tournament losses at Oklahoma were swirling in his head. But he wasn't talking about those losses. Sampson didn't believe OU would lose to No. 15-seeded Illinois-Chicago, but the thought did cross his mind.

He didn't mention it to the team. He talked about the team's eight-game winning streak and the scouting report on the Flames.

When he was later asked about a *Sports Illustrated* article, calling him a snake-bit coach, Sampson didn't flinch.

"I think snake bit is good term for that," Sampson said. "Our teams have been a little snake bit, I wouldn't disagree with that. But we have been just good enough to make it a lot of years. I look at Gonzaga [first-round loser] and Cincinnati [second-round loser] this year. Sometimes you have to be good. Sometimes you have to have a little luck with your seed, draw, or matchup. Sometimes you lose a key player. But I think that's fair."

The team bussed down from Norman to Dallas and watched Sampson's favorite movie, *The Patriot,* during the 190-mile trip. Then, Sampson decided he would bring former OU coach Billy Tubbs to the team's practice in Dallas. Tubbs, who had resigned as the TCU head coach, had taken the Sooners to their previous Final Four in 1988 and lost to Kansas in the NCAA title game.

"I meant it as a gesture but also as information," Sampson said.

Tubbs talked about the distractions of girlfriends and hangers-on and family.

"They're on vacation; they want to come down and enjoy the games," Tubbs said. "But you have to make sure you stay focused and get away from all of that. Get done with the ticket stuff early."

Tubbs told the Sooners they wouldn't play against a team that was better coached, more disciplined, played better defense, and was better at rebounding. He told the Sooners to play the way they have all year and not to change anything.

"You'll be in the Final Four," Tubbs said.

Tubbs had the team mesmerized. All of the Sooners' managers wanted to get pictures of him and get his autograph.

"It was a touching moment for Billy and the program he put on the map," Sampson said. "Billy Tubbs put the program on the map. I didn't. If it had not been for Billy Tubbs, I would never have come to Oklahoma. He showed other coaches you could win at Oklahoma."

Sampson said his team was "very jittery" in the first round of the NCAA Tournament. But McGhee continued to star and recorded his 13th double-double of the season with 26 points and 12 rebounds in the Sooners' 71-63 victory over Illinois-Chicago in the first round. The 15th-seeded Flames led 7-4, but one of only two OU three-point baskets of the game tied the score. OU never trailed again.

McGhee, originally from Aurora East High School in suburban Chicago, had a field day against his hometown team.

"Since that time [high school] he has gotten into Oklahoma's program, and he decided he wants to be a pro," Illinois-Chicago coach Jimmy Collins told *The Daily Oklahoman.* "Make no mistake about that. He is a pro. He's not just an inside player. He plays outside. He makes passes. He plays sound defense. He is a professional basketball player."

Oklahoma led by 15 points in the first half and settled for an eight-point half-time lead. The Sooners had control of the game but made only two of 18 three-point shots. The Flames shot just 33.3 percent overall and 22.7 percent from three-point range.

Oklahoma expected to beat Illinois-Chicago. There was no celebration in the locker room after the game. The team watched the first half of the Hawaii-Xavier game and then went back to the hotel. Sampson and his assistants scouted the second game.

"I thought we would play Hawaii because they were up 12 at half time," Sampson said of the first-round game the Musketeers rallied to win in the second half. "Xavier played a lot like us. They were an image of us. They had a great inside player in David West. They had a great wing in Romain Sato. And they have a great point guard in Lionel Chalmers. They were a well-coached team and very disciplined. And they had great role players. They were very much like Oklahoma."

Sampson elected to double-team West with McGhee and 6-10 Jabahri Brown. That at least slowed down West, the 6-8, 232-pound junior who averaged 18.3 points and 9.8 rebounds. Sato scored 16 of his team's first 18 points. West finally got going and added 18 points and eight rebounds but didn't overwhelm OU. Chalmers was held in check, 1 for 12 from the field, with only two assists and three turnovers.

"We didn't get beat by a good team," Xavier's first-year coach Thad Matta said. "We got beat by a great team."

Sampson's scoring triangle (guard Ebi Ere, McGhee, and Price) produced 57 points. A 9-0 run, with McGhee scoring six points midway through the second half, put the game out of reach, 78-65. Oklahoma made 24 of 28 free throws to win the game. Selvy was strong with nine rebounds off the bench.

"We expected to win the Xavier game," Sampson said. "We got to the locker room, we were advancing to another site. We would have

Forward Aaron McGhee became the Sooners' top scoring option
during the second half of the 2001-02 season. Photo by Jerry Laizure.

been disappointed if we had not won two games. And the first thing we do after we get on the bus and go home, is we go eat at McDonald's. That's what our kids wanted to do.

"I always tell them, 'Don't forget where you came from.' And they say, 'Coach, we can't forget where we came from. We have to go to McDonald's.'"

So, instead of eating at a full-service restaurant, his players were getting sacks of Big Macs and Quarter-Pounders, Cokes, and fries. Sampson was talking on his cell phone doing interviews with CBS, Fox Sports Net, and ESPN in the parking lot of a McDonald's off Interstate 35 on the way back to Norman. People were honking their horns at the victorious Sooners.

The next two days were a blur getting ready to go to San Jose and play Arizona in the Sweet 16 at the Compaq Center. But there was a growing concern by Sampson about his father's health. Mr. Ned and his wife, Eva, had traveled to Norman to see Lauren and Kellen in late February. Mr. Ned liked to watch Kellen play games with the Norman High School basketball team.

But Kelvin could tell Mr. Ned, who walks with a cane, wasn't feeling well because he spent most of his time in bed. Even when Mr. Ned would attend Sooner basketball practices, Kelvin would see him nodding off. After dinner in the evenings, he would sit in a recliner and fall asleep. Mr. Ned was complaining of headaches. And after Oklahoma got back from the first two rounds of the NCAA Tournament in Dallas, for a couple of days Mr. Ned hardly came out of his room at the Sampsons' sprawling two-story Norman home.

Later Kelvin Sampson would learn fluid on the brain affected the side of the brain that controls sleep.

But Mr. Ned, 72, was on the team plane to San Jose for the three-hour ride. Kelvin told Mr. Ned if he didn't feel well, he could skip the practice. "But he is not going to miss anything," Sampson said. "I think if I was walking downtown, he would want to go with me."

After the plane landed and the official OU party went to the team hotel, the team bus headed for San Jose City College for the Sooners' practice on March 19. The bus had to park about a quarter of a mile from the entrance to the gymnasium.

Dr. Brock Schnebel, the Sooners' team physician, and Kellen followed behind Mr. Ned, who had a seizure or some kind of mini-stroke.

"We were fortunate Dr. Schnebel was with us," Oklahoma Athletic Director Joe Castiglione said. "Mr. Ned was sort of veering when he got off the bus. We knew something was not right."

"It was like a car with a flat tire," Sampson said. "He fell against the fence and couldn't straighten up. But he made it to the gym and sat down. He was pale without any color.

"I had a hard time getting him into the arena," Dr. Schnebel said. "He didn't want to go to the hospital."

Mr. Ned, who suffered from lupus and had a major stroke in 1982, wouldn't get in the ambulance. But he would get in the car, and he was driven to the hospital early in the evening.

Mr. Ned was admitted to O'Connor Hospital and eventually placed in the intensive care unit. CAT scans were performed on his brain. When Kelvin arrived following practice, there were IVs in Mr. Ned's arm, an EKG was in place, and wires were attached to his head. At about 11:30 p.m., the neurosurgeon had reviewed the X-rays, brain scans, and CAT scans. Kelvin's mother was there as well to hear the news.

"The fluid on the brain had created such pressure, the brain had shifted," Sampson said. "Everything that was supposed to be aligned with the brain was all out of kilter. They had to get that fluid off or there could be a major stroke or aneurysm."

Sampson called his top assistant, Lopes, and told him he had to handle the film session that evening back at the team hotel. The OU players were told Coach Sampson's father had a health issue and he would remain with his father at the hospital.

Dr. Schnebel assisted Dr. Marshall Rosario in the one-hour operation, a subdural hematoma. They drained the blood buildup on the brain by drilling two holes in the skull. Dr. Halverstadt, Kelvin's close personal friend who sits on the bench during games, and his mother, Eva, stayed in an outer room until 3 a.m. when they were allowed to see Mr. Ned following the surgery.

Kelvin returned to the hospital at 8:00 a.m. Wednesday morning. Doctors reported the surgery had been successful in shifting the brain back to its proper place. Kelvin missed a morning practice again. But he had confidence in his staff and players.

"I thought my mother and father needed me a lot more than my team did at that point," Sampson said.

On Wednesday afternoon Sampson and the Sooners went to the Compaq Center for a practice and interview sessions with the media.

Word filtered through the media that Sampson's father was in the hospital, and Sampson was asked how he was doing. Finally, when a question was asked about his upbringing, Sampson broke down for about one minute, but he composed himself and went on answering questions.

"It was always amazing how my father had stayed in the background and never took the credit," Sampson said. "I think one of his greatest thrills was to watch our team play basketball. After he had a stroke in 1982, he just couldn't do what he used to do. It took a lot out of him. It was almost like he was done coaching. I think God put me on this earth to coach so he could enjoy it.

"But here we were at our greatest moment and our best chance to go to a Final Four. I was afraid he wasn't going to be able to see it. He had gone through so much to get here. I knew he wasn't going to be able to go to the Arizona game. It just seemed unfair. I got emotional."

Sampson had a long-time association with Arizona coach Lute Olson. Sampson had lost 15 straight games to Olson at Washington State from 1987-94 before he beat him the first time in 1999 in the first round of the NCAA Tournament when the 13th-seeded Sooners upset the fourth-seeded Wildcats. Sampson called it his most significant victory at Oklahoma.

"Even at Washington State when they were winning, Kelvin was doing a great job," Olson said. "It's a lot easier to get it done in Norman than in Pullman [Wash.]. He's a hard worker, a quality guy. And he does things the right way... I am happy to see them surviving to this point."

Before the game, Sampson and Olson met at half court. Sampson had always viewed Olson as a role model because of the Arizona coach's work ethic.

"The first thing he asked was how was Karen," Sampson said. "I couldn't get her attention in the stands at first. She absolutely adores Lute. Lute, Bobbi [Olson's late wife], Karen, and I go way back."

There was a role reversal in San Jose. For the first time Sampson was favored in a game against Arizona.

"It was a little different for me," Sampson said. "It was like going outside without your raincoat. I liked that feeling. Our quickness, athleticism, and our toughness bothered them. I felt that would be the difference in the game. Arizona plays a lot like Kansas. They are a freewheeling finesse team that can really, really score. We tend to do well against teams like that."

Not in the first half.

The Sooners trailed Arizona, 37-33, at half time and needed a pick-up. Price scored 22 of Oklahoma's 33 first-half points against Arizona's zone, while McGhee was in foul trouble. Arizona shot 56.5 percent in the first half and had out-rebounded the normally tenacious Sooners by three. In the second half Oklahoma's defense limited Arizona to 29.4 percent shooting, and the Sooners dominated the boards.

At half time Sampson exploded on his assistant coaches in a room adjacent to the locker room, loud enough for the players to hear. Hollis kidded later he always wondered what Sampson said to his assistants before he addressed the team.

"We were giving them [the Wildcats] too much respect," Sampson said. "I said respect your opponents, but don't over respect them. My assistant coaches didn't do a good job of telling me what I wanted to hear."

The Sooners, however, got some kind of half-time message.

Ere scored all 14 of his points in the second half. McGhee scored 19 of his 21 in the final 20 minutes when the Sooners used an 11-0 run to erase a four-point deficit and take a 51-44 lead with 11:40 remaining. It would end up being Arizona's second lowest scoring game of the season and lowest in 26 games.

Selvy came off the bench to score 10 of his 15 points. Defensively, Selvy also was switched to Arizona's Luke Walton, who finished with only nine points in the game, nearly six below his average.

"Selvy likes challenges like that," Sampson said. "He can guard any position on the court. He's a unique kid. He really doesn't have a position. When Selvy was on the floor, I always went to some kind of trap to take advantage of his strengths. He could change the game when he came in. Selvy was not a very good shooter. But he was a good scorer. His greatest strength was when the ball hit the rim—he could go get it."

"Their quickness was evident," Olson said. "When we did get a good look [in the second half], they were so quick to get there and pressure the shot, what had looked like a good shot was a challenged shot by the time we got it off."

Price, who made six three-point shots against Arizona, placed in his shoe a clipping of a story in which Arizona's Salim Stoudamire

Forward Daryan Selvy became a valuable bench player for
the Sooners during the 2001-02 season. Photo by Jerry Laizure.

said he didn't know why people "boosted Price up to be Michael Jordan." Price outscored Stoudamire, 26-8. "I am not a trash talker," Price said. "But I brought my A game. I still have it [the story] in my shoe."

Oklahoma won its 11th straight game to set up the West Region final meeting against Missouri, which had upset UCLA in the other semifinal. It would be an all Big 12 final for the right to go to the Final Four in Atlanta. "I think at this point, if we hadn't gone to the Final Four, this team would have been crushed," Sampson said.

Mr. Ned was still unable to go to the Missouri game and wouldn't attend any of the rest of the NCAA Tournament games.

"He was in and out," Sampson said. "He was in pain and was getting morphine for his incisions. That was Thursday. He watched the Arizona game on TV. But on Friday he wasn't passing neurological exams. I knew he wouldn't be able to go to the Missouri game on Saturday."

Missouri coach Quin Snyder had been under fire for the Tigers' performance during the regular season when they struggled to a sixth-place finish in the Big 12 and barely made the NCAA Tournament. On January 21 Oklahoma defeated Missouri, 84-71, at Norman in an ESPN Big Monday game.

"In our minds we are playing a No. 1 seed and one of the elite teams in the country," Snyder said. "They do a great job of getting in the lane and breaking you down for shots. In addition they're great in transition. They can all handle the pass. They really find each other. And they're a great offensive rebounding team."

The Tigers, however, had a new lease on life in the NCAA Tournament, pulling upsets of Miami (Fla.), Ohio State, and UCLA as senior guard Clarence Gilbert had lifted his play to a new level.

"Missouri was much better than the first time we played them, but so were we," Sampson said. "Rush and Gilbert had never beaten us. Nobody on the current Missouri team had. Usually a team gets its personality from one player. They got their personality not from Kareem Rush, but Gilbert. He was their most intense, toughest hard-nosed player. But Rush was their star.

"I studied four tapes on Missouri...Iowa State (in the Big 12 Tournament), Miami (Fla.), Ohio State, and UCLA. This team was focused. Rush was playing at a high level. Gilbert was their engine. Arthur Johnson was a beast inside. The player playing the best was

Rickey Paulding. We were always talking about our triangle. They had a rectangle."

But Sampson was already in uncharted territory. And he wanted to go further.

"This was our opportunity to make a statement about our program to the nation," Sampson said. "How many chances do you get to do that? We had always been a program that had the 'if' and the 'but' beside its name. 'If they could ever do this. They did this, but....' This was our chance to take the if and the but away from Oklahoma basketball. I wanted this game desperately for a number of reasons. But I wanted it for our program. It was our chance to be on the national stage. Being one of the elite is what we lacked. We had to take that next step. It wasn't a huge leap. For some people to get to the Final Four, it's like crossing time zones and area codes. For us I never thought it was a huge leap."

Either Missouri or Oklahoma would become the first Big 12 Conference team to make the Final Four since the league was established in 1996-97 because Kansas was playing in the Midwest Region final the following day.

Missouri would lead only briefly on a couple of occasions in the first half of what was a foul fest. There were 54 fouls called in the game. Seven Oklahoma players had three or four fouls, but none fouled out. The Tigers, despite never trailing by more than 10 points in the second half, could never take the lead in the final 20 minutes of the Sooners' 81-75 victory, which was their ninth straight over the Tigers.

McGhee, in foul trouble, scored only four points in the first half. He scored a basket early in the second half but picked up his fourth foul and didn't surface again until he made a jumper with 5:04 remaining in the game to push OU ahead, 65-58. He scored nine points down the stretch and fouled out Missouri center Arthur Johnson with 2:53 remaining.

Rush's three-pointer brought Missouri within 70-67, with 2:43 remaining. But McGhee answered with another one 28 seconds later for a 73-67 lead. It became a free throw shooting contest after that. And Oklahoma is the Big 12's best at that.

"The key thing in that game was when to put Aaron back in," Sampson said. "I remember putting him back into the game, and I told Aaron we are going to go to you right away. We have this play called curl. We have an inside entry pass to Aaron. As soon as he got back into the game, we went right to him and he scored. That put us ahead 65-58. That was a big turning point. Aaron then hit a big three to put us ahead 73-67, with just more than two minutes left after Rush had made a three."

Oklahoma had cut off Missouri's head, Gilbert, who finished his career making only 1 of 16 shots. Gilbert had been prophetic in his assessment of the Sooners a few days earlier.

"Kansas, they are the best team in the Big 12, but they are not the toughest," Gilbert said. "There's a difference. Oklahoma, they may not be as good as Kansas, but they are tougher. They beat you up and wear you down. Kansas is talented and very good. But Oklahoma, they are tougher."

Oklahoma coach Kelvin Sampson led the cheer, "Final Four, Final Four, Final Four" and thrust his arm in the air. During a television interview he was excited. "This is for everybody at Montana Tech, Washington State, and Oklahoma," Sampson said of two of his previous head coaching jobs before arriving at OU in 1994-95.

Price, who Arizona's Olson had called one of the most underrated players in college basketball earlier in the week, was named the West Region's Most Outstanding Player. In the victory over Missouri, Price led OU with 18 points and was a major part of a defensive effort on Gilbert.

In four NCAA Tournament games, Price was averaging 18.3 points, had connected on 12 of 25 three-point shots, and had made 11 of 12 free throws.

Of course, that didn't surprise Sampson. In the Amateur Athletic Union (AAU) 17-and-under National Tournament, Price's Shreveport team made it to the finals and won the national title game in 1998 against a New Jersey team that included Duke's Jason Williams.

"Hollis willed his team to the win," Sampson said. "They played Chris Duhon's [who also went to Duke] team in the state championship. And Hollis was the MVP of the state championship. He expects to win. He goes out and wins big games. He has no fear. He attacks fear."

Sampson realized the importance of the moment. There had been many great coaches such as Kansas State's Jack Hartman, Oregon State's Ralph Miller, and Missouri's Norm Stewart who never made the Final Four during their illustrious coaching careers. Purdue's Gene Keady and Georgia State's Lefty Driesell still haven't.

Kelvin Sampson celebrated winning the NCAA West Region title after an 81-75 victory over Missouri. Photo by Lisa Hall/OU Athletic Media Relations.

The other thing that flashed through his mind was that he would be practicing on Friday at the Final Four. He had always dreamed of having his team in those practices at the Final Four when thousands of people were watching. As a young coach, Sampson always went to the Final Four and watched those Final Four practices the day before the semifinals.

"It is a validation, but it is unfair to say you are not a great coach if you never make it to the Final Four," Sampson said. "Not all programs are capable of making it. There are 10 programs in the Pac-10. And Washington State is probably 10th. I felt as good taking Washington State to the tournament as I do taking OU to the Final Four. OU is a school that should get to the Final Four. A lot of great coaches don't have the opportunity to coach at schools that have the resources to get to the Final Four."

Before the Sooners left San Jose, they had two stops to make. First, the Sooners went by O'Connor Hospital to visit Mr. Ned, who wouldn't board the team plane. He was improving from the emergency brain surgery, but he would stay in San Jose until midweek. Dr. Halverstadt would set up a private plane to fly Mr. Ned directly from San Jose to Atlanta. Dr. Havlerstadt would fly back out to San Jose to help with the transfer.

McGhee gave Mr. Ned the nets from around his neck, the same nets the team had cut down at the Compaq Center after winning the West Region title only a couple hours before.

"When we went in, for a man who had surgery on his head, had fluid taken out, he was the happiest person I have ever seen," said Ere. "I mean, he was smiling."

After visiting Mr. Ned, the team bus stopped at McDonald's for another post-game celebration.

"Our players say, 'Coach, we don't have any McDonald's All-Americans but we eat at McDonald's,'" Sampson said. "We don't have kids who require a shoeshine stand. They don't need lettuce and tomato on their hamburger. They are just solid, easy guys to coach."

Once they were back in Norman, one of Sampson's first calls on Sunday was to his buddy Michigan State coach Tom Izzo, who had been to the Final Four three straight years: "What did you do differently the second time than the first?"

Izzo's reply: "Tickets done by Monday."

"That was the first thing out of his mouth," Sampson said. "He was talking about player tickets. Tom did a great job telling me about media. He told me you don't have to do every radio show. He told me your Sports Information Director is your best friend that week. Tom tried to do a good job preparing me. But you have to experience it to know. He said stay focused on the game and don't change anything. But we didn't talk about Indiana. I didn't feel like it was right to ask him about Indiana because he was in the same conference."

Marquette coach Tom Crean, an assistant for Izzo in 1999 when the Spartans were in the Final Four, watched practice on Wednesday in Norman before the Sooners headed to Atlanta the next day. "I had you guys picked to go to the Final Four a month ago," Crean told the Sooners, "because I think you are that good."

The media already had descended on Norman. The CBS crew wanted total access to everything. But Sampson wouldn't let CBS into the locker room or film room. He allowed them to follow Price and McGhee around campus. Every day Sampson had a press conference before practice.

"This was Yankee Stadium...I had more beat writers from Indianapolis than I had from Oklahoma," Sampson said. "We came out one day at practice and there were 25 cameras the first 10 minutes of practice before I made them leave. We hadn't ridden this horse before."

The Oklahoma-Indiana game had some interesting subplots.

Davis, who is black, and Sampson, a Lumbee, would be the first two minority coaches to play in the Final Four. Only four minority head coaches had reached the Final Four before 2002 but had not faced each other in a game there: Arkansas' Nolan Richardson, Minnesota's Clem Haskins, Kentucky's Tubby Smith, and Georgetown's John Thompson.

Sampson said Richardson, Thompson, and George Raveling, who coached at USC, Iowa, and at Washington State before Sampson, were his role models as minority coaches.

"They gave me hope," Sampson said. "I thought, 'I can do this one day.'"

In turn, Davis, in only his second season at Indiana after replacing Bob Knight, received hope from Sampson, who wrote him a letter his first season. "I always followed him because of the letter he wrote," said Davis, who still has the letter.

"Mike was almost frighteningly honest in his interviews," Sampson said. "I just felt the need to reach out to him. I don't know why. I got out the pen and paper and wrote him the longest letter during his first season. It might have been after the game he was self-deprecating. He may have made the statement he didn't know if he deserved this job. He was saying things every coach thinks about but shouldn't say."

Sampson told Davis to develop a system or philosophy because "when it is broken you will know how to fix it. I said when your team wins give the players the credit. But something my father told me—be careful how you take the blame [when the team loses]."

Early during Final Four week, Sampson was receiving congratulatory faxes and e-mails of his own from buddies, friends, and coaching associates, including Minnesota coach Dan Monson, who said he is one of those young coaches who attends those Final Four practices. But at the same time Sampson was watching video of Indiana and worrying.

"Indiana was not going to beat itself," Sampson said. "Some teams we could make them turn the ball over a lot. Kansas had 20 turnovers. Indiana was tough, smart, and was going to dictate pace of play.

"Indiana made only 2 of 10 three-point shots against Duke. So we weren't buying into this thing, if you shut down their three-point shooting, you would beat them. The big thing for Indiana was offensive rebounding. And rebounding was one of our strengths. I thought that would be neutralized."

Much of the pre-game coverage focused on the left ankle injury of Indiana guard Tom Coverdale. Would he play or wouldn't he? But on Thursday at the Sooners' last full practice before meeting Indiana, Oklahoma point guard Quannas White suffered an injury to his left ankle.

"I knew it was serious because he never came back to practice," Sampson said. "When it leaked out someone asked me if that was some psychological ploy to get into Indiana's head. I said, 'I don't want to get into Indiana's head. I want my point guard with a healthy ankle.'"

As the game started, Sampson said he could tell White was not 100 percent, not even close. White couldn't move laterally or accelerate.

"And the problem with him not being able to accelerate I had to play Hollis too much at point guard," Sampson said. "Our team was not made that way. Our team was set up all year long for Quannas to be our point guard. Hollis was so much more comfortable with the ball not in his hands and having to run the offense."

This was evident. The fact Price had to handle the point and Indiana's face Dane Fife, an excellent defensive player, took him out of the game offensively. Price wound up making only 1 of 11 shots.

"Fife did a great job," Hollis said. "He was so physical. I usually get around that, but tonight I couldn't."

After missing several shots early, Sampson barked at Price not to pass up more shots. "Be a star!"

"I thought he was deferring," Sampson said. "I told him to have the courage to succeed or fail. Our team is not set up for Ebi or Aaron to take all the shots. We need you, Hollis."

Despite Hollis's problems, Oklahoma still was in a position to take a big lead in the first half. The Indiana offense was going nowhere. OU led 17-9. Then Indiana forward Jeff Newton, from Atlanta, came into the game and played what Davis called the game of his life and caused Oklahoma to get into foul trouble with his inside play. Newton scored a career-high 19 points.

"We had a chance to put them way," Sampson said. "I thought one of the things was we got less aggressive on defense when we got into foul trouble. Jabahri Brown reverted back to the Kansas game in Lawrence. The Newton kid really kept Indiana in it. I thought the first half we could have been up 10-15 points if he had not played so well. He played good against Duke, too. So that wasn't a total shock."

Indiana made a three-point basket as the buzzer sounded to end the first half, slicing OU's lead to four. Even then, Price missed a couple of wide open three-point shots late in the first half which could have put OU in the driver's seat.

Sampson second-guessed himself for not playing reserve Blake Johnston more at the point guard and leaving Hollis at wing. Reserve guard Jason Detrick made only one of six shots, but he had been battling an ankle injury since February 16. It had not been reported in the media. "He was never 100 percent," Sampson said. "That happened right after the Kansas State game at home. He was getting treatment around the clock. And he even got a shot before the games."

Those critical of Sampson's coaching in the final game wondered why he didn't press. But with two guards with gimpy ankles, OU really wasn't in any better position to press than Indiana was with Coverdale. "Defensively we do what we do," Sampson said. "We don't press anybody. Remember the game was tied at 60. It was not a matter of what defense we were going to play."

Despite McGhee fouling out with 4:40 remaining, Oklahoma scrambled back to tie the score at 60 on a basket by Selvy with 3:24 remaining. And Selvy had a chance to put OU ahead at the 3-minute mark but missed the front end of a 1-and-1.

Newton then answered with a layup and so did reserve guard Donald Perry to give IU command of the game. During the last 3:24, Oklahoma only scored four points. The Indiana bench was key, out-scoring OU's 41-12. Oklahoma was eliminated from the NCAA Tournament by a team from the state of Indiana for a third straight season.

"Hollis shooting 1-for-11, Quannas going 0-for-5, and Selvy shooting 2-for-10—none of that individually hurt us," Sampson said of players' shooting. "But what really hurt us, it was collectively all on the same day. With our foul trouble and shooting percentage (36.4), we couldn't overcome that. I give Indiana credit. They just didn't beat themselves and they made every critical three-point shot. They were 6-for-6 in the second half.

"Then we came back and tied the score at 60. I said this was typical Oklahoma basketball. We were still going to win this thing. We said that in the huddle, right before Selvy shot his 1-and-1. If we could have gotten a two-point lead and stopped them from scoring on the next possession, all of a sudden the personality of the game changes. We just could never get over the hump."

Epilogue

It was early April in Norman, Oklahoma. Normally, that's time for spring football. But this past spring, the Sooners' nationally prominent football team had to take a backseat to the men's and women's basketball programs, which both made the 2002 Final Four.

For men's coach Kelvin Sampson, early April 2002 meant a whirlwind of events after his initial Final Four appearance and the school's first in 14 years: tapings for rewrite of his book, *Kelvin Sampson: The OU Basketball Story*, recruiting, watching the Portsmouth Invitational future pro tournament, and moving his offices from the bowels of Lloyd Noble Center to a new practice facility.

In early April he sat in his brand new office overlooking the Sooners' new practice facility, which adjoins Lloyd Noble Center. He has one of the twins. The women's basketball program has the same setup on the other side of the building. Sampson will be able to merely look down during the off-season and see if his players are working out.

Sampson's face was worn. There were small bags under his eyes. He hadn't slept much during the previous five weeks. Sampson had a contentment that the Sooners' program reached the Final Four in his eighth season here. But he also had a sense of an opportunity lost.

The Sooners fell to Indiana, 73-64 in the Final Four semifinals in Atlanta. The eventual NCAA champions, the Maryland Terrapins, lost to OU, 72-56, way back in December. Kansas, the other Final Four team, split with the Sooners this season. OU's basketball team could have NCAA champions beside its name for the first time in school history.

"You just don't know if you are ever going to get back to the Final Four," said Sampson who was named the Chevrolet Coach of the Year and National Association of Basketball Coaches Division I Coach of the Year. "You can say you are going to get back the next year. It is not that easy. I know that. I remember watching Bob Huggins' team at Cincinnati in 1992. I thought they would be back. We had a great opportunity. I was disappointed Indiana didn't get our best shot. We didn't play good. I was disappointed in the way we played and the finality of it all.

"Always we were trying to get to the destination, but in the end it's the journey that counts. I got a little melancholy in the locker room. I was a little sad. I had a wide range of feelings. I didn't get as emotional as I might have because I was mad we didn't play better. But I started feeling for our seniors, Aaron McGhee and Daryan Selvy. We rode their backs."

Sampson, who had not made it past the Sweet 16 as a coach before the 2001-02 season, allowed himself another look back at the Indiana game in which guard Hollis Price had a poor shooting night, McGhee fouled out, and the Hoosiers shot brilliantly from three-point range in the second half.

"I think back to the Indiana game," Sampson continued. "With the score tied, 60-60, Selvy missed that one-and-one. And the thought ran through my mind maybe I should have had them more at the free-throw line at the end of practice. You always question yourself as a coach. That is why free throws are so important."

But nine days after that game, as boxes were being moved into his office and entire pieces of furniture carted by, Sampson was excited about the future, which will not include his assistant coach of nine years, Ray Lopes.

Terry Evans, the Sooners' director of basketball operations during the 2001-02 season, also is leaving to become head basketball coach at Central Oklahoma.

During the Sooners' Final Four run, officials from Boise State and Fresno State came to the OU campus to interview Lopes for their vacant head coaching jobs. Oregon State and De Paul were also interested in hiring Lopes, who took the Fresno State job and will succeed legendary coach Jerry Tarkanian.

"My top assistant always sits in the front seat beside me on the bus," Sampson said. "Jason Rabedeaux [now head coach at UTEP] sat in the front seat for five years at Oklahoma and the last four years I was at Washington State. The last three years here it has been Ray. Ray has been to nine consecutive NCAA Tournaments, won two Big 12 Tournament titles, went to a Sweet 16, and made a Final Four. He has been a big part if it. You are sad to see your coach go. Your program always takes a hit. But on the other hand I was more happy for him. He gave me nine great years and he was so loyal. I always knew Ray had my back.

"When Jabahri Brown found out Ray was leaving, he wept uncontrollably," said Sampson. "Ray made the initial contact with him. Ray made his formal announcement to the team after the championship game in Atlanta. Some were sad and they were crying a little bit. But they believed this was his destiny."

And what will the Sooners' destiny be during the 2002-03 season? OU only loses McGhee and Selvy to graduation. That means OU returns four starters and seven of its top nine players. The backcourt returns intact with guards Hollis Price and Quannas White, high school teammates from New Orleans. Brown is back at center, and 6-5 Ebi Ere is at the other guard spot.

Jason Detrick will be the first guard off the bench. But Blake Johnston, a redshirt freshman in 2001-02, showed he could provide valuable minutes as well. The seventh player in the mix from last season will be 6-9 Jozsef Szendrei, the Sooners' fourth post player. In addition, 6-8 sophomore Johnnie Gilbert (medical redshirt in 2001-02) and 6-9 freshman Matt Gipson, a Texan who sat out last season, will bolster the frontcourt.

The Sooners will add three new players, two of which will come from one of the top high school classes in the state's history: 6-8 Kevin Bookout from Stroud, Oklahoma, and 6-5 DeAngelo Alexander from Midwest City, Oklahoma.

"DeAngelo is the best high school guard that we have signed," Sampson said. "I know that includes Hollis, but DeAngelo is almost 6-5 and weighs 210. I know his talent level is high. I know he will come in here and be a good player. What you don't know about is his toughness. And there's always a risk in recruiting local kids because you don't know how they will be influenced by people around them. If DeAngelo will come here and focus on us and let us coach him and not get coached outside our program, I think he will have a great career here.

"As for Bookout, his high school coach said you get one of these kids every 50 years. Then he amended himself and said one every 100 years. He is 6-8 and weighs in the 250s. He is the United States' top Olympic hopeful in shot and discus in 2008."

In mid-April Sampson was also on the trail of another guard, whose signing would complete the Sooners' roster for the 2002-03 season.

"This is the first year I have been at Oklahoma where we have nucleus coming back in the frontcourt and the backcourt," Sampson said. "This year we have nucleus of posts back and all of our guards. We red-shirted two really good post guys. Gipson has the ability to make us a very good team in time. He will just be a freshman. But with Gilbert, Kevin Bookout, and Jabahri, we don't have any seniors. They will all be back the following year.

"I think our program has risen to the point people expect us to win," Sampson said. "For us to be a national program we have to be a Sweet 16, Elite Eight, or a Final Four team more than just this past year. That's where the challenge is. But I think we are now on people's radar."

McGhee came into Sampson's office and was greeted and congratulated by the OU office staff for being named the MVP at Portsmouth.

Down the hall, Oklahoma assistant coach Bennie Seltzer was preparing for the first team meeting since the Final Four.

"I am going to get chewed out for not working out the players," Seltzer said with a smile. "It has been nine days since our last game. But I have taken one for the team."

Sampson peered out his office window at the new men's practice floor below. "This may not be good, because I will be able to see out there, and if they aren't working out and shooting I will be mad." Shortly after Sampson made the statement, Blake Johnson was walking up the tunnel with a basketball and a buddy to work out at the new facility.

Sampson continued, "Before this past NCAA Tournament, Hollis said, 'Coach, I am tired of you going to the Final Four every year by yourself. We want to go with you.' Well, I am going next year and I want to take them with me. It would be sweet redemption, wouldn't it? You know there are going to be a lot of failures between now and then. And there will be a lot of obstacles. After last season was over, I was ready for a break. After this season, I can't wait for October."

And that journey that Kelvin Sampson knows so well will begin anew.

A Thank You from Kelvin Sampson

I have worked with many wonderful people during my nineteen seasons as a head coach. This group spans presidents to secretaries at Montana Tech, Washington State, and Oklahoma.

I want to thank my president at Montana Tech, Fred DeMoney, and my president at Washington State, Dr. Sam Smith. My current president, David L. Boren at Oklahoma, has been of great help and inspiration to me.

I have worked with and maintained good relationships with seven athletic directors: Forrest Wilson and Mick Delaney at Montana Tech; Dick Young and Jim Livengood at Washington State; Donnie Duncan, Steve Owens, and Joe Castiglione at Oklahoma.

Special thanks go to my assistant coaches: Mike Carle, Mark Watts, John Thatcher, Moose Petritz (trainer) at Montana Tech; Kip Motta, Dave Harshman, Tim Kelly, Mark Adams, Donnie Newman, Jason Rabedeaux, Lynn Mitchem, Ray Lopes, Bobby Champagne, Brian Sanders (trainer), Dan Ruiz (trainer) at Washington State; Lopes, Rabedeaux, Champagne, Bennie Seltzer, Jim Shaw, Dan Shell, Dan Hare, Josh Prock, Terry Evans, and Alex Brown (trainer) at Oklahoma. I want to salute all my former and current managers and secretaries, including current office manager Renee Forney.

I couldn't have made it at Montana Tech without Vic Burt, a friend forever. My former coaches at Carolina Military Academy, Pembroke High School (my father, Coach Ned), and at Pembroke State (Lacey Gane and Joe Gallagher) helped me develop as an athlete, coach, and person. My father, Coach Ned, mother Eva, and sisters Ursula, Karen, and Suzanne were always there for me.

The three most special people in my life are my wife, Karen, and children, Lauren and Kellen.

When I came home from basketball practice at Washington State, Lauren would meet me at the door with her blanket and book. I would read her a story every night. Eventually I read to her class at school. I enjoyed that so much. It was a tremendous opportunity to share with the community in Pullman. And we brought that school reading program to Norman when I became coach of the Sooners. It started with Lauren and her book at Washington State.

And now Lauren is a junior at OU and a member of the Chi Omega Sorority, and Kellen is a senior at Norman High School. I couldn't be prouder of them and Karen, who has been behind me every step of the way.

Working with Joe Castigilone has been one of my career highlights. I have always put athletic directors in two categories. They are either inhibitors or facilitators. And Joe is a facilitator. He is an athletic director who will not only challenge you in his own unique way but also be there to support you along the journey. Joe has been there to hold the ladder while I climbed up to cut down the nets after we

The Sampsons (from left to right): Kelvin, Lauren, Karen, and Kellen.

have won two consecutive Big 12 Tournament Championships and the NCAA West Region in San Jose, California. It is very special when that person holding that ladder is not only your boss but also one of your best friends.

Thank you Joe!

Kelvin Sampson
Spring, 2002

Appendix

The Kelvin Sampson Log

Montana Tech	Overall	Conference*	Place
1981-82	7-20	1-14	6th
1982-83	22-9	10-5	3rd
1983-84	22-7	11-4	1st
1984-85	22-9	12-3	1st

Montana Tech record: 73-45 (four seasons)
Frontier League

Washington State	Overall	Conference*	Place
1987-88	13-16	7-11	6th
1988-89	10-19	4-14	8th
1989-90	7-22	1-17	10th
1990-91	16-12	8-10	T-5th
1991-92	22-11	9-9	T-5th NIT
1992-93	15-12	9-9	T-5th
1993-94	20-11	10-8	4th NCAA

Washington State record: 103-103 (seven seasons)
Pac-10

Oklahoma	Overall	Conference	Place	
1994-95	23-9	9-5*	3rd	NCAA
1995-96	17-13	8-6 *	3rd	NCAA
1996-97	19-11	9-7+	6th	NCAA
1997-98	22-11	11-5+	T-2nd	NCAA
1998-99	22-11	11-5+	T-2nd	NCAA
1999-00	27-7	12-4+	T-3rd	NCAA
2000-01	23-7	12-4+	T-2nd	NCAA
2001-02	31-5	13-3+	2nd	NCAA

Oklahoma record: 187-74   (eight seasons)
*Big Eight
+Big 12

Kelvin Sampson facts:

- Oklahoma has a 104-16 home record (86.7 percent winning percentage) in eight seasons under Sampson.

- The Sooners have played in four of the six Big 12 Tournament title games, winning the crown in 2001 and 2002 and finishing second in 2000 and 1998.

- Sampson's Sooners have a 68-28 Big 12 regular-season record, second best only to Kansas (80-16).

- Sampson's Sooners (29-19) are one of only three league teams with a winning record in Big 12 road games. Kansas (36-12) and Texas (27-21) are the others.

- Sampson celebrated his 300th career victory with a 93-65 victory over Texas Tech on February 23, 2000, in Norman.

- The eleven largest home crowds in Oklahoma history have all come during the Kelvin Sampson era at Oklahoma. The top crowd in OU home history is 13,280 vs. Oklahoma State on February 12, 2000.

Index

Index

Stewart, Dwight, 65
Stewart, Norm, 126
Stone, Renzi, 149, 150, 158,
    159-160, 161, 166-167,
    181-182
Szendrei, Jozsef, 220, 225, 237-238,
    265

T

Teegins, Bill, 199
Tubbs, Billy, 98-99, 103, 104, 211,
    246

U

Underwood, John, 99-100, 104-105

V

Vaughns, Brian, 43

Vik, David, 64
Vitale, Dick, 203

W

Walls, Jaquay, 185
Warmenhoven, Joey, 64, 84
Washington State, 47-71
Webster, Jeff, 112
White, Quannas, 216, 219-220,
    222-224, 225, 230-231, 234,
    260
Wiley, Evan "Hootie," 132, 145, 160,
    161-162
Williams, Roy, 99, 103, 123-124,
    167-168, 244
Withers, Bud, 56